Back to Work: Canada

IMPROVING THE RE-EMPLOYMENT PROSPECTS OF DISPLACED WORKERS

OECD
BETTER POLICIES FOR BETTER LIVES

Please cite this publication as:
OECD (2015), *Back to Work: Canada: Improving the Re-employment Prospects of Displaced Workers*, OECD Publishing, Paris.
http://dx.doi.org/10.1787/9789264233454-en

ISBN 978-92-64-23323-2 (print)
ISBN 978-92-64-23345-4 (PDF)

Series: Back to Work
ISSN 2306-3823 (print)
ISSN 2306-3831 (online)

Photo credits: Cover © Bull's Eye/Imagezoo/Inmagine LTD

Corrigenda to OECD publications may be found on line at: *www.oecd.org/about/publishing/corrigenda.htm*.

Foreword

OECD labour markets are characterised by their dynamism. Each year, more than 20% of jobs, on average, are created and/or destroyed, and around one-third of all workers are hired and/or separate from their employer. These large job and worker flows are driven by a continuous process of labour reallocation, both across industries and between declining and growing firms within the same industry. This reallocation is an important source of productivity gains, since more productive firms expand at the expense of less productive firms and earnings rise on average for workers changing jobs, particularly workers who voluntarily quit one job in order to move to another. However, high job turnover is also a source of insecurity for workers, especially those who are displaced from their jobs because their employer downsizes its workforce or goes out of business altogether. A common challenge facing OECD governments is thus to nurture labour market dynamism while keeping the adjustment costs that are borne by displaced workers as low as possible.

To address this issue the OECD Employment, Labour and Social Affairs Committee is carrying out a thematic review of policies to help workers who lose their jobs for economic reasons or as a result of structural change to move back into work. Nine countries participate in this review: Australia, Canada, Denmark, Finland, Japan, Korea, New Zealand, Sweden and the United States.

This report on Canada was prepared by Gwenn Parent and Shruti Singh under the supervision of Christopher Prinz and Paul Swaim. Statistical assistance was provided by Sylvie Cimper and Agnès Puymoyen, editorial assistance by Gabriela Bejan, with contributions from Marc Gendron (Employment and Social Development Canada – ESDC). It is the third country report prepared in the context of this thematic review supervised by Mark Keese. The report benefited greatly from discussions with various Canadian experts, officials, employer federations, trade unions, academics and businesses during an OECD mission to Canada in June 2013, and from detailed comments provided by ministries and organisations at the federal level, and from the two provinces covered in the report, Ontario and Quebec.

Table of contents

Boxes

Figures

Tables

Acronyms and abbreviations

ALFS	Annual Labour Force Statistics
ALMP	Active labour market programme
ARTT	*Aménagement et réduction du temps de travail* (Quebec)
CAD	Canadian dollars
CANSIM	Canadian Socioeconomic Information Management system (Statistics Canada)
CAR	*Comité d'aide au reclassement* (Quebec)
CCAJ	Connecting Canadians to Available Jobs
CIS	Client Information Session
CJF	Canada Job Fund agreements
CJG	Canada Job Grant
CPMT	*Commission des partenaires du marché du travail* (Quebec)
CREC	*Comité d'aide au reclassement à entrées continues* (Quebec)
CSP	*Contrat de sécurisation professionnelle* (France)
CTA	Career Transition Assistance
EAS	Employment Assistance Services
EBSM	Employment Benefits and Support Measures
EEITI	Extended Employment Insurance and Training Incentive
EI	Employment Insurance
EICS	Employment Insurance Coverage Survey
EO	Employment Ontario
EPL	Employment protection legislation
ESA	Employment Standards Act
ESDC	Employment and Social Development Canada
GDP	Gross domestic product
GFC	Global financial crisis (of 2008-09)
HRSDC	Human Resources and Skills Development Canada
ILO	International Labour Organization
JCP	Job Creation Partnerships

LMA	Labour Market Agreement
LMDA	Labour Market Development Agreement
LMI	Labour Market Information
LMP	Labour Market Partnership
LWF	Longitudinal Worker File
MESS	*Ministère de l'Emploi et de la Solidarité sociale* (Quebec)
MTCU	Ministry of Training, Colleges and Universities
NAICS	North American Industry Classification System
NOC	National Occupational Classification
NRR(s)	Net Replacement Rate(s)
P/Ts	Provinces and territories
PES	Public employment service (employment services network, for example Employment Ontario or *Emploi-Québec*)
RRTS	Rapid Re-employment and Training Service
SC	Second Career
SD	Skills Development
SERRÉ	*Soutien aux entreprises à risque de ralentissement économique* (Quebec)
SITI	Severance Investment for Training Initiative
SLID	Survey of Labour and Income Dynamics
STW	Short-Time Work
TIOW	Targeted Initiative for Older Workers
TWS	Targeted Wage Subsidies
WEPP	Wage Earner Protection Program
WI	Wage Insurance
WS	Work-Sharing

Executive summary

Workers who are involuntarily displaced from their jobs, as firms close or downsize in response to fluctuations in demand and production, face substantial economic and social costs. Around 2.2% of Canadian workers with at least one year of tenure are involuntarily displaced every year. About half are re-employed within one year and almost two-thirds within two years. However, many have to accept significant wage cuts and/or an often involuntary shift to part-time or temporary jobs. Older displaced workers face the poorest re-employment prospects, and those with long tenure bear the largest wage losses.

Overall, Canada has a sound set of policies and programmes to minimise the adverse consequence of displacement. Measures to avoid unnecessary redundancies in periods of weak economic activity are well-developed and play a useful role. Most of the emphasis is placed on early intervention measures for workers affected by mass layoffs and, especially, Employment Insurance benefits and employment services *after* workers have become unemployed.

Notwithstanding a relatively favourable policy set-up, areas of weakness exist. Programmes offering intensive adjustment assistance are not universal, leaving some displaced workers with insufficient re-employment support. In particular, early intervention services that could accelerate the adjustment process are too often not available to workers affected by small-scale and individual displacements or, more generally, to workers receiving advance notice or a large severance package. More could also be done to combine adequate financial support to older long-tenured displaced workers with effective re-employment measures.

The OECD recommends that policy makers in Canada:

- Improve the effectiveness of early intervention services in the case of mass dismissals, while extending these services as much as possible to workers affected by small-scale and individual displacements.
- Connect people receiving severance pay to employment services earlier by delinking such services from eligibility for Employment Insurance benefits.
- Experiment with several policy options to address large and persistent earning losses borne by older long-tenured workers, including through wage insurance to moderate wage losses.
- Promptly assess displaced workers' needs and provide those who need it with greater access to more intensive re-employment counselling and retraining.

Assessment and recommendations

Displaced workers bear an important share of the costs resulting from structural adjustments of the economy, in particular during recessions

Job displacement – defined as involuntary job loss due to economic reasons such as firm closure or downsizing – affects many workers over the course of their working lives. Around 2.2% of Canadian workers with at least one year of tenure are displaced on average every year. Once displaced, some workers find suitable new jobs relatively quickly while others experience long periods of unemployment. In Canada, just under half of displaced workers are re-employed within one year after displacement, and almost two-thirds are re-employed within two years. In an international comparison, re-employment rates for displaced workers are lower in Canada than in Australia, New Zealand, Sweden and the United States, about the same as in Japan and Korea, and well above the re-employment rate in France.

Even displaced workers who find a new job within the first year tend to experience important earning losses. One in five displaced workers face hourly wage cuts of 25% or more. On average, real annual earnings fall by 60% in the year following displacement, not taking benefit payments into account. This reflects the combined effects of three components: a lower hourly wage in the new job (around 2% decline compared with the previous hourly wage); fewer annual working hours after displacement due to unemployment; and fewer working hours in the new job. The latter two taken together represent the equivalent of almost seven months of the previous annual wage in the year following displacement. The brunt of these costs are borne by older long-tenured workers who face significantly greater challenges finding new jobs after displacement than other displaced workers, and when they do find a new position, they face significantly higher and longer-lasting wage losses. Job quality along a number of other dimensions also tends to be lower in the post-displacement job. For example, there is a shift into involuntary part-time and temporary jobs.

While job displacement is an important source of insecurity for workers, it is also an inescapable part of a dynamic labour market. Accordingly, an important policy priority could be to try to limit the adjustment costs associated with displacement whilst encouraging efficiency-enhancing labour reallocation.

The labour market system is difficult to navigate for displaced workers

The responsibility for income support and employment in Canada is divided between different jurisdictions. The federal government provides *Employment Insurance* (EI) to eligible displaced workers, while re-employment support for displaced workers is delivered by the provinces and territories and co-funded by the federal and the provincial levels. This setup can lead to a number of problems if the governments do not put in place co-ordination mechanisms to reach potential clients as early as possible. One consequence is that job-search monitoring and sanctioning of jobseekers for the non-fulfilment of requirements is in different hands than the provision of job-search assistance and services. This can delay access to re-employment services while also making it more difficult to implement an efficient activation strategy that conditions the provision of re-employment assistance on active job search. Problems can also arise because training provision differs from province to province, implying differences in certification practices which can be a significant barrier to greater mobility between booming and declining provincial economies.

Significant design and delivery responsibilities have been transferred to provinces and territories (P/T) under various labour market agreements, allowing P/Ts to design and deliver programmes and services according to local needs. Improved co-ordination between federal and provincial governments in the implementation and delivery of re-employment support could be pursued within existing systems. Even though a first step has been made in most P/Ts in bringing together re-employment services for recipients of Employment Insurance benefits and of social assistance, bringing the delivery of EI benefits and employment services closer together would be particularly beneficial. Delivering all services in a "one-stop-shop" either relying on Service Canada or on the provincial/territorial Public employment service (PES), would be ideal but is not a precondition for improved co-ordination of a fragmented system. Further efforts to improve labour market information and to reconcile differences in occupational standards across provinces would facilitate the geographic mobility of the unemployed.

Employment protection is not very restrictive, and the Canadian authorities responded well during the global financial crisis

Compared with their counterparts in other OECD countries, Canadian employers face relatively few legislative or regulatory restrictions on layoffs that are deemed necessary. While this makes Canadian workers potentially more vulnerable to job loss, the displacement rate is not especially high and the light-touch approach to regulating hiring and firing also promotes higher labour mobility with most unemployed workers finding their way back into jobs relatively quickly. Employment protection rules are also well-designed in that employers planning mass layoffs face additional requirements to provide their employees and labour market authorities with additional advance notification. This provides an opportunity to explore alternatives to layoffs and, when displacements cannot be avoided, it allows the affected workers and local labour market authorities to start early in preparing for a smooth adjustment.

The federally-run Work-Sharing (WS) programme provides a useful incentive for employers confronting a temporary reduction in business activity to retain valuable employees by temporarily reducing working hours, and paying workers a partial unemployment benefit for unworked hours. During the recession that followed the global financial crisis (GFC), the Canadian Government and P/Ts reacted very quickly to increase access by: offering temporary flexibilities; extending the maximum duration during which the WS benefit would be paid; and reducing associated administrative burden. Like Short-Time Work schemes in other OECD countries the WS programme enabled jobs to be preserved in Canada.

Overall the WS operates relatively well albeit further improvements can be made to minimise associated deadweight and displacement costs. Unlike in most OECD countries, Canadian firms do not bear any direct cost relating to the number of workers using the scheme. While this feature should help to encourage firms to participate in the scheme, shifting a modest share of the direct costs towards employers may make employers more careful to enrol only workers they are quite sure they will wish to retain after the subsidy ends. Further research and engagement with employers may be required to determine the appropriate employer share in costs and to determine what factors may contribute to programme uptake.

Well-developed early intervention policies following mass dismissals should be extended to individually dismissed workers

When mass layoffs are announced, considerable priority is given to adjustment support to workers early on via the so-called *transition* or *rapid response* services to facilitate their transition into new jobs. These early intervention services provided by Action centres in Ontario through programmes such as the Adjustment Advisory Program and *Comité d'aide au reclassement* (CAR) in Quebec are typically organised by public employment services working closely with the employer, labour representatives and other stakeholders to provide job-search assistance, career counselling and personal counselling to displaced workers to deal with the stress of job loss. Despite the potential benefits associated with early intervention, however, co-operation is not always forthcoming from employers.

Even when employers co-operate, the services offered before the layoff can be quite limited because of organisational difficulties. Employers are sometimes reluctant to co-operate with authorities to go beyond basic informational meetings during the notice period, for example by offering re-employment services, since doing so could disrupt production. Similarly, the public employment services are reluctant to intervene too extensively early on in the process, because some announced layoffs never occur due to unexpected improvements in sales or other factors. Participation in such services also remains voluntary, providing few incentives to some displaced workers such as older workers who are likely to be in receipt of large severance payments and other workers who may hope their jobs can be saved and hence may be reluctant to participate in active job search or retraining.

An additional challenge is to extend early intervention programmes to workers who are dismissed individually and therefore miss out on tailored adjustment support early on. Quebec is an exception. Workers affected by individual or small-scale displacements in Quebec can be referred to a reclassification committee known as the *Comité d'aide au reclassement à entrées continues* (CREC), designed to meet the distinct needs of this group that are not met by core labour market programmes. This appears to be a promising approach, but its effectiveness is difficult to assess in the absence of rigorous evaluation.

Addressing wage losses of older and long-tenured displaced workers

Most Canadian displaced workers with stable work histories have relatively good access to income support from the EI system whilst they look for new jobs. But benefit durations, at around ten months, are shorter than in other OECD countries and, as a result, displaced workers experiencing long spells of unemployment are at risk of a sharp fall in their living standards. While the shorter benefit payment duration potentially encourages more rapid re-employment, it may also increase the risk of poverty among the more vulnerable displaced workers, especially given the strict eligibility criteria for "last-resort" benefits such as social assistance. Thanks to the recent temporary increase in the duration of unemployment benefit, protection for unemployed workers increased during the global economic recession.

One particular concern is the adequacy of EI benefits for two (overlapping) groups: older and long-tenured workers. Older displaced workers are particularly at risk of exhausting their EI entitlement before they become re-employed while their long-tenured counterparts experience the largest wage losses after displacement; the average wage loss is three times larger for workers with long tenure. In addition, the current design of EI – notably the requirement to exhaust severance pay awards before becoming eligible for EI benefits – disadvantages this latter group as they are most likely to be in receipt of sizeable severance payments. While this requirement is not a disadvantage from an income adequacy perspective, the resulting delay in EI benefits can in turn leave long-tenured jobseekers without effective re-employment support during extended periods of unemployment as they are not required to register with employment services during this period.

The federal government took temporary steps to improve the accessibility to EI and related employment support for long-tenured workers in 2009 during the GFC. The *first* measure, *Extension of Employment Insurance Benefits for Long-Tenured Workers*, extended the duration of EI by up to 20 additional weeks. The *second* measure known as *Career Transition Assistance* (CTA) offered two types of benefit packages. The first option extended the maximum duration of EI benefit receipt to up to two years, conditional upon participation in training. The second option allowed earlier access to EI to workers using all or part of their severance pay package to invest in training. While the CTA was a promising initiative to expand income support and expedite re-employment support to the sub-group of displaced workers incurring the biggest losses, the take-up was very low.

Policy makers in Canada may wish to consider two alternative policy options to help address issues related to wage losses among older long-tenured displaced workers. The *first* is to extend duration of EI payment with a replacement rate that falls with the duration of unemployment. This can be a useful policy tool where individual search behaviour is an important influence on the likelihood of finding a job but income adequacy during unemployment is also a central policy consideration. *Another option* is to pilot several versions of a *Wage Insurance* (WI) scheme (an earnings subsidy that replaces a fraction of the difference between the wage in the old and the new job to workers who accept new jobs at lower pay) which is increasingly advocated as a good way to compensate part of the persistent earnings losses faced by some displaced workers, particularly older long-tenured workers. While WI is attractive in theory, there is limited experience available with large-scale schemes and the prudent approach would be to conduct pilot studies along the lines of the Earnings Supplement Project some years ago. Pilots should combine wage insurance with targeted job-search assistance and retraining options, a combination that reduces earnings losses by improving re-employment prospects and compensating some of the loss that remains. Such a combination has also led to improved take-up of similar earning supplement schemes in the past.

Providing effective re-employment support to find good-quality jobs quickly

Some displaced workers, especially those involved in mass layoffs, will benefit from the services offered before actual displacement by an Action centre (Ontario) or a CAR (Quebec). Some other displaced workers involved in smaller layoffs in Quebec can also benefit from the services offered by a CREC. But many displaced workers – especially those involved in small-scale or individual layoffs – will only have access to basic job-search assistance and will be left on their own to make use of the job-matching resources available through Service Canada or the local employment service agencies and providers. Furthermore, the interaction between severance payments and eligibility to EI means that some of these displaced workers are likely to delay their contact with Service Canada, and most likely also with the PES, until long after they become unemployed. This could delay their access to even basic re-employment support, such as job-matching services. These delays could help to explain why 52% of displaced workers do not find a job in the first year after displacement.

Policy makers therefore face two main challenges. The first challenge is to reach displaced workers earlier in their unemployment spell. A considerable share of displaced workers has not had to look for a job in many years. These workers would benefit from the early provision of information on the income support system, as well as about mainstream employment services and targeted programmes available to help them find a suitable new job. Such information sessions should explain the potential benefits of using self-service job-search support and offer basic training on how to use such support and how to prepare CVs. Follow-up could be encouraged by requiring participants in these information sessions to register with the PES.

The second challenge is to identify displaced workers who face above-average adjustment difficulties and to improve their access to more intensive employment support, while avoiding that unnecessarily intensive (and expensive) services are provided to jobseekers not needing them. Systematic early needs assessment for displaced workers can help to achieve this goal, especially when the outcome of the assessment is formalised in an individual action plan that can lead to early intervention when specific barriers to re-employment have been identified.

Needs assessment can also help in identifying training needs and targeting training subsidies to those with the biggest barriers. This is particularly relevant for the recently implemented *Canada Job Fund* (CJF) agreements with P/Ts, which include the delivery of the *Canada Job Grant* (CJG) to directly connect skills training with employers and help Canadians gain the skills required for available jobs. CJF provides incentives to employers to train individuals currently employed, underemployed or unemployed who could be a good fit for the firm with some level of training. Nevertheless, CJG risks subsidising training that is provided already as employers can also apply to train current employees who require training or retraining for either their current job or another position in the organisation. Tight targeting of publicly-funded training to vulnerable groups of workers and low-skilled unemployed who often miss out is critical for the success of the agreement, while also making sure to appeal to smaller companies that may lack the resources to provide training. For that reason, funding under the CJF also supports a broad range of employment services by helping those at the margin of the labour market by giving priority to individuals who are not eligible for EI and low-skilled employees. In addition, small businesses may benefit from flexible arrangements of the CJG.

In recent years, the federal and provincial governments have made considerable efforts to reach out to groups of displaced workers in greater need of re-employment support and training, especially older long-tenured workers which face larger barriers and suffer higher losses than their younger counterparts. Some of these programmes have shown considerable potential to fill the gap in the provision of more intensive re-employment services to displaced workers, provided they are made permanent and achieve adequate scale. For example, the *Second Career* programme in Ontario which provides additional adjustment assistance for older or long-tenured workers affected by economic restructuring and the *Targeted Initiative for Older Workers* (TIOW) programme that supports unemployed older workers with their reintegration into the labour market. The targeting of these programmes and the range of services that they offer differ somewhat, but they illustrate how a well-designed co-ordinated package of income and re-employment support can help reduce the adjustment costs associated with displacement. However, these schemes are often of a temporary nature with no guarantee that they will be continued in the future and, for some of them, have reached relatively few displaced workers, or in the case of TIOW, prior to Budget 2014, only applied to communities that have high unemployment or rely to a large extent on single industries.

Extra re-employment services for displaced workers are likely to be particularly desirable during an economic downturn, when the number of workers experiencing layoffs increases and their job-search prospects deteriorate. It is important that governments quickly scale up Active Labour Market Programmes (ALMPs) in a recession, while also shifting the mix of services away from immediate job placement towards more general types of training and counselling. Following the global financial crisis, the federal and provincial governments successfully reoriented and expanded existing employment and training programmes in an effective manner. That model should be held ready for future downturns.

Key policy recommendations

Easing the navigation of displaced workers through the multi-layered institutional system providing re-employment support

- Improve the co-ordination between federal and provincial governments in the design, implementation and delivery of re-employment support. Employment services need to be more client-oriented.

- Make steps towards bringing federal delivery of EI benefit and provincial delivery of employment service operations closer together. Co-location of federal and provincial services would be a first step but in the medium run a "one-stop-shop" structure, as put in place in many other OECD countries, would be ideal.

- Promote geographic mobility through the timely provision of labour market information and a reconciliation of differences in occupational standards across provinces.

Improving the effectiveness of prevention and early intervention measures

- Enhance the effectiveness of early intervention services offered to displaced workers affected by mass dismissals by raising incentives to co-operate for employers, employment services and workers who have been notified that they will be displaced.

- Experiment with extending early intervention services to workers affected by small-scale and individual displacement. For example, consider expanding permanent services such as the Comité d'aide au reclassement à entrées continues currently in use in Quebec.

- Connect people receiving severance pay to employment services earlier by delinking such services from eligibility for Employment Insurance benefits.

- Increase obligations for workers to actively search for a new job and register with the PES during their notice periods or as soon as workers are dismissed irrespective of whether they are in receipt of severance payments. Non-compliance should have consequences for access to *Employment Insurance*.

- Engage with employers to determine the appropriate employer share in the costs of the *Work-Sharing* programme and to determine what factors may contribute to programme uptake.

Key policy recommendations *(cont.)*

Addressing income adequacy needs of older long-tenured workers while maintaining work incentives

- Consider extending the duration of Employment Insurance benefits with a net replacement rate that falls with the duration of unemployment (similar to degressive benefit schemes that exist in several other OECD countries). Such extensions however should be accompanied by systematic monitoring of job search and mandatory participation in active labour market programmes.

- Develop and implement *Wage Insurance* pilot schemes for displaced workers with a focus on combining wage insurance with job-search support and other labour market programmes.

Providing early and effective re-employment support to displaced workers who need more intensive help

- Deliver systematic early information to displaced workers on income support, mainstream employment services and targeted programmes available to help them find a suitable new job. Make registration to the PES during these information sessions compulsory.

- Implement systematic early needs assessment for displaced workers, formalised in an individual action plan that can lead to an early intervention when specific barriers to re-employment have been identified.

- Expand the access of older long-tenured displaced workers to more intensive job-search assistance, case management and training, building on the experience with *Second Career* and the *Targeted Initiative for Older Workers.*

- Increase expenditures on active labour market programmes and strengthen the activation of displaced workers. Stand ready to ramp up ALMP spending, particularly for general skills training, should a deep economic downturn occur.

Chapter 1

Job displacement in Canada and its consequences

This chapter examines the prevalence and consequences of job displacement in Canada. Overall labour market performance has been relatively strong in recent years, due both to a longer-run trend improvement and greater resilience to the global financial crisis. Nonetheless, structural adjustment pressures are quite strong in the labour market and 2.2% of employees with at least one year of job tenure were displaced annually during 2000-10. Displaced workers are a very diverse group, but certain workforce groups are over-represented among them, including men, less-educated and blue-collar workers. There are significant adjustment costs associated with displacement, including the earnings losses associated with the time required to become re-employed and the lower wage on average in the new job. These losses are especially large for older and long-tenured workers. One source of these losses is that displaced workers sometimes become re-employed in different occupations that do not make full use of their skills.

As a basis for the policy analysis in the following chapters, this chapter analyses the incidence and consequences of job displacement in Canada, defined as involuntary job loss due to economic reasons such as firm closure or downsizing. The chapter is organised as follows: the next section reviews recent labour market developments in Canada. The following documents the incidence of job displacement. The third section discusses the re-employment prospects of displaced workers, while the next section analyses the costs they face when finding a new job in terms of wages losses and lower job quality. The last section focuses on changes in occupation and skills used on the job.

The Canadian labour market context

Recent labour market performance has outpaced that seen in many other OECD countries

The labour market in Canada has performed relatively well in recent years, partly due to a boom in natural resources exports.[1] Since 2000, the employment rate has climbed from a level lying between the OECD average and the US rate to being substantially higher than either (see Figure 1.1). Consequently, Canadian unemployment has transitioned from being above the US and OECD-average levels to being below both of these benchmarks during the global financial crisis (GFC) and up to 2013. Real wage growth has also been quite strong (see Figure 1.2). Despite this overall strong performance, the 2007-14 appreciation of the currency has intensified structural adjustment pressures in certain sectors, particularly manufacturing, raising concerns about displaced workers.

The Canadian labour market also exhibited greater resilience in 2009 than it had shown during the recession in the early 1990s.[2] Nevertheless, the GFC did result in substantial job losses and the unemployment rate remains slightly above its pre-crisis level. The unemployment rate (ILO definition) was 7.0% in the second quarter of 2014 (slightly below the OECD average at 7.5%), down from a peak of 8.5% in the third quarter of 2009. According to the 2014 *OECD Employment Outlook*, the recovery will continue in Canada bringing unemployment down to 6.5% by the end of 2015, still moderately above its pre-crisis level of 5.9%.

While overall unemployment in Canada has declined significantly since reaching its recessionary peak late in 2009, the share of the unemployed who have been out of work for a year or longer is still much higher than it was before the GFC (12.7% in 2013 as compared with 7.4% in 2007), although still much lower than in the United States and most European countries, and the number of long-term unemployed persons has more than doubled.[3] Experience in a number of OECD countries indicates that this group, which may contain a considerable number of displaced workers, often requires additional assistance to benefit from an improving labour market (OECD, 2013a).

Figure 1.1. **Employment and unemployment rates in Canada, the United States and the OECD area, 2000-14**

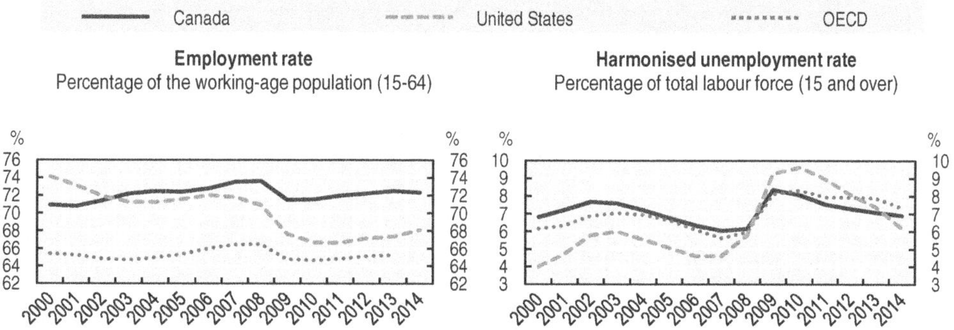

Note: For additional information on harmonised unemployment rates, see http://www.oecd.org/std/labour-stats/44743407.pdf.

Source: OECD Short-term Labour Market Statistics Database, www.oecd.org/statistics/ for harmonised unemployment rates; and *OECD Online Employment Database*, www.oecd.org/employment/database for employment rates.

StatLink http://dx.doi.org/10.1787/888933238470

The relatively strong resilience displayed by the Canadian economy and labour market in the wake of the GFC appears to have been the result of a number of positive factors.[4] Policies to support hard hit sectors like the automobile industry[5] also helped to offset the negative demand shock, as did strong private investment in the energy and mining projects and federal investments in infrastructure.[6]

Labour market policies, such as the federal Work-Sharing programme, also helped limit the job losses resulting from temporarily low production levels. Average weekly hours worked fell by about half an hour between 2007 and 2009 (resulting from cuts in overtime[7] and Work-Sharing, see Figure 1.2), reducing the pressure for layoffs. As will be discussed in Chapter 3, OECD analysis suggests that work-sharing programmes enabled a significant number of jobs to be preserved in a number of OECD countries during the GFC and probably also in Canada, even though take-up was much lower than in the much discussed case of *Kurzarbeit* in Germany.

Figure 1.2. **Change in real earnings[a] and hours worked[b] of dependent employees[c] in Canada, 2001-14**

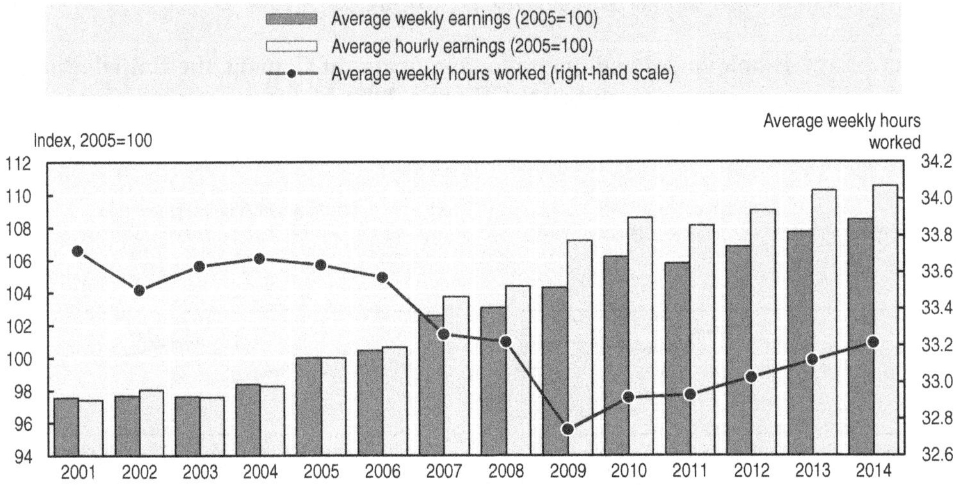

a) The earnings data, which include overtime pay and are based on gross taxable payroll before source deductions, are deflated using the consumer price index (CPI). Average weekly earnings are derived by dividing total weekly earnings by the total number of employees and average hourly earnings by dividing average weekly earnings by average weekly hours worked.

b) Average hours worked refers to the average of actual hours worked (including overtime) during the reference week in all jobs by employees who are currently working.

c) The data cover all industrial sectors except those primarily involved in agriculture, fishing and trapping, private household services, religious organisations and the military personnel of the defence services. Workers employed by businesses that could not be assigned a North American Industry Classification System (NAICS) code were excluded from the calculations.

Source: OECD estimates based on data from the Survey of Employment, Payrolls and Hours (SEPH), http://www23.statcan.gc.ca/imdb/p2SV.pl?Function=getSurvey&SDDS=2612.

StatLink *http://dx.doi.org/10.1787/888933238488*

Canadian employers appear to have gone to unusual lengths to preserve jobs during the recession, even when they did not participate in Work-Sharing. Employers may have anticipated possible labour shortages after the crisis (Burleton et al., 2013) and preferred to retain their most valuable employees through the economic downturn, rather than dismissing them and facing hiring difficulties after the crisis. Indeed, labour shortages were felt in some regions and sectors even during the crisis period (mining and energy in Alberta for example). The Canadian population is also ageing quickly and a large share of older workers will retire in the next decade, leading to forecasts of labour shortages that will particularly affect certain occupations (e.g. management) and sectors (e.g. public administration and education). Anticipation of these demographic changes by employers may also have helped to limit the fall in employment during the crisis in Canada.

Structural adjustment pressures are quite strong in the Canadian labour market

While overall employment in Canada grew from 14.8 million in 2000 to 17.8 million in 2014, this growth was not spread evenly across different industries. Indeed, manufacturing employment fell by 615 000 during this 14-year period (see Figure 1.3, Panel A), with more than half of that decline occurring since 2007. As a result, manufacturing now represents less than 10% of total employment, whereas it accounted for almost 16% in 2000. A number of factors contributed to declining employment in manufacturing, including the US "dot-com" recession at the beginning of this period, the sharp rise in the value of the Canadian dollar (CAD) in 2003, increased competition from low-wage countries such as China and weak global growth since the GFC. Agricultural employment also fell between 2000 and 2014 by a little more than 115 000 jobs.

By contrast, services, construction and mining provided substantial new employment opportunities. The service sectors accounted for the largest employment gains (3.0 million jobs over the period). Nonetheless, employment growth in mining and construction is likely to have been particularly important for production workers displaced from manufacturing, given the greater similarities in job skill requirements and employment conditions. Employment in the mining and energy sectors expanded by almost 170 000 jobs between 2000 and 2014,[8] while the construction sector grew by more than 550 000 jobs.

According to the Canadian Occupational Projection System (ESDC, 2013), job creation is projected to slow over the next decade (2013-22) in the primary, construction and services sectors, while employment in manufacturing is expected to stabilise (Figure 1.3, Panel B). Therefore, the employment distribution is projected to shift somewhat further towards the services and construction sectors. Changes in the industry composition of employment are only the visible tip of the iceberg of overall labour reallocation, as gross flows of labour across firms are huge in comparison with these net changes in stocks (Riddell, 2009). In Canada and the United States, roughly 10% of all jobs are destroyed each year while a comparable number of new jobs are created (Davis and Haltiwanger, 1999; and Baldwin et al., 1998). Even though job reallocations caused by sectorial shifts are small compared with job reallocation within sectors (Balakrishnan, 2008), the job displacement associated with shifts in the industry mix of employment tends to result in greater adjustment difficulties for the affected workers and is thus of particular importance for labour market policy.

Figure 1.3. **Employment by broad economic sectors**

A. Employment levels by sectors,[a] 2000 and 2014

Percentage of total employment[b]

B. Employment growth by sectors,[c] 2003-22

Average annual growth, percentages

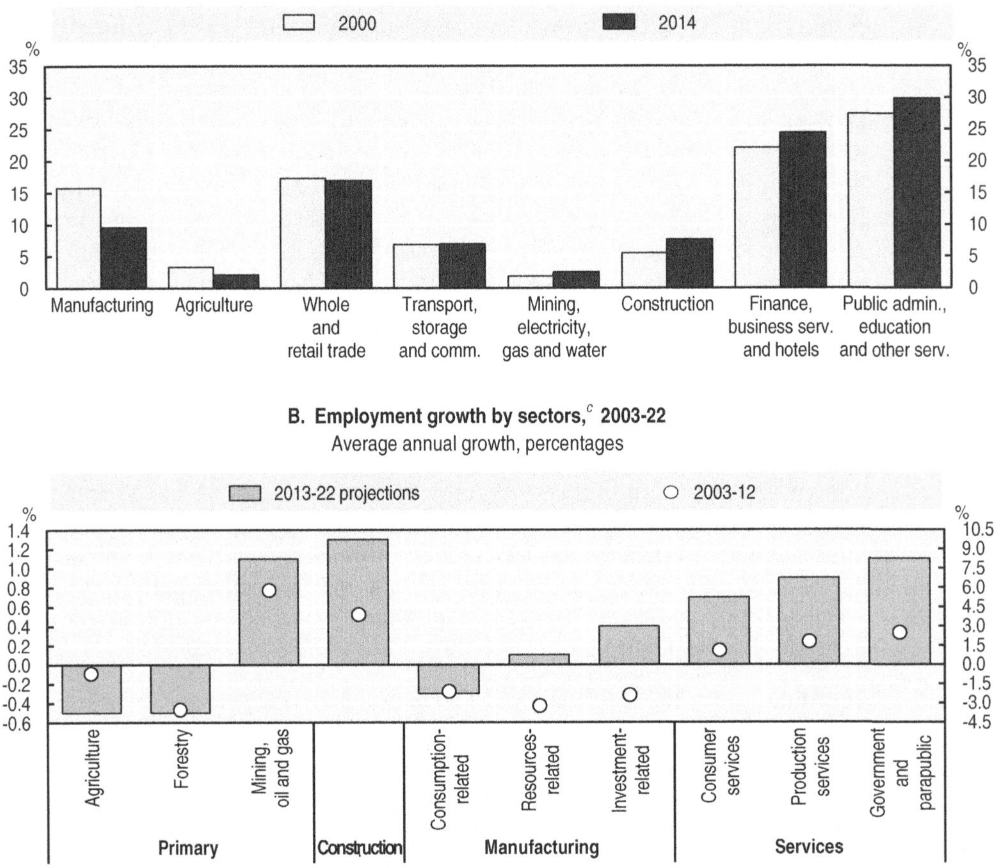

a) Economic activities classification based on Revision 3 of the International Standard Industrial Classification (ISIC). Figures differ from the one published by Statistics Canada, which uses the North American Industry Classification System (NAICS) rather than the ISIC one.

b) Sectors are ranked by ascending change over 2000-13.

c) Economic activities classification used is the NAICS.

Source: OECD Employment by Activities and Status (ALFS) Dataset, a subset of the *OECD Annual Labour Force Statistics* (ALFS) *Database*, http://dotstat.oecd.org/Index.aspx?DataSetCode=ALFS_POP_LABOUR for Panel A; and ESDC – Employment and Social Development Canada (2013), *Canadian Occupational Projection System projections – Industrial Scenario (2013-22)*, http://occupations.esdc.gc.ca/sppc-cops/content.jsp?cid=52&lang=en&preview=1#fig1 for Panel B.

StatLink *http://dx.doi.org/10.1787/888933238496*

Displaced workers: Incidence and characteristics

Job displacement – defined as involuntary job loss due to economic reasons such as firm closure or downsizing – has affected a significant number of workers each year since at least the late 1970s and many of these workers have experienced large and persistent earnings losses following permanent layoffs, especially long-tenured workers. The rest of this chapter provides a portrait of Canadian displaced workers and how they fare in the labour market.

Defining and measuring job separations

There are two main data sources available to study job separations in Canada. The first is the Longitudinal Worker File (LWF),[9] and the second is the Survey of Labour and Income Dynamics (SLID),[10] which is used in this report. For a comparison of the incidence of displacement using different data sources, see Morissette and Qiu (2012). So as to allow comparisons with other OECD countries, the empirical analysis adopts the internationally harmonised definition of displacement that was adopted in OECD (2013b).[11]

Labour turnover is high in Canada

In all OECD countries, labour turnover is high, particularly for recently hired workers, and job displacement represents only a modest share of all job separations. Figure 1.4 presents summary data on the average annual incidence of job separations in Canada during the period 2000-10,[12] differentiating between workers with less than a year of job tenure at the beginning of the year and those with a year or more of tenure. The many possible reasons for leaving a job are grouped here into four categories: i) job loss for economic reasons or dismissal (the displacement definition that will be examined in detail below for workers with more than one year of tenure in their previous job); ii) workers whose seasonal or temporary jobs ended; iii) other job separators who remained active in the labour market (predominantly, workers who voluntary quit their job in order to begin or search for another job, or who want to change their working conditions); and iv) a residual group of job separators who either withdraw from the labour force or for whom the reason for separating was not reported. The following patterns emerge:

- Nearly one-half of all workers with less than one year of tenure on their job will leave that job in the next year (46.7%), as compared with one in four workers who already had a year or more of tenure (25.4%). Very high turnover among low tenure workers is due to the seasonal/temporary nature of some jobs and the many reasons that a worker or employer can conclude that a new "job match" is not worthwhile pursuing.

- Job separations for economic reasons/dismissals account for only a modest share of all separations, both in the first year following hiring (6 percentage points of the 46.7% separation rate) and after a year or more of tenure (2.2 percentage points of the 25.4% separation rate). The ending of temporary and seasonal jobs accounts for nearly as many job separations among newly hired workers as do separations for economic reasons/dismissals, but this is not an important source of separations for workers with a year or more of tenure.

Any attempt to differentiate job leavers into displaced workers and other job separators is somewhat arbitrary. Nonetheless, it seems reasonable to consider workers who have already been in a job for at least a year and who then lose that job due to economic reasons, such as a plant closing or downsizing, as corresponding closely to the group of workers who experience involuntary job loss due to changing economic conditions and are potentially at risk of experiencing significant adjustment difficulties. In the rest of this review, only the first three of the four types of job separations that were defined above are analysed. The comparison group "other job separations" used in the rest of this review includes the ends of seasonal and temporary jobs, and other separations into a new job or job search.

Figure 1.4. **Annual average rate of job separations by reason, 2000-10**

Percentage of employees[a]

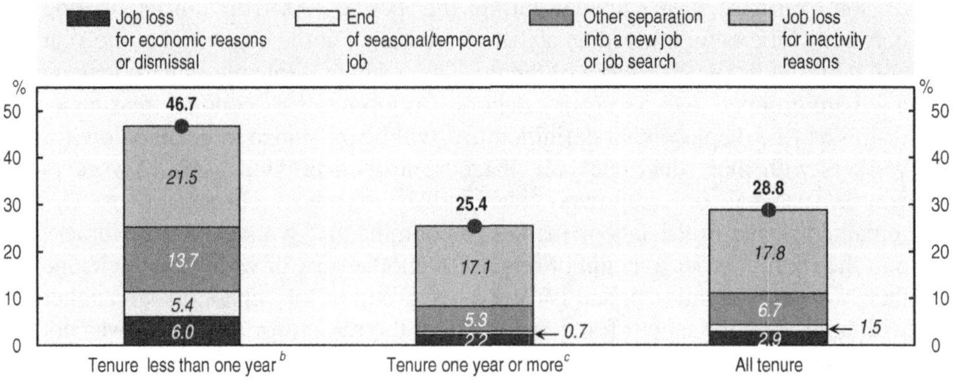

a) Employees in public administration, defence, community, social and personal service activities and extra-territorial organisations are excluded from these calculations.

b) Salaried workers with short tenure (less than one year) represent 16% of the sample.

c) Salaried workers with medium-long tenure (one year and over) represent 84% of the sample.

Source: OECD calculations based on data from the Survey of Labour and Income Dynamics (SLID).

StatLink http://dx.doi.org/10.1787/888933238503

Job displacement increased substantially during the GFC

Job displacements are defined as job separations where the reason given for leaving the previous job is economic (e.g. redundancy, layoff, business slowdown, lack of work, firm closure, mass dismissal, etc.) or dismissal for cause.[13] To avoid picking job separations that happen soon after hiring and may be the result of the firm and employee deciding they are not well-matched, the definition of job displacement and other job separations is restricted to workers with at least a year of job tenure. Figure 1.5 presents annual data on job displacement between 2000 and 2011 in Canada and the United States for workers with one year or more of tenure.

Figure 1.5. **Displacement rates in Canada and the United States, 2000-11**

Percentage of employees with one year or more of tenure

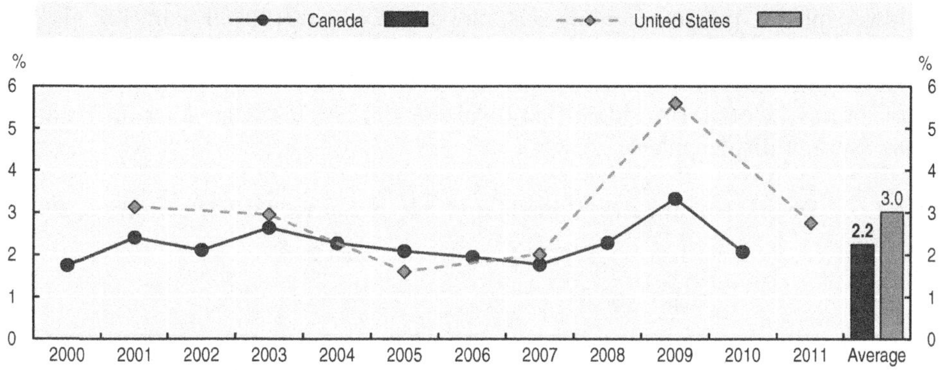

Source: OECD calculations based on data from the Survey of Labour and Income Dynamics (SLID) for Canada, and data from the US Census Bureau, Current Population Survey, the CPS Displaced Worker Supplement for the United States.

StatLink http://dx.doi.org/10.1787/888933238519

These annual data clearly indicate that the incidence of job displacement is counter-cyclical, increasing during recessions and decreasing when growth is strong. In particular, the displacement rate reached a recessionary peak of 3.3% in 2009, nearly double the 1.8% rate in 2007. As was noted above, the recessionary increase in the unemployment rate – and especially the incidence of long-term unemployment – has only gradually receded since reaching their recessionary peaks in 2009. By contrast, the displacement rate had already fallen back to 2.1% in 2010. Other types of separations show very different cyclical patterns. Job losses due to the ending of seasonal and temporary jobs are essentially acyclic and remained stable at around 0.7% every year since 2000. Job separations for other (mostly voluntary) reasons are pro-cyclical since it is easier to find a new and better job when the labour market is relatively tight and there is a lot of hiring. The share of workers separating to move to another job declined from an average of 5.6% during 2000-08 to less than 4% in 2009, when the labour market opportunities were particularly poor.

The incidence of displacement in Canada is near the international average…

Displacement rates in Canada lie in the lower-middle part of the range of rates calculated for seven OECD countries where displacement is defined in the same way as is done here for Canada and implemented using more or less comparable household survey data (see "self-defined displacement" in Figure 1.6). In these countries, displacement rate ranges from 1.4% in Japan to 4.3% in Korea. With rates near 2%, Canada and France have a lower-middle position within this range (OECD, 2013b). Figure 1.6 also presents displacement rates for seven countries that were calculated using employment data for firms to estimate which workers lost their jobs as part of a mass layoff ("firm-identified displacement"). This is a rather different measure of displacement.

Figure 1.6. **Displacement rates, Canada and selected other OECD countries, 2000-10**

Percentage of employees aged 20-64 who are displaced from one year to the next

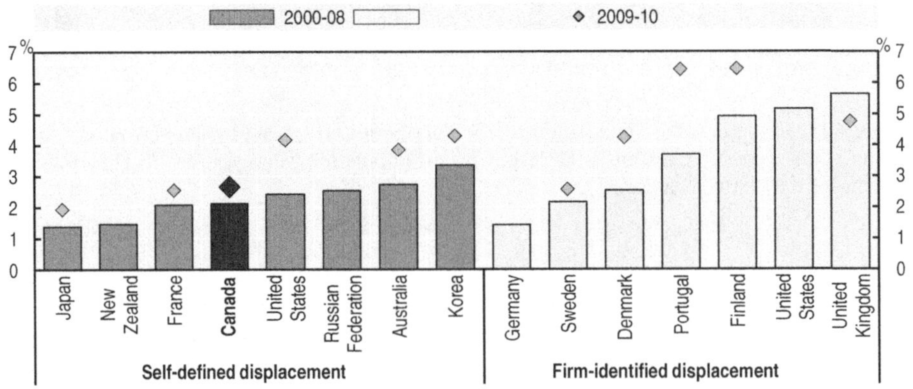

Note: See Annex 4.A1 of OECD (2013) for details on the samples, years and definitions used for each country.

Source: OECD (2013), "Back to work: Re-employment, earnings and skill use after displacement", Final Report, Directorate for Employment Labour and Social Affairs, OECD Publishing, Paris, October, www.oecd.org/els/emp/Backtowork-report.pdf.

StatLink http://dx.doi.org/10.1787/888933238529

Thus, the relatively low level of employment protection in Canada (see Chapter 3) does not translate into particularly high levels of job displacement as might have been expected. Even though the legal restrictions on dismissing workers are relatively light, employers appear to make extensive use of alternative adjustment mechanisms when reducing staffing levels, including relying on voluntary attrition, the expiration of temporary contracts and temporary layoffs.[14]

... with large regional disparities

Across provinces for 2000-08, higher-than-average unemployment rates are clearly associated with higher-than-average displacement rates (Figure 1.7). This pattern suggests that displaced workers often live in regions where job opportunities are relatively scarce; raising the possibility that migration to areas with more buoyant labour markets could improve the prospects of displaced workers for getting back into suitable jobs quickly.

Figure 1.7. **Displacement and unemployment rates across provinces, 2000-08**

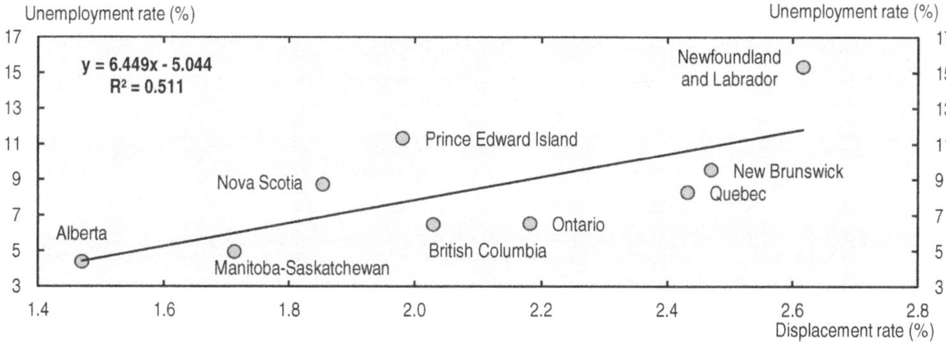

Source: OECD calculations based on data from the Survey of Labour and Income Dynamics (SLID) for displacement and *Statistics Canada Key Socioeconomic Database* (CANSIM), http://www5.statcan.gc.ca/cansim/a01?lang=eng for unemployment rates (average of monthly unemployment rates over the period 2000-08).

StatLink http://dx.doi.org/10.1787/888933238536

Large regional differences in labour market performance represent a long standing concern in Canada that has recently been heightened by the natural resources boom in the west (Parliamentary Budget Officer, 2014). In 2013, unemployment rates ranged from around 4% in Alberta and Saskatchewan, where many employers express concern about skill shortages in construction and mining, to double-digit levels in New Brunswick,

Prince Edward Island and Newfoundland and Labrador. The unemployment rates in Ontario and Quebec are 7.7% and 7.8%, respectively, slightly above the national average of 7.5%. Minimising disparities in regional labour markets and skills mismatches is thus an important issue for labour market policies in Canada. As such, policies that facilitate labour mobility across P/Ts, as well as intra-provinces, are of particular interest. However, the characteristics of displaced workers, such as how well their skills profile matches job openings elsewhere and the extent to which linguistic, cultural, and institutional barriers limit their geographic mobility, probably mean that migration is only a viable option for some of them.

How do displaced workers differ from other job separators and job stayers?

Relative to other job separators, displaced workers in Canada are disproportionately male, older and with greater job tenure (Figure 1.8). These differences by age and tenure reflect the greater tendency for younger and short-tenured workers to voluntarily quit their current job for the purpose of accepting or searching for a new job that better suites their needs and aspirations. Compared with other job changers, displaced workers may thus lose considerably more firm-specific human capital. They may also not have any recent job-search experience with and thus may be more in need of job-search assistance than other job changers. Job stayers look very much like displaced workers in terms of their ages, but have even more job tenure. For example, 42% of job stayers have ten or more years of tenure, consistent with the risk of displacement tending to fall as job tenure rises.

Displaced workers are less educated than either other job separators or job stayers. The relatively lower educational attainment of displaced workers reflects, in part, the over-representation of older and blue-collar workers in this group. Nonetheless, displaced workers should not be considered to be generally poorly educated. One-half of all displaced workers have a post-secondary education while only 18% have less than a high school education.

Figure 1.8. **Selected characteristics of displaced workers compared with other job separators[a] and job stayers, 2000-10**

Percentage of all workers in each group

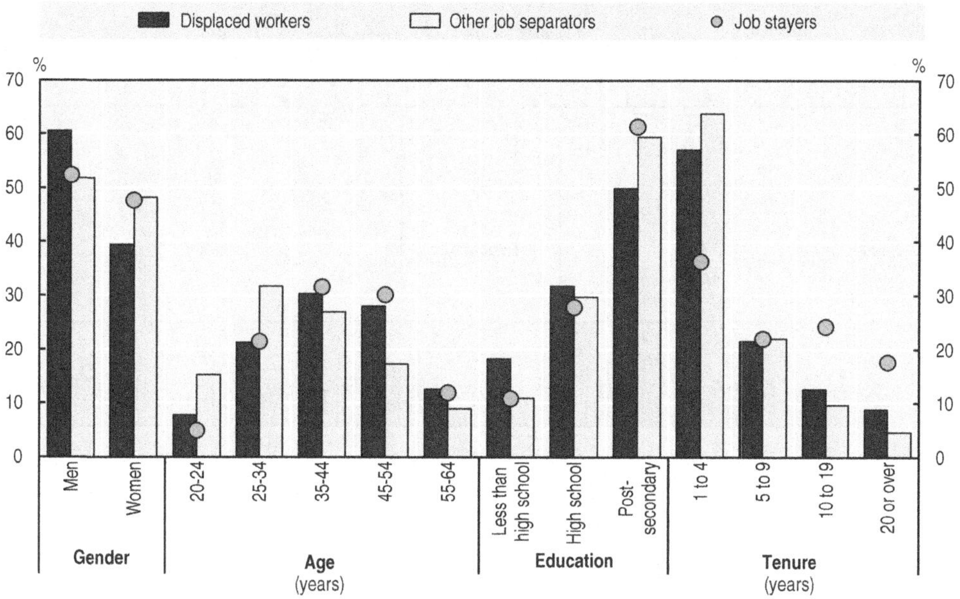

a) Other job separators include workers whose seasonal/temporary jobs ended as well as those leaving their jobs to begin or search for another job.

Source: OECD calculations based on data from the Survey of Labour and Income Dynamics (SLID).

StatLink *http://dx.doi.org/10.1787/888933238547*

Who is more at risk of being displaced?

Some groups of workers experience a higher displacement rate than others. For example, Figure 1.9 shows that men have a higher displacement rate (2.4%) than women (1.8%). Age differences tend to be small, except that displacement rates were somewhat higher for young adults (aged 20-24 years), particularly during the 2009-10 recessionary period. By contrast, displacement rates fall sharply with educational attainment and job tenure. They also differ significantly across broad industrial sector (being particularly high in construction and to a lesser extent in manufacturing)[15] and occupation (being particularly high in manual occupations, including crafts and the skilled trades).

Figure 1.9. **Displacement rates by characteristics, 2000-10**

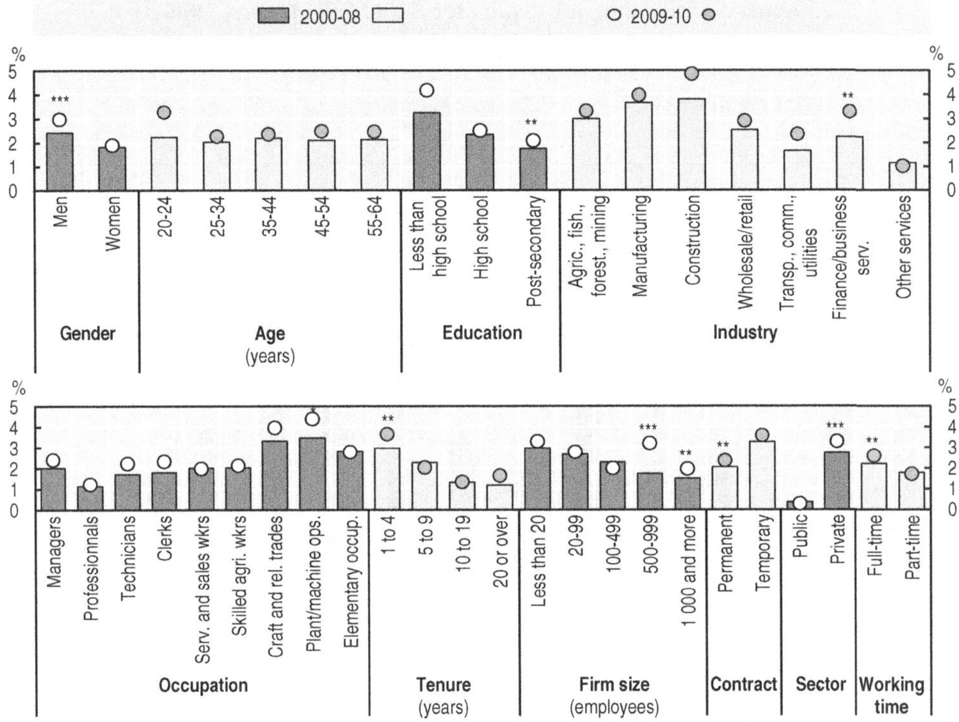

***, **, * Indicate that the difference between pre-crisis (2000-08) and crisis period (2009-10) is significant at the 1%, 5% and 10% levels, respectively.

Source: OECD calculations based on data from the Survey of Labour and Income Dynamics (SLID).

StatLink http://dx.doi.org/10.1787/888933238556

The simple comparison of displacement rates provided by Figure 1.9 is not a reliable guide as to which factors determine which workers will be displaced in a causal sense. Multivariate analysis isolating the causal effect of different worker and job characteristics from compositional effects (e.g. the concentration of men in high displacement jobs) provides a different picture (see Annex Figure 1.A1.1): men are not more at risk of being displaced than women, all other things equal, nor are low-skilled who are just more likely to be employed in higher risk sectors. On the other hand, the risk of job displacement rises with age beyond age 34 whereas long-tenured workers have a lower probability of displacement (-0.9 percentage points). Tenure typically rises with age and thus depresses displacement rates for older workers. However, older workers with relatively short job tenure are particularly vulnerable to being displaced. The type of job held also influences the risk of displacement. Workers in agriculture and the manufacturing sector are the most at risk of displacement, as are employees in small firms (less than 20 employees).

Labour market outcomes following displacement

One displaced worker out of two gets back into work within one year…

Just under half of Canadian displaced workers are re-employed within one year after displacement, and almost two-thirds are re-employed within two years (see Figure 1.10, Panel A).[16] The re-employment level of displaced workers then stabilises with no further increase within the third year after displacement and even a small decrease in the fourth year (down to 60%). Other job separators have significantly better re-employment perspectives than displaced workers (see Figure 1.10, Panel B). Almost 70% of this group are in employment within a year following job loss, as compared to only 48% of displaced workers. Two years after the job separation, this re-employment gap narrows from 21 to 6 percentage points.

The first-year re-employment gap between displaced workers and other separators is near the national average in British Colombia, Ontario, Quebec, and in the three Maritime provinces (Prince Edward Island, Nova Scotia and New Brunswick). However, the gap is much smaller in Alberta and, to a lesser extent, Manitoba, where unemployment rates are very low and the re-employment rate is high for both categories of job separators. The gap is also relatively small in Newfoundland and Labrador, where the unemployment rate is very high and re-employment perspectives are nearly as poor for other job separators as they are for displaced workers. This complex pattern suggests that it may be more useful for labour market programmes to single out displaced workers for extra re-employment assistance in regions with intermediate levels of unemployment, than in regions with very low or very high unemployment.

International comparisons of re-employment rates of displaced workers suggest that there could be some scope for improvement in Canada (Figure 1.10, Panel C).[17] Re-employment rates are significantly higher in Australia, New Zealand and the United States and some of the European countries such as Finland and Sweden. However, Canada performs better than France. Re-employment rates fell during the "Great Recession" in all countries where pre- and post-crisis rates could be compared, but less so in Canada. The first-year re-employment rate of Canadian displaced workers fell by 4 percentage points during the GFC (from 49% in 2000-08 to 45% in 2009-10), whereas it dropped by 17 percentage points in the United States over the same period (from 58% to 41%), for example.

Figure 1.10. **Re-employment rates after displacement, 2000-10**

Percentages

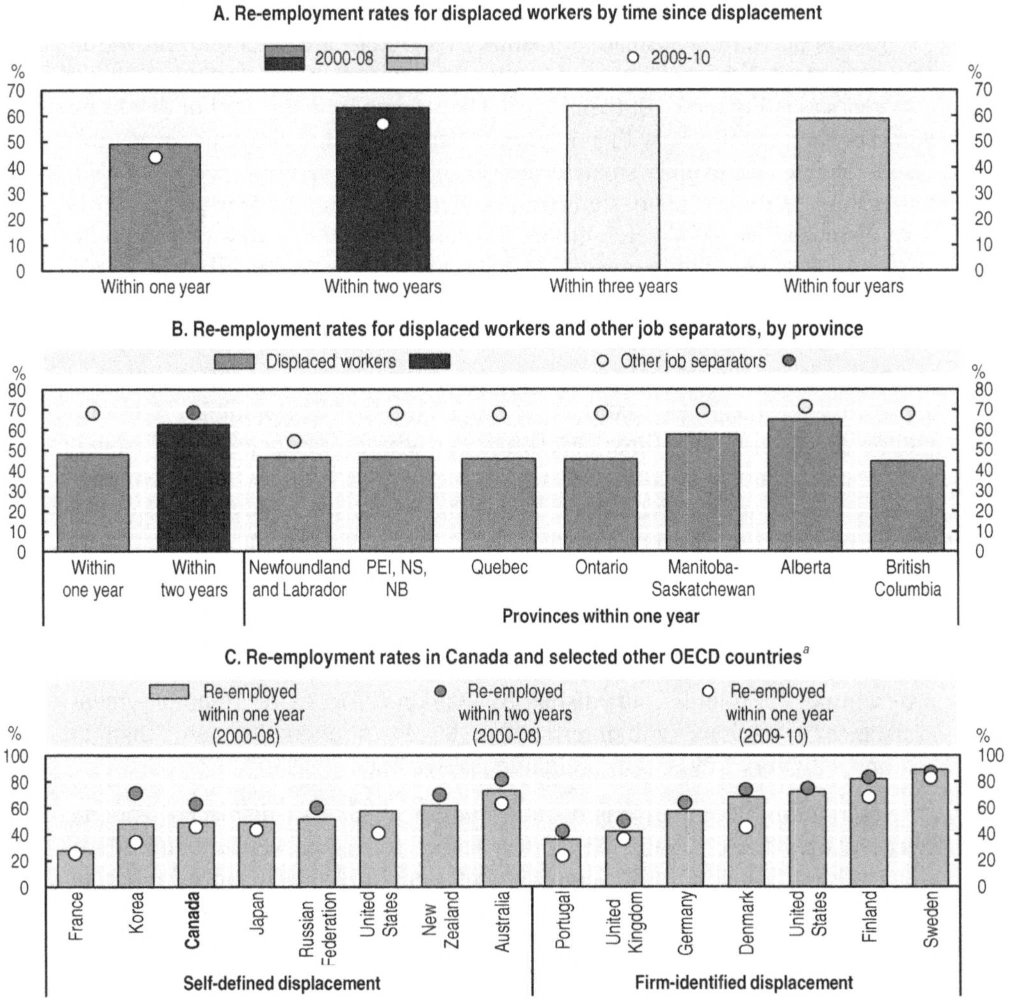

Note: NB: New Brunswick, NS: Nova Scotia, PEI: Prince Edward Island.

a) Data for Germany are for 2004. For Australia, Canada, France, Korea, New Zealand and the Russian Federation, data refer to workers displaced due to economic reasons, end of a temporary contract or for cause. For other countries, data refer to workers displaced due to a mass layoff or firm closure. For full details of the data sources and methodology, see OECD (2013).

Source: OECD calculations based on data from the Survey of Labour and Income Dynamics (SLID) for Canada; and OECD (2013), "Back to work: Re-employment, earnings and skill use after displacement", Final Report, Directorate for Employment Labour and Social Affairs, OECD Publishing, Paris, October, http://www.oecd.org/els/emp/Backtowork-report.pdf.

StatLink http://dx.doi.org/10.1787/888933238563

... but older and long-tenured displaced workers struggle to find new jobs

The probability of re-employment after displacement varies considerably across different groups of Canadian workers. In particular, the first-year re-employment rate is higher for men than for women, it increases with education and decreases with age and job tenure (see Figure 1.11). Long-tenured workers (20 years and over) have been particularly affected by the worsening economic conditions, as their re-employment rate fell by 12 percentage points during the GFC (from 46% in 2000-08 to 34% in 2009-10). Workers displaced from manufacturing and finance faced the worst re-employment perspectives. Surprisingly, the re-employment rate of workers displaced from manufacturing and construction rose during the crisis. This could be due to the construction and mining boom, which increased the re-employment opportunities for workers displaced from these sectors or others with occupations requiring similar skills.

Figure 1.11. **Re-employment rates of displaced workers by characteristics, 2000-10**

Percentages

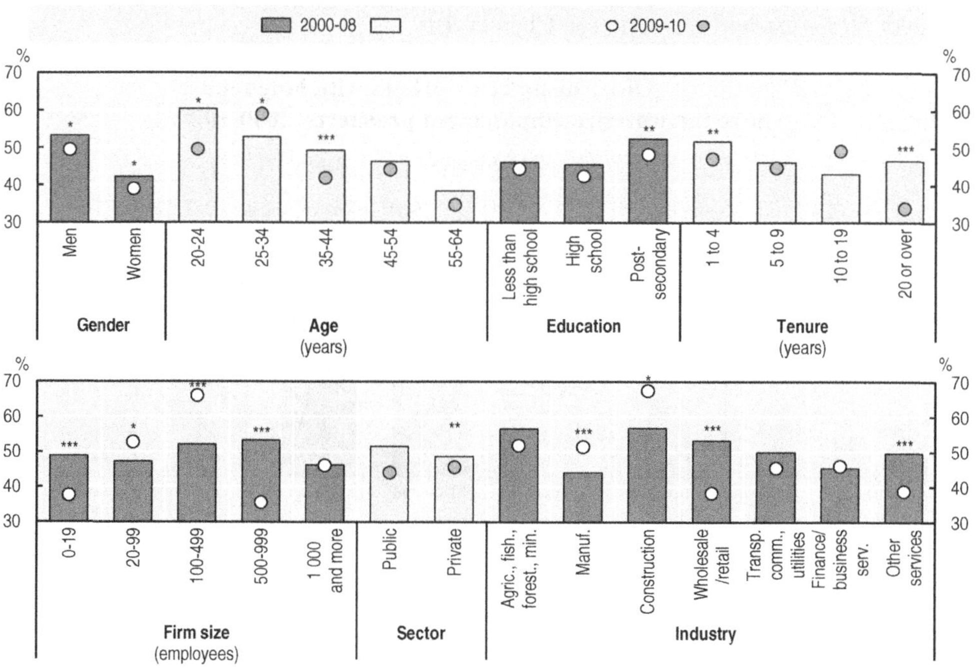

***, **, * Indicate that the difference between pre-crisis (2000-08) and crisis period (2009-10) is significant at the 1%, 5% and 10% levels, respectively.

Source: OECD calculations based on data from the Survey of Labour and Income Dynamics (SLID).

StatLink http://dx.doi.org/10.1787/888933238573

Differences in average re-employment rates can conceal compositional effects that obscure which factors causally determine re-employment success. Controlling for other characteristics, only gender and age remain highly significant determinants of re-employment probabilities (Figure 1.A1.2). Women are around ten percentage points less likely to be re-employed within a year of displacement than their male counterparts, while workers aged 55-64 have a probability of re-employment that is 14 percentage points lower than workers aged 25-34. For both groups, this may reflect greater barriers to finding a suitable new job but also a greater propensity to withdraw from the labour force.

The gap in re-employment rates between prime-age workers with long job tenure and older workers with long tenure is large (52% and 32%, respectively), suggesting that the impact of long job tenure on re-employment varies with age (Figure 1.12). A follow-up study among older workers who exhausted regular EI in the 1990s illustrated that among those aged 45-59 (who are not eligible for Canada Pension Plan benefits), about one-quarter have "retired" within five years post-displacement[18] (Finnie et al., 2011), raising the issue of the adequacy of income support for older long-tenured workers (see Chapter 4).

Figure 1.12. **Older displaced workers with long tenure have the worst re-employment prospects, 2000-10**

Percentages

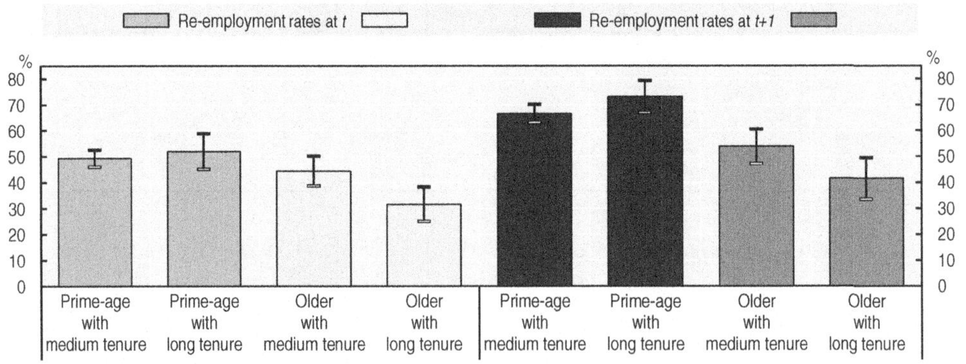

Note: The whisker symbol represents the 95% confidence interval.

Source: OECD calculations based on data from the Survey of Labour and Income Dynamics (SLID).

StatLink http://dx.doi.org/10.1787/888933238583

What happens to non-employed displaced workers?

An understanding of the situation of displaced workers who do not find re-employment could be a help in identifying policies that can prevent long-term unemployment and permanent labour market withdrawal after displacement. In the first year following displacement, 60% of the displaced workers who are not in employment are unemployed and actively looking for a job (Figure 1.13). Very few retire or pursue education (Frenette et al., 2011), although this varies by age, with young workers more likely to be studying full-time after displacement and older workers more likely to retire. Women are less likely to search actively for a new job after displacement and more likely to withdraw from the labour force than men, although not predominantly through retirement or education. The percentage of displaced workers becoming unemployed was higher in 2009-10, when labour market conditions were relatively poor, than during 2000-08. Two years after displacement, only 37% of displaced workers who are *not in employment* are still actively searching for work.

Figure 1.13. **Main activity after displacement, 2000-10**

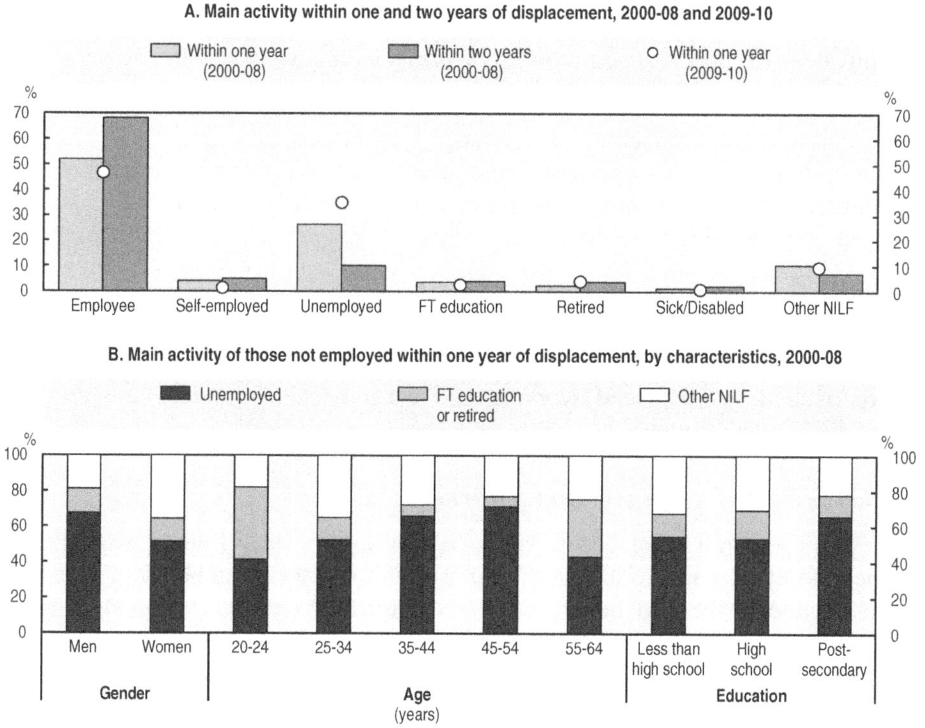

Note: FT: Full time; NILF: Not in the labour force.

Source: OECD calculations based on data from the Survey of Labour and Income Dynamics (SLID).

StatLink http://dx.doi.org/10.1787/888933238590

Change in wages and job characteristics following displacement

For the one-half of the displaced workers who find a new job within one year, wages and other employment conditions tend to be poorer in the new job than in their pre-displacement job.

Displacement leads to important losses in earnings…

According to SLID data (2000-10), even displaced workers who find a new job within the first year tend to experience important earning losses. One in five displaced workers face hourly wage cuts of 25% or more. On average, real annual earnings[19] fall 60% in the year following displacement, not taking benefit payments into account (Figures 1.14 and 1.15) and still remain 24% below its pre-displacement level two years after displacement. This fall in annual earnings reflects the combined effects of three components: a lower hourly wage[20] in the new job (displaced workers face a 1.9% decline compared with previous hourly wage); fewer annual working hours after displacement due to unemployment; and fewer working hours in the new job. The latter two taken together represent the equivalent of almost seven months of previous annual wage in the year of the displacement.

The earnings trajectory of displaced workers differs significantly from that for other job separators and, even more so, from job stayers (Figure 1.14). By contrast with displaced workers, other job losers experience a 7.6% increase in the hourly wage, rather than a decrease. However, both groups experience a large drop in annual earnings in the year following job separation. Other job separators experience a 43% decrease in real terms, because the time spent out of work represents 5.7 months earnings at previous annual wage. While large, this is smaller than the loss experienced by displaced workers and earnings also bounce back more rapidly for this group.

… especially for long-tenured workers

Long-tenured displaced workers face a significantly higher wage loss once they find a new position than those with shorter job tenure: an almost 6% decline in the real hourly wage, as compared with a 0.8% decline for their medium-tenured counterparts, and a 61% decline in annual earnings. The earnings losses following displacement are also more persistent for this group. Analysing the cost of displacement in Canada over the last three decades (1978-2008), Morissette, Qiu and Chan (2013) find that even five years after displacement, high-seniority workers and individuals with a formerly stable labour market attachment still experience annual earnings losses ranging from 10% to 18% compared with their previous job.

Figure 1.14. **Earnings before and after displacement compared with the earnings of other job separators and job stayers,[a] 2000-10**

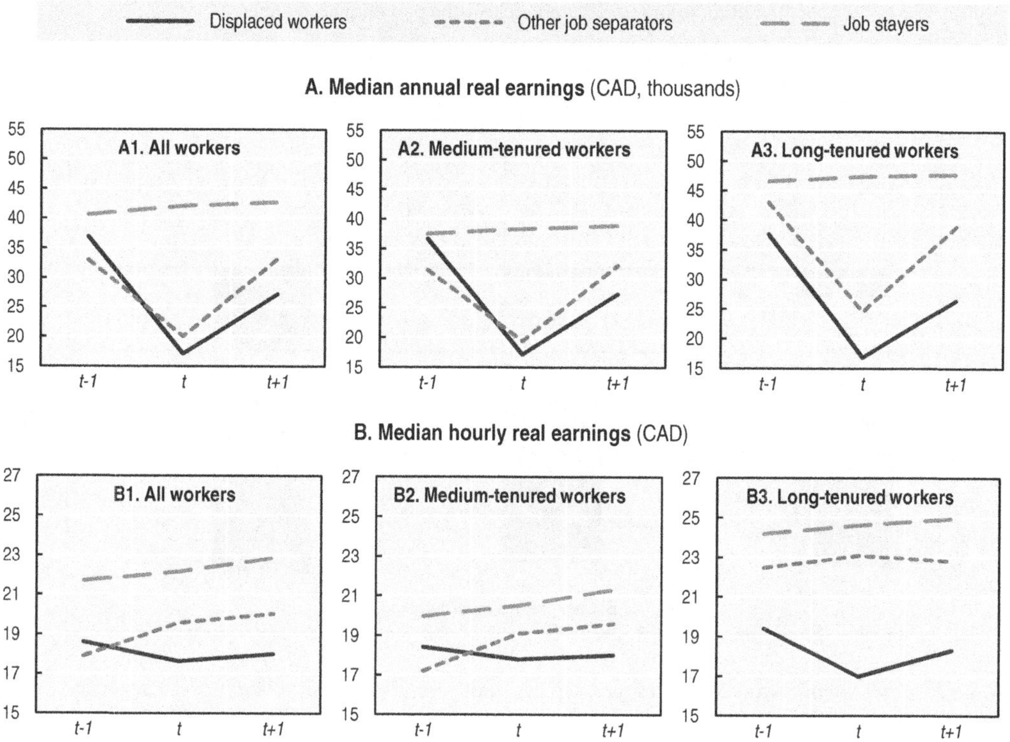

Note: CAD: Canadian dollars. *Medium-tenured* workers: one to nine years in previous job. *Long-tenured* workers: ten years and over.

a) The time period *t-1* corresponds to the year prior to displacement, year *t* to the year of displacement and year *t+1* to the second year following displacement.

Source: OECD calculations based on data from the Survey of Labour and Income Dynamics (SLID).

StatLink http://dx.doi.org/10.1787/888933238601

Figure 1.15. **First-year changes in earnings for displaced workers and other job separators, 2000-10**

Median hourly and annual earnings percentage changes

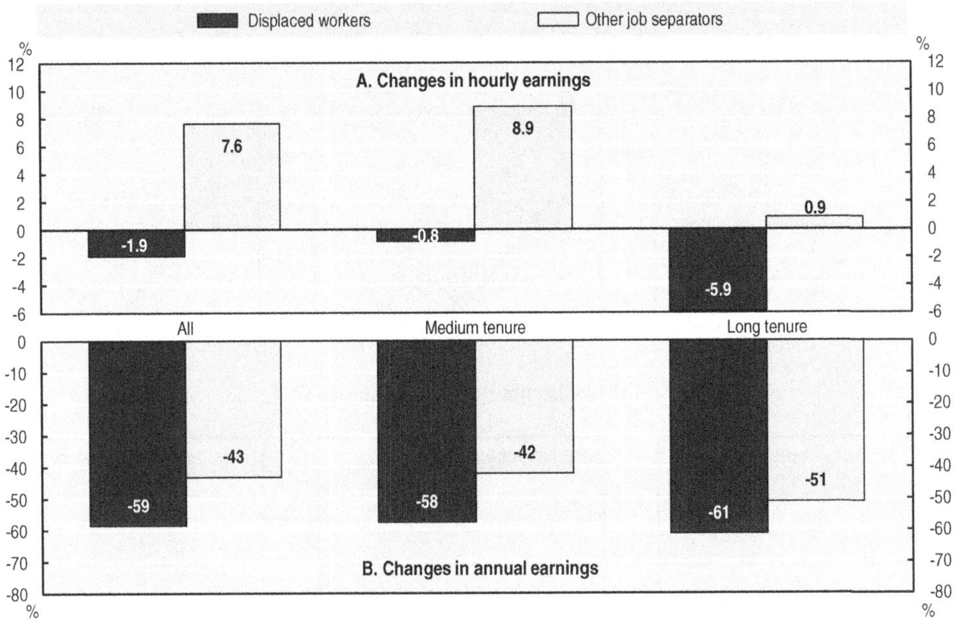

Note: Medium-tenured workers: 1 to 9 years in previous job. *Long-tenured* workers: 10 years and over.

Source: OECD calculations based on data from the Survey of Labour and Income Dynamics (SLID).

StatLink http://dx.doi.org/10.1787/888933238619

Looking more closely at the distribution of individual wage gains and losses reveals how almost all displaced workers experience a decline in annual earnings in the displacement year (see Figure 1.16). Only 10% experience no loss, while this is the case for more than 20% of other job separators. The first decile of the earnings change distribution (i.e. the 10% of displaced workers who suffered the greatest earnings losses) experienced annual earnings declines of 90% during the displacement year. Hourly wage changes indicate that fewer than 40% of other job separators became re-employed in a new job with a lower hourly pay than on the previous job, while this is the case for around 60% of displaced workers in the displacement year. The majority of job stayers experience small increases in both hourly and annual earnings.

Figure 1.16. **Cross-worker distribution of first-year earnings changes, by labour mobility status, 2000-10**

Percentage change in earnings between year *t-1* and year *t*

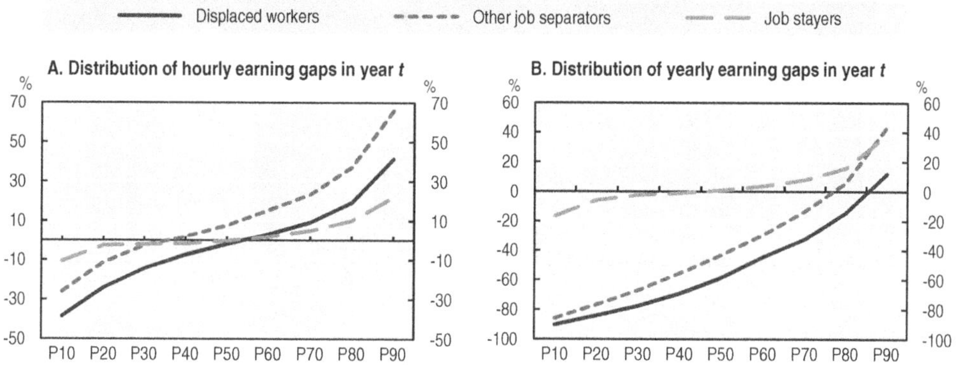

Source: OECD calculations based on data from the Survey of Labour and Income Dynamics (SLID).

StatLink http://dx.doi.org/10.1787/888933238621

Job quality worsens after displacement

Figure 1.17 shows that job quality also tend to worsen. Once re-employed, displaced workers are less likely to have permanent contracts (69%) than they were prior to displacement (87%), but more likely to work part time (15% compared with 9%). A lower proportion of displaced workers (14%) perceive their new job as a managerial position after displacement compared with their pre-displacement jobs (20%), and a lower share is covered by a Supplementary Pension Plan on their new job than was the case on their pre-displacement job (26% compared with 34%).[21] A small decrease in union membership also occurs.

Figure 1.17 also shows that both displaced workers and other job separators show considerable mobility across industry and occupation. Among re-employed displaced workers, 50% move to a different industry and 55% change occupation. This mobility across sectors and occupations probably explains a significant part of their wage loss, as these workers lose the wage premia they previously enjoyed for their industry and occupation-specific skills (see also Morissette et al., 2013). Geographic mobility appears to be quite low in Canada for displaced workers. Less than 1% of re-employed displaced workers move to a different province, compared with 3.5% among other job separators.

Figure 1.17. **Job characteristics of the re-employed displaced workers, 2000-10**

Percentages

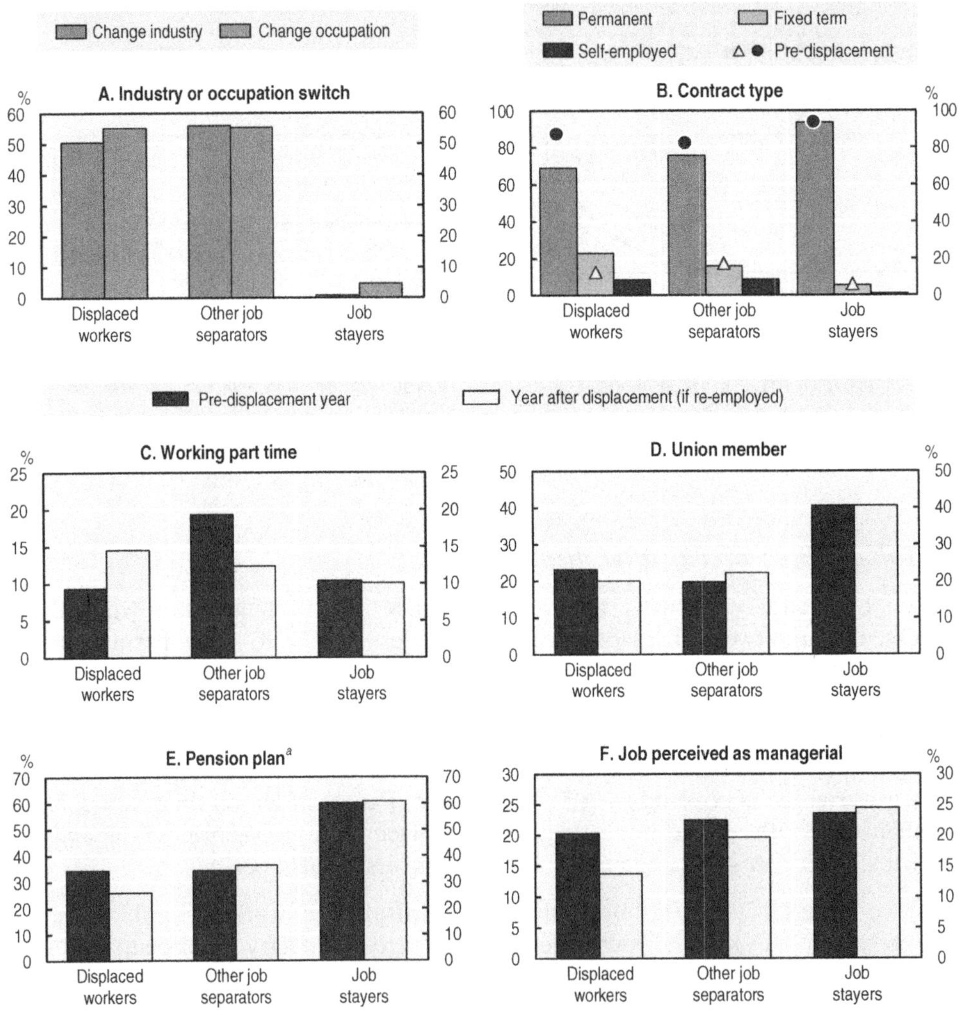

a) Pension plan: Person is covered by a pension plan connected with this job during the reference year [excluding *Canada Pension Plan* (CPP) and *Quebec Pension Plan* (QPP), deferred profit sharing plans or personal savings plans for retirement].

Source: OECD calculations based on data from the Survey of Labour and Income Dynamics (SLID).

StatLink http://dx.doi.org/10.1787/888933238630

How is skill use affected by job displacement?

Much of the research literature on job displacement attributes a significant share of wage losses upon re-employment to the loss of firm, industry and occupation-specific human capital. Similarly, Gendron (2011) finds that involuntary occupational movers in Canada suffer a wage penalty which increases with the distance in terms of skills requirements between the previous and new occupation. This section analyses changes in skill use between the pre- and post-displacement jobs, as this may explain part of the earnings losses associated with displacement as well as provide some indication of potential training needs. The analysis is based on the methodology used and explained in details in OECD (2013a).[22]

Occupational changes and changes in skill requirements

The typical set of skills used by displaced workers in their pre-displacement job is very different from the one used by the average employee (Figure 1.18). Displaced workers tend to use less interpersonal, verbal and cognitive skills than other employees in Canada. Conversely, displaced workers make much more use of craft and physical skills. OECD (2013a) highlighted similar skills gaps between all employees and displaced workers for other OECD countries, but Canada (along with Korea) stands out for the size of these skills differences.

Figure 1.18. **Skill use before displacement, 2000-10**

Difference in pre-displacement skill use between displaced workers and all employees[a]
(units of a standard deviation)

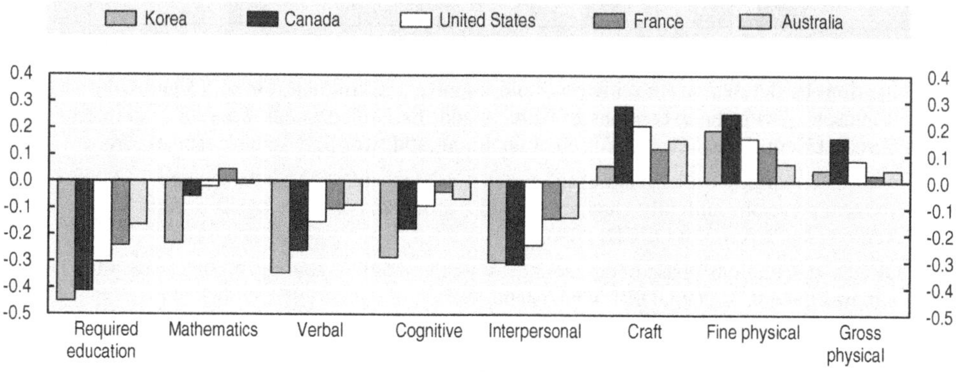

a) Skill requirements are measured by indices with mean zero and unit standard deviation (see Box 4.3 in OECD, 2013). This figure reports the difference in skill requirements between displaced workers and all employees.

Source: OECD calculations based on countries with similar source of data in OECD (2013), *OECD Employment Outlook 2013*, OECD Publishing, Paris, http://dx.doi.org/10.1787/empl_outlook-2013-en.

StatLink http://dx.doi.org/10.1787/888933238649

Figure 1.19 shows that 62% of the re-employed displaced workers change occupation in Canada, the highest level of the five OECD countries studied in OECD (2013a). If human capital were completely occupation-specific, this would imply important losses in skills used after displacement. However, the same skill often can be used in many occupations, and the three skills-related measures defined in OECD (2013a) (i.e. based on changes in the ranking of key skills at work, as well as changes in the intensity with which key skills are required at work) show that only a small proportion of displaced workers move to occupations with very different skill requirements.[23] In Canada, skill-based measures indicate that only 20 to 30% of displaced workers switch skills. OECD (2013a) also assesses how skills switches may explain post-displacement earning losses.[24]

Figure 1.19. **Changes in occupation and skills set after displacement, 2000-10**

Percentage of displaced workers who change occupation[a] and skills set[b]

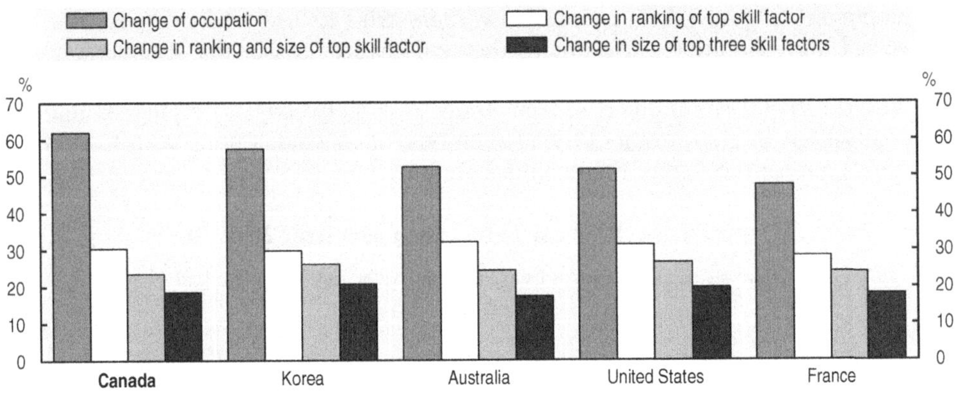

a) Occupation is defined at the International Standard Classification of Occupations (ISCO-88) two-digit level, with the exceptions of Canada and the United States where it is defined using the US Census Occupational Classification at the three- and two-digit levels, respectively.

b) For skills set changes, the ranking of the top factor is considered to have changed if it has fallen by at least two positions and only changes in skill factor sizes of at least half a standard deviation are considered (see Box 4.3 in OECD, 2013).

Source: OECD calculations based on countries with similar source of data in OECD (2013), *OECD Employment Outlook 2013*, OECD Publishing, Paris, http://dx.doi.org/10.1787/empl_outlook-2013-en.

StatLink http://dx.doi.org/10.1787/888933238650

Professional downgrading following displacement

Skill switches do not necessarily lead to professional downgrading. Some of the displaced workers who are re-employed in occupations with different skill requirements than their previous job may be moving to jobs with higher skill requirements.[25]

In Canada, approximately 6% of the re-employed displaced workers experience a skill switch accompanied by a professional downgrading and the same share experience a professional upgrading. Professional downgrading is more frequent in other OECD countries with comparable data, up to 8% in the United States and 12% in Australia, whereas professional upgrading happens about as often as in Canada (OECD, 2013a). This suggests that only a relatively small proportion of Canadian displaced workers suffer large human capital losses, but for them, the losses are likely to be important.

On average, displaced workers in Canada experience significant losses in verbal and interpersonal skills, more limited losses in mathematics and cognitive skills, and significant increases in craft and physical skills (Figure 1.20). The same qualitative pattern is observed in all of the other countries studied in OECD (2013b). In contrast, non-displaced job movers experience significant gains in all skill use categories, except in fine and gross physical skills. In particular, the new jobs held by voluntary movers make considerably greater use of their cognitive and social skills.

Figure 1.20. **Changes in skill use after displacement, 2000-10**

Average change in each skill factor (units of a standard deviation)

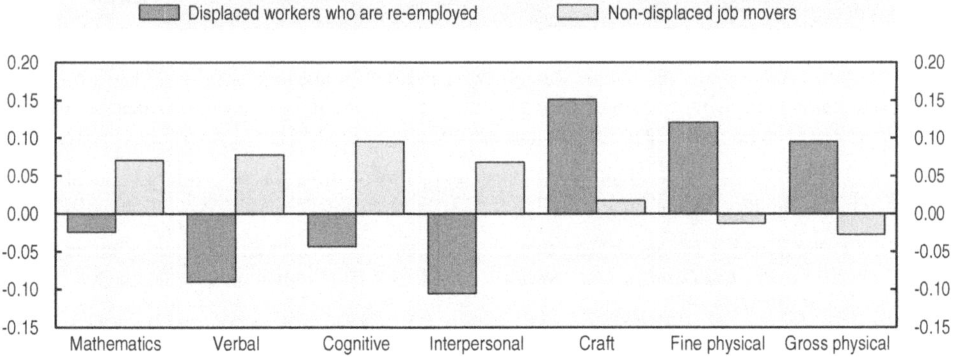

Source: OECD calculations based on data from the Survey of Labour and Income Dynamics (SLID).

StatLink http://dx.doi.org/10.1787/888933238668

Who is the most affected by skill losses after displacement?

In Canada, women are markedly more likely to experience skill switches – both downgrading and upgrading – than men (Figure 1.21). Professional downgrading is higher for young individuals than for prime-age or older displaced workers. Those with a low level of education experience skill switches less frequently, in particular skill upgrading. Improving the ability of low skilled displaced workers to retrain and access jobs in new sectors and new occupations is a major policy challenge. As expected, industry movers are significantly more likely to experience skills downgrading. Interestingly, they are also much more likely to experience skills upgrading.

Figure 1.21. **Skill switches[a] of displaced workers by nature of the switch and socio-demographic characteristics,[b] 2000-10**

Percentages

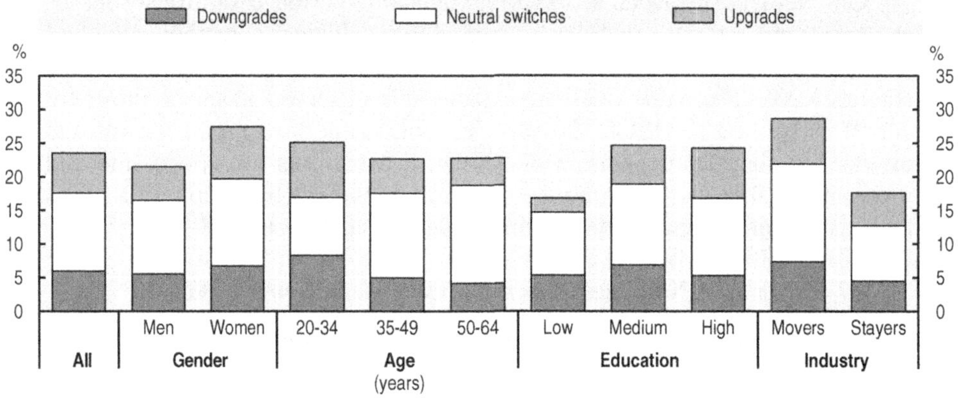

a) All skills switches are based on switch measure 2. Professional downgrading (upgrading) is defined as a skill switch accompanied by a fall (rise) in required years of education of at least one year; the remainder of the skill switches are defined as neutral (see Box 4.3 in OECD, 2013).

b) For education: *Low:* Less than secondary education; *Medium:* Secondary education; and *High:* Post-secondary education.

Source: OECD calculations based on data from the Survey of Labour and Income Dynamics (SLID), and OECD (2013), *OECD Employment Outlook 2013*, OECD Publishing, Paris, http://dx.doi.org/10.1787/empl_outlook-2013-en.

StatLink *http://dx.doi.org/10.1787/888933238670*

The analysis in this section confirms that among displaced workers who are re-employed within one year, about one in four find a job in an occupation that has significantly different skill requirements than they used on their prior job. In some cases, these changes represent large losses of human capital (or, at least the employment thereof) that in turn imply large and persistent losses of earnings potential.

Conclusion

Compared with most OECD countries, the Canadian labour market has performed quite well in recent years and showed considerable resilience during the 2008-09 GFC. Nonetheless, structural adjustment is a constant feature, as reflected in the fact that an average of 2.2% of Canadian workers with at least one year of job tenure were displaced annually during 2000-10. This displacement rate places Canada a little below the average of the seven countries the OECD has studied using approximately comparable data.

The incidence of displacement does not show any clear secular trend. However, it is clearly counter-cyclical and rose from 1.8% in 2007 to 3.3% in 2009 as the effects of the GFC were felt in the Canadian labour market. The displacement rate had already fallen back to 2.1% in 2010, as the recovery got underway. By contrast, large regional differences in displacement rates appear to be quite persistent, with above-average displacement rates being found in provinces where overall unemployment is also above the national average. Displacement rates are also relatively high in manufacturing, and blue-collar occupations. Helping individual displaced workers to reintegrate into appropriate jobs is thus closely connected to the challenge to reduce regional imbalances and skills mismatches.

Slightly less than one-half of all displaced workers are re-employed within one year, while almost two-thirds are re-employed within two years. Re-employment rates are lower for women (withdrawing more often from the labour market) than for men and also tend to decline with age and rise with education. Older displaced workers with long-job tenure experience the greatest difficulties in re-entering the labour market and face significantly higher and longer-lasting wage losses. Displaced workers show considerable mobility across occupations and industries, but much less across provinces. Overall re-employment rates for displaced workers are lower in Canada than in many other OECD countries.

Even displaced workers who become re-employed within the first year experience important earning losses. On average, real annual earnings fall 60% in the year following displacement. Since the hourly wage falls a much smaller 2%, it appears that much of the short-run loss in earnings reflects time out of work. Job quality along a number of other dimensions also tends to be lower in the post-displacement job. Compared with the jobs they lost, displaced workers are less likely to: have permanent employment contracts; work full time; hold managerial positions; or receive non-monetary compensation such as complementary pension plans on their new jobs.

The adjustment experience of displaced workers is very diverse but there are some regular patterns within all of this diversity that can help to target labour market programmes towards the workers facing the greatest barriers to successful adjustment.

It is inevitable that a considerable number of workers will be displaced every year in a flexible labour market. Indeed, the associated reallocation of workers from declining firms and sectors to growing firms can contribute to economic dynamism and growth. However, the costs can be high for the affected workers and governments have to consider how best labour market programmes can help displaced workers to maintain their living standards while finding suitable new jobs as quickly as possible.

Notes

1. An improvement in the economic performance of Quebec was also due to important infrastructure investments.

2. Unemployment peaks respectively reached 8.3% in 2009 and 11.4% in 1993, despite a sharper GDP contraction in 2009 (-2.8%) than in 1991 (-2.1%). Exploiting data covering a long time period including several previous recessions, the Parliamentary Budget Officer (2012) finds that Canada's labour market was not as negatively affected in the most recent downturn as it was during downturns in the 1980s and the 1990s.

3. The rise in long-term unemployment has been uneven across provinces. In Quebec, long-term unemployment remained quite stable between 2007 and 2010, and increased since 2011 to reach a level close to the national average (12.1%) in 2012/13. Ontario experienced the most significant increase in long-term unemployment since 2007/08 (+7.5 percentage points), reaching the highest level of all Canadian provinces in 2012/13 (CEIC, 2014).

4. Expansionary fiscal and monetary policy helped to cushion the fall in aggregate demand, as did the move by the federal government to provide guaranties to the financial system that helped prevent a sharp tightening of credit availability.

5. The Canadian automobile industry is extremely interdependent with its supply chain: for ten direct jobs in auto assembly, there are 36 jobs in motor-vehicle parts industry, manufacturing as well as non-manufacturing sectors (such as engineering, financial services, wholesale trade or transportation). Therefore, a shock to the supplier base caused by production disruptions at one of Canada's automakers would pose a

systemic risk and have negative implications for the long-term competitiveness of Canada's automotive sector. As a result, the governments of Canada and Ontario worked in partnership with the government of the United States to support the automobile sector. Combined support by Canadian governments, provided through loans and other instruments to General Motors and Chrysler, totalled about CAD 13.7 billion. The Department of Finance estimated that approximately 52 000 Canadian jobs were protected by this support to the automotive industry (Government of Canada, 2010).

6. This construction and mining boom, unseen in previous recessions, led to 675 000 job creations between 2000 and 2013 and might explain part of the greater resilience of the Canadian labour market during the most recent recession. Strong demand in the construction and mining sectors created many retraining opportunities for laid-off manufacturing workers, who suffered 592 000 job destructions over the same period.

7. The decline in the average weekly hours worked in Canada began before the crisis due to the cuts in overtime, and in the case of Quebec, the 2005-07 decline was equivalent to the one seen during the 2007-09 crisis period (around 30 minutes).

8. The strong employment growth in mining is concentrated in a few provinces in Western Canada (Saskatchewan, Alberta and British Columbia) and Newfoundland and Labrador, but limited in Quebec and Ontario.

9. LWF is a longitudinal administrative data set consisting of a 10% random sample of all Canadian workers. It provides a large sample that is highly representative of the Canadian population, but changes in the definition of mass layoffs make it difficult to analyse displaced workers in a coherent and comparable way over time.

10. This is a longitudinal household survey that allows workers to be followed over time and provides information on individual, job and firm characteristics. One limitation of the SLID data is that it provides relatively small samples of displaced workers. Overall patterns in the incidence of displacement and its consequences for affected workers can be analysed with reasonable reliability, but estimated differences in these patterns for very specific groups within the workforce and by regions should be interpreted with some caution. SLID data was also discontinued by Statistics Canada, and longitudinal estimates are only available up to and including 2010.

11. The sample is restricted to employees aged 20-64 years. Unpaid workers and multiple job holders (prior to displacement) are also excluded from the sample, as are employees in the public administration, defence,

community, social and personal service activities and extra-territorial organisations. No firm size threshold was applied as for other countries using the same self-defined definition of displacement.

12. These and all subsequent estimates in this chapter are based on confidential data from Statistics Canada's Survey of Labour and Income Dynamics (SLID). All computations on these micro data were prepared by Marc Gendron of Employment and Social Development Canada (ESDC) and Agnès Puymoyen and Gwenn Parent of the OECD Secretariat. The OECD Secretariat would like to thank Statistics Canada for allowing access to data. We also deeply thank Marc Gendron for the empirical work he performed on these data and for his investment in the project. The responsibility for the use and interpretation of these data is entirely that of the OECD Secretariat.

13. The latter reason typically would not be considered as representing job displacement, but was included since this type of separation could not be differentiated from economic dismissals for some of the countries studied.

14. Temporary layoffs are not considered as job displacement in the analysis reported here, if the worker is recalled by the same employer within the year.

15. Morissette and Qiu (2012) provide a comparative analysis of separations rates and worker reallocation in Canada using three data sets: LWF, Labour Force Survey (LFS) and SLID. Based on this detailed analysis, LWF estimates of permanent layoffs are fairly similar to those obtained from SLID using a layoff definition that includes end of contracts and of seasonal jobs (corresponding to our group of comparison). Therefore, results from Morisette, Qiu and Chan (2013) are not comparable with the present analysis.

16. Morisette, Qiu and Chan (2013) find significantly higher re-employment rates, with around 80% of workers laid off during the mid-2000s finding a paid job in the following year. In addition to the reasons listed above, the population included in MQC only considers workers 25-54 year old, leaving behind the hard to place older workers (55-64 years old displaced workers) who represent 13% of our sample and suffer from a significantly lower re-employment rate (38%).

17. OECD (2013a) describes the methods and data used in detail.

18. Retired in this evaluation refers to individuals that rely on pensions as their primary source of income.

19. This analysis is based on the total real annual earnings from the job in the reference year.

20. The hourly wage is calculated at the end of the reference year or at the end of the job, if it ended during the reference year. The amount includes tips, bonuses and commissions. For respondents who reported their wage

or salary at this job as an hourly amount, the value is taken directly. For respondents who reported their wage or salary on some other basis, the amount is converted to an hourly "implicit" rate using information provided like number of months worked, number of weeks worked and number of hours per week usually worked.

21. In addition to the public pension scheme that has near universal coverage of the workforce – *Canada Pension Plan* (or the *Quebec Pension Plan* in Quebec province) – employers can provide a *Supplementary Pension Plan*.

22. Since SLID data does not contain direct measures of skill use, data on occupations before and after displacement is linked with detailed information on skill requirements by occupation from the O*Net data source, allowing skill use and its changes after displacement to be studied. Following the methodology used and detailed in OECD (2013a), each occupation is associated with measures of required maths, verbal, cognitive, interpersonal, craft, and gross and fine physical skills and a measure of the number of years of education required. Once skill requirements are attached to each occupation, comparisons between occupations before and after displacement are relatively simple (see OECD (2013a) for more details about the methodology and definitions of skill switches used in this section).

23. Poletaev and Robinson (2008) find that wage losses following displacement in the United States are more closely associated with switching skill portfolios than switching industry or occupation per se.

24. Based on four countries – Denmark, Finland, Portugal and the United Kingdom –, the analysis shows that in all of these countries, changes in skills play a crucial role on earning losses. Displaced workers experiencing no change in skills-set (with or without changing industry) tend to experience the lowest earning penalties following displacement.

25. As explained in OECD (2013a), the measures of skills switching presented in Figure 1.19 are based on the ranking and changes in value of mathematics, verbal, cognitive, craft, interpersonal, gross physical and fine physical skills requirements. One way to disentangle between downgrading and upgrading skill switches is to measure the level of education required in their previous job, as well as their post-displacement job. A positive change in the number of years of education required between both jobs (of at least one year) is a signal that the person has moved up to a higher-level job while a negative change in required education points to a move down the career ladder.

References

Balakrishnan, R. (2008), "Canadian firm and job dynamics", *IMF Working Papers*, No WP/08/31, February, http://www.imf.org/external/pubs/ft/wp/2008/wp0831.pdf.

Baldwin, J., T. Dunne and J. Haltiwanger (1998), "A comparison of job creation and job destruction in Canada and the United States", *Review of Economics and Statistics,* Vol. 80, No. 3, pp. 347–356, August.

Burleton, D., S. Gulati, C. Mc Donald, S. Scarfone (2013), "Jobs in Canada. Where, what and for whom?", Special Report, TD Economics, October, http://www.td.com/document/PDF/economics/special/JobsInCanada.pdf.

CEIC – Canada Employment and Insurance Commission (2014), *2012/13 EI Monitoring and Assessment Report*, Canada Employment Insurance Commission, Employment and Social Development Canada [ESDC], March, http://www.esdc.gc.ca/en/reports/ei/monitoring2013/index.page?&_ga=1.233996382.1385248077.1426040236.

Davis, S.J. and J. Haltiwanger (1999), "Gross job flows", in O. Ashenfelter and D. Card (eds.), *Handbook of Labor Economics*, pp. 2711–2805, Elsevier, Amsterdam.

ESDC – Employment and Social Development Canada (2013), *Canadian Occupational Projection System projections – Industrial Scenario (2013-22)*, http://www23.hrsdc.gc.ca/c.4nt.2nt@-eng.jsp?cid=52&lang=en&preview=1#fig15.

Finnie, R., D. Gray, I. Irvine and Y. Zhang (2011), "The income sources for long-term workers who exhaust employment insurance benefits", Mowat Centre Employment Insurance Task Force Background Paper, Mowat Centre for Policy Innovation, School of Public Policy and Governance, University of Toronto, http://www.mowateitaskforce.ca/sites/default/files/Finnie.pdf.

Frenette, M., R. Upward and P. Wright (2011), "The long-term earnings impact of post-secondary education following job loss". Statistics Canada, Analytical Studies Branch – *Research Paper Series*, No. 334, March, http://www.statcan.gc.ca/pub/11f0019m/11f0019m2011334-eng.pdf.

Gendron, M. (2011), "The consequences of occupational mobility in Canada: How does a change of skills required by an occupation affect wages?", Information Note, HRSDC, Labour Market Policy Directorate, Canada.

Government of Canada (2010), *Canada's Economic Action Plan: A sixth report to Canadians*, September, http://www.fin.gc.ca/pub/report-rapport/2010-09-27/pdf/ceap-paec-2010-09-eng.pdf.

Morissette, R. and T. Qiu (2012), "Worker flows in the longitudinal worker file and other Canadian data sets", Statistics Canada, Social Analysis Division, mimeo, 10 April.

Morissette, R., H. Qiu and P.C.W. Chan (2013), "The risk and cost of job loss in Canada, 1978-2008", *Canadian Journal of Economics,* Vol. 46, Issue 4, pp. 1480-1509, November.

OECD (2013a), *OECD Employment Outlook 2013*, OECD Publishing, Paris, http://dx.doi.org/10.1787/empl_outlook-2013-en.

OECD (2013b), "Back to work: Re-employment, earnings and skill use after displacement", Final Report, Directorate for Employment Labour and Social Affairs, OECD Publishing, Paris, October, http://www.oecd.org/els/emp/Backtowork-report.pdf.

PBO – Parliamentary Budget Officer (2014), "Labour market assessment 2014", Office of the Parliament Budget Officer, 25 March, http://www.pbo-dpb.gc.ca/files/files/Labour_Note_EN.pdf.

PBO (2012), "An assessment of Canada's labour market performance", Office of the Parliamentary Budget Officer, 29 October, http://publications.gc.ca/collections/collection_2012/dpb-pbo/YN5-44-2012-eng.pdf.

Poletaev, M. and C. Robinson (2008), "Human capital specificity: Evidence from the dictionary of occupational titles and displaced worker surveys, 1984-2000", *Journal of Labor Economics*, Vol. 26, No. 3, July, pp. 387-420.

Riddell, W.C. (2009), "Economic change and worker displacement in Canada: Consequences and policy responses", Canadian Labour Market and Skills Researcher Network, *CLSRN Working Papers*, No. 33, July.

Database references

OECD Employment by Activities and Status (ALFS) *Dataset*, a subset of the *OECD Annual Labour Force Statistics* (ALFS) *Database*, http://dotstat.oecd.org/Index.aspx?DataSetCode=ALFS_POP_LABOUR.

OECD Online Employment Database, www.oecd.org/employment/database.

OECD Short-term Labour Market Statistics Database, www.oecd.org/statistics/.

Survey of Employment, Payrolls and Hours (SEPH), Statistics Canada, http://www23.statcan.gc.ca/imdb/p2SV.pl?Function=getSurvey&SDDS=2612.

Statistics Canada Key Socioeconomic Database (CANSIM), http://www5.statcan.gc.ca/cansim/a01?lang=eng.

Survey of Labour and Income Dynamics (SLID), confidential data, Statistics Canada, http://www23.statcan.gc.ca/imdb/p2SV.pl?Function=getSurvey&SDDS=3889.

Annex 1.A1

Supplementary figures

Figure 1.A1.1. **Marginal effect of selected characteristics on the likelihood of being displaced, 2000-10**

Percentage points

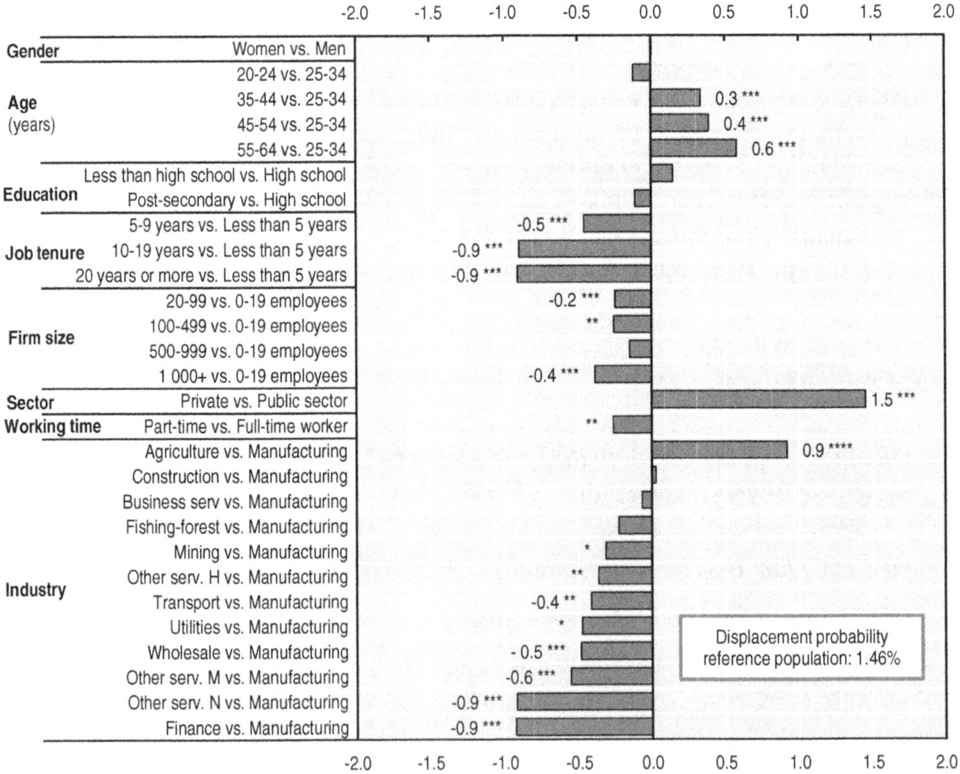

Source: OECD calculations based on data from the Survey of Labour and Income Dynamics (SLID). Marginal effects (in percentage points) of a logit estimation. Explained variable: displacement in year *t*. Explainable variables included in the estimation, but not displayed in the figure: occupation, rural/urban area, student, type of contract, province, year dummies. Non-permanent job can be either seasonal job, temporary term or contract job (non-seasonal), casual job, or work done through a temporary help agency.

StatLink http://dx.doi.org/10.1787/888933238681

Figure 1.A1.2. **Marginal effect of selected characteristics on the likelihood of re-employment, 2000-10**

Percentage points

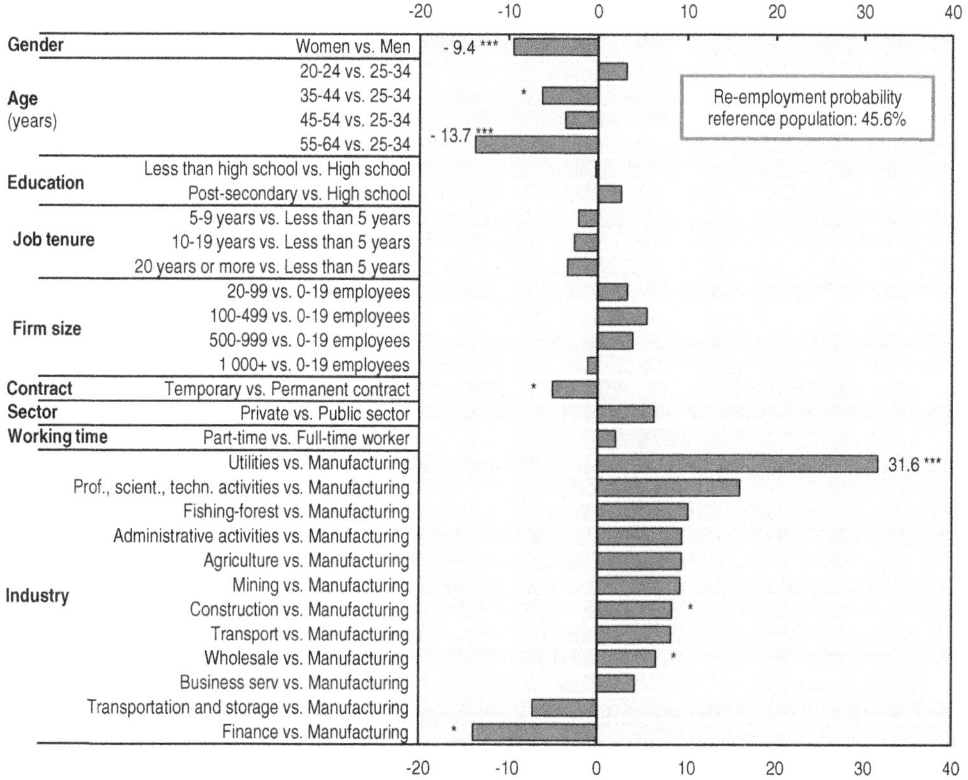

Source: OECD calculations based on data from the Survey of Labour and Income Dynamics (SLID). Marginal effects (in percentage points) of a logit estimation. Explained variable: re-employment within the same year than displacement. Explainable variables included in the estimation, but not displayed in the figure: occupation, rural/urban area, student, province, year dummies.

StatLink http://dx.doi.org/10.1787/888933238691

Chapter 2

Institutional setup of employment services in Canada

Canada is characterised by an institutional setting that combines a federal jurisdiction with 13 provincial and territorial jurisdictions. The OECD recommends promoting employment services more client-oriented than the existing system-oriented ones, improving the co-ordination between Federal and provincial governments in the implementation and delivery of employment services and considering gathering the delivery of Employment Insurance benefit and employment services in a "one-stop-shop" place. These changes would ease their way for unemployed and, among them, displaced workers to navigate the fragmented employment and skills system.

This chapter presents a brief overview of the institutional setup of labour market services in Canada. It looks at the division of responsibilities between the federal government and the provinces and territories, different ways employment and skills services are delivered to the unemployed in Canada, and the main issues arising from this institutional setting.

Division of responsibilities and budget between the federal government and the provinces and territories

Canada is characterised by a deeply rooted institutional setting combining a federal jurisdiction with 13 provincial and territorial jurisdictions. The federal government administers the *Employment Insurance* (EI) programme, which provides assistance to individuals who are laid off or are unable to work due to specific life circumstances and helps the unemployed across the country find employment (CEIC, 2014). The Canadian EI programme is funded by contributions from workers and employers and consists of two parts: EI-Part I provides income support benefits to eligible unemployed individuals and can be considered as the passive side of the labour market programme; EI-Part II provides active support such as job-search assistance and training, as well as the information and guidance necessary to find new and suitable employment (CEIC, 2014).

Part I of the EI programme provides temporary financial assistance to workers who have lost their job through no fault of their own while they look for work or upgrade their skills (see Chapter 4). The federal government is responsible for administering EI-Part I and Service Canada is in charge for delivering EI benefits to eligible unemployed workers (among many other responsibilities). Since its creation in 2005, Service Canada offices (and its web site) have been the place where Canadians go to get information on and access to a broad range of programmes, services and benefits provided by the Government of Canada. For example, Service Canada is the door displaced workers enter when claiming EI benefit.

Part II of the EI programme provides support to unemployed workers through active measures intended to help them prepare for, find and maintain employment. At the end of the 1990s, the federal government began decentralising the responsibility of delivering employment services through bilateral *Labour Market Development Agreements* (LMDAs, see Box 2.1) negotiated with the provinces and territories (P/Ts). The agreements were signed by the provinces and territories between 1996 and 2009 (Quebec 1997, Ontario 2007). Two sets of individually-negotiated agreements between each P/T and the Government of Canada now govern the decentralisation of the public employment service (PES). LMDAs provide funding and guidelines for provincial and territorial labour market programmes and employment services delivered to individuals who are (or recently were) eligible for EI (e.g. income benefits). Though not funded from EI sources, *Labour Market Agreements* (LMAs) renewed since through the *Canada Job Fund* (CJF) agreements, provide funding and guidelines for provincial and territorial labour market programmes and services for the unemployed who are not eligible for EI.

Box 2.1. **Agreements to foster employment service provision**

The Government of Canada funds employment services and skills development through different types of agreements that are negotiated with P/Ts:

- The **Labour Market Development Agreements** (LMDAs) provide federal funding for the P/Ts to design, deliver and manage skills and employment programmes for *EI-eligible* unemployed workers including active EI claimants and former claimants (who have had an EI claim in the last 36 months, or for whom a claim for maternity or parental benefits has been established within the 60 preceding months).
- While programme design and delivery are left to P/T authorities, it is specified that these funds should be used to promote the quick re-entry of the EI-eligible unemployed into jobs and the development of a skilled labour force that corresponds to employers' needs. The federal government provides annually around CAD 2 billion through LMDAs. In order to enhance the availability of training during the recession, the Budget 2009 allocated an additional CAD 1 billion over two years.
- From 2007 to 2014, the **Labour Market Agreements** (LMAs) provided federal funding to support skills development for unemployed workers who did not qualify for EI (such as long-term unemployed who have been out of work for a prolonged period of time). Through the LMAs, the Government of Canada also provided funding for P/T labour market programmes and services to employed persons who did not have a high school diploma or recognised certification, or had low literacy and essential skills. The federal government allocated annually CAD 500 million to LMA programming. An additional CAD 500 million over two years was allocated in Budget 2009 in training support through the LMAs, as a response to the recession. These agreements expired on 31 March 2014.
- The Government of Canada has renewed and transformed LMAs agreements with P/Ts into new **Canada Job Fund (CJF) agreements** to help equip Canadians with the skills and training they need to fill available jobs. These new six-year agreements (2014-20) include the Canada Job Grant (CJG) initiative (see Box 5.1) and aims at ensuring greater employer involvement in training decisions. Through the CJF agreements, the federal government continues to provide funding for a broad range of employment programmes and services designed and delivered by P/Ts and targeting the same public as former LMAs.

Box 2.1. **Agreements to foster employment service provision** *(cont.)*

- The **Labour Market Agreements for Persons with Disabilities** (LMAPDs) provide federal funding for the P/Ts to deliver programmes and services designed to improve the employment situation for persons with disabilities by enhancing their employability, increasing the employment opportunities and building on the existing knowledge base (sharing of information and best practices). The federal government provides annually around CAD 218 million to help approximately 300 000 persons with disabilities giving them access to over 100 programmes delivered by P/Ts.

Agreements between the federal government and P/Ts have been renegotiated several times. The federal government also reaffirmed in its Economic Action Plan 2014 that it would seek to renegotiate the terms and conditions of the LMDAs with all P/Ts to strengthen the alignment of training with labour market demand. The exact form and scope of the changes will emerge through discussions to be held with P/Ts, but the federal government has already identified areas of improvement including: increased emphasis on employer driven training, earlier engagement of the unemployed, serving a broader public and greater accountability and transparency to ensure they are receiving a return on their investment in EI. ESDC is expecting to have retooled amending agreements in place by 2015.

Source: CEIC – Canada Employment and Insurance Commission (2014), "EI monitoring and assessment report 2012/13", Employment and Social Development Canada, March, http://www12.hrsdc.gc.ca/servlet/sgpp-pmps-pub?lang=eng&curjsp=p.5bd.2t.1.3ls@-eng.jsp&curactn=dwnld&pid=7982&did=1, and ESCD website, http://www.esdc.gc.ca/eng/jobs/training_agreements/cjf/index.shtml.

Programmes delivered under EI-Part II are called Employment Benefits and Support Measures (EBSM, see Annex 5.A1 for further details). Each P/T is given funds by the federal government through LMDAs to design and administer these Active Labour Market Programmes (ALMPs) in a way that addresses their unique labour market challenges and priorities (these programmes delivered by P/Ts are in fact called "EBSM-similar" programmes in Canada, but will in the rest of this review be referred to as EBSM programmes or ALMP for simplicity).[1]

P/Ts are now the main actors in the area of employment policies at the regional and local levels, even though the general strategic orientations and guidelines continue to be set at the federal level, which also monitors and evaluates how the funds are used and to what extent they fulfil the federal objectives. In addition to the federal funds coming from the Government of Canada, P/Ts also dedicate specific funding to employment services. In practice, even though the financing is different between LMDAs, CJF agreements and P/Ts employment services, some of these programmes can be quite similar in their content despite the fact that LMDA-funded training and skills development programmes are restricted to EI claimants while the others are devoted to non-EI claimants. This EI/non-EI segmentation of programmes from the accounting and monitoring point of view illustrates how the Canadian institutional setting might be seen as *system*-oriented rather than *client*-oriented (see the final section of the chapter).

Delivery of employment services

All jurisdictions across Canada are moving toward more client-oriented and cost-effective delivery of re-employment services, although in very different ways across provinces and territories. Three basic models for EBSM delivery are emerging: some jurisdictions have completely transferred re-employment service delivery to third-party service providers (e.g. Ontario), while other jurisdictions emphasise the government's role in service delivery (e.g. Quebec). A third group of jurisdictions has implemented a mixed model, where third-party providers and P/T government jointly organise the delivery of EBSM (Figure 2.1). The following describes how employment services and skills training are delivered at the federal level and in Ontario and Quebec in greater detail, including by providing an overview of the main providers of employment services in these three jurisdictions.

Figure 2.1. **Employment services delivery in Canada**

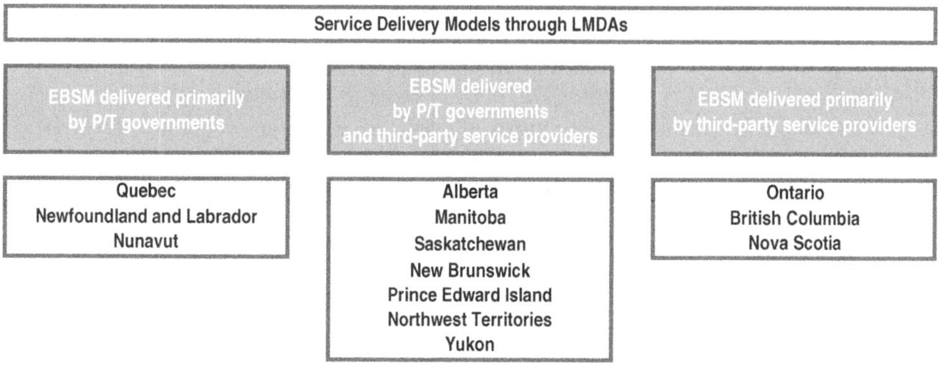

Note: LMDAs: Labour Market Development Agreements. EBSM: Employment Benefits and Support Measures. P/T: Province and territory.

Source: CEIC – Canada Employment and Insurance Commission (2014), "EI monitoring and assessment report 2012/13", Employment and Social Development Canada, March, http://www12.hrsdc.gc.ca/servlet/sgpp-pmps-pub?lang=eng&curjsp=p.5bd.2t.1.3ls@-eng.jsp&curactn=dwnld&pid=7982&did=1.

Federal employment and skills system

OECD (2014) provides a comprehensive presentation of Federal, Ontario's and Quebec's employment and skills system. At the federal level, Employment and Social Development Canada (ESDC, formerly known as HRSDC) is responsible for the labour market and social policies nationwide, involving the direct provision of services to workers in the federal jurisdiction – which covers specific sectors nation-wide (e.g. transportation, banking, communication, energy and mining) and accounts for around 10% of total employment – and via some pan-Canadian ALMPs that are intended to address national priorities (e.g. Aboriginal programming, persons with disabilities) or programmes targeted to specific populations (e.g. older workers, immigrants). Service Canada provides direct services to the Canadian population at over 600 service locations across the country (e.g. Employment Insurance).

Quebec employment and skills system

In 1997, Quebec was the first Canadian province to sign a Labour Market Development Agreement with the federal government, making the Government of Quebec fully responsible for public employment services in the province. The Ministry of Employment and Social Solidarity (*Ministère de l'Emploi et de la Solidarité sociale* – MESS) is responsible for implementing and delivering employment services including active labour market policies while the Ministry of Education formulates policies and programmes to support training.

Emploi-Québec was created in 1998 following the establishment of the LMDA. Within the MESS, this public agency is responsible for the delivery of employment services and social assistance services to individuals as well as services to employers. *Emploi-Québec* services are delivered by 130 service points or local employment centres (*centre local d'emploi*) and points of service in 17 administrative regions (CEIC, 2014). *Emploi-Québec* supplies, among other services, placement and labour market information (LMI).

As discussed in Box 3.1, Quebec has set up the *Commission des partenaires du marché du travail* (CPMT), which brings together key decision makers representing employers, employees, training institutions, community organisations and some ministries involved in economic and social issues. The CPMT plays a key role in terms of investment and training decisions on skills development with key players in the labor market. It advises the provincial government on employment- and training-related issues. At the local level, *Emploi-Québec* works with 17 regional councils of labour market partners, which examine labour market issues specific to their regions and recommend an action plan addressing local needs to the CPMT (see Chapter 3). These councils also adapt *Emploi-Québec* measures and services to regional needs and co-ordinate the employment services delivered by the local employment centres in their respective regions [see OECD (2014) for further details].

Ontario employment and skills system

Ontario signed their Labour Market Development Agreement with the federal government in 2007. This agreement led to the creation of an employment and training system called *Employment Ontario* (EO), managed by the Ministry of Training, Colleges and Universities (MTCU). EO brought together employment and training services from the federal and provincial government into one coherent and comprehensive service delivery system relying upon private (mostly non-profit) sub-contractors to deliver all ALMPs, including basic case management, job-search assistance and training. EO's network of service providers relies on 170 third-party providers located in more than 400 points of service across Ontario (CEIC, 2014).

Despite some heterogeneity among sub-contractors, all EO agencies are meant to offer a single entry door for all employment and training services: in all EO offices, students, jobseekers as well as employers can have access to information, services and many programmes similar to the federal EBSM. Jobseekers self-refer to these third-party providers but with limited prior information on their specialisation (online self-service based information)[2] and on the type of services offered by each one of them, leading to a weak primary orientation towards employment services. After a first assessment of the unemployed person's needs, caseworkers can refer this client to another EO provider and/or recommend specific courses to the unemployed person. In limited circumstances, the MTCU must approve the training or programme recommended to the client.

Through *Employment Ontario*, jobseekers have access to two levels of services (OECD, 2014). Any client entering an employment service provider office will have access to unassisted services (e.g. self-services), including job-search assistance such as filling out applications or completing a curriculum vitae as well as job matching. Clients who require more intensive services in finding a job will be provided with assisted services. EO also manage provincial programmes to support workplace training and workplace preparation, including apprenticeship, career and employment preparation, and adult literacy and basic skills. *Ontario Works* is administered by the Ministry of Community and Social Services and aims at helping people in financial need find sustainable employment and achieve self-reliance through the provision of employment services and financial assistance. Adults receiving financial assistance under *Ontario Works* are required to participate in approved employment assistance activities as a condition of eligibility for assistance.

OECD recommendations to address Canadian institutional issues

As identified in previous OECD reviews, Canada faces governance issues arising from its multi-layered institutional framework that might affect those who do not find their way back into jobs (OECD, 2010).

Governance issues arising in employment services delivery

The federal government funds and administers EI benefits and a large share of ALMPs, but these programmes are largely designed and delivered by the P/T employment services. On the one side, this devolution of ALMP delivery to P/Ts has given sub-national governments more flexibility to tailor ALMPs to meet local needs, while also achieving economies of scale by consolidating what had previously been parallel systems of federal and P/T labour market programmes serving similar clients in the same places. On the other side, this decentralisation has created new challenges, since there is now no easy way for ESDC to ensure that the ALMP funding provided to P/Ts is spent in accordance with national policy priorities.

A system-oriented institutional framework rather than a client-*oriented one, uneasy to navigate for displaced workers…*

Canada's *system* focus in operational policy making has produced a fragmented set of income support and employment services that are difficult for clients to navigate and access. One of the weaknesses for displaced workers to navigate in the complex Canadian system is the multitude of agencies they have to deal with at different stages: CAR/CREC/Action centres in the case of mass dismissals during their notice period (see Chapter 3); Service Canada for their Employment Insurance claim (see Chapter 4) and in rare cases for the monitoring of their job search and potential sanctions in the case of non-compliance (see Chapter 5); Ontario Works in Ontario for social assistance recipients; and a variety of private providers under Employment Ontario or *Emploi-Québec* local agencies for re-employment support (see Chapter 5). Income support and employment services for displaced workers (and all other unemployed people) are administered in federal and provincial silos.

From the perspective of the client, if Service Canada seems to be well identified as the income support delivery agency (as also administering all other administrative aspects of the Canadians), it might be unclear for them to know what kind of employment support is available to them. As already identified in OECD (2010), because provincial and federal agencies do not work in a joint way when dealing with common clients (despite some local improvements for example with the co-location of some Service Canada agencies with

EO providers), it is up to the client to try to work out what is available. There is no roadmap or obligation for clients to follow a given sequence or process to access the available support. The model in place in Canada today is therefore *system*- rather than *client*-focused.

… and difficult to monitor and evaluate

Governance issues also arise within the P/Ts where the PES makes extensive use of private sub-contractors to deliver services. Maintaining central accountability while allowing local service providers to tailor their programmes to diverse local needs can be an organisational challenge. This requires efficient accountability and proper evaluation of the effectiveness of the programmes. Some governance mechanisms are in place to ensure national policy priorities are included in ALMP funding, including meetings between jurisdictions (Forum of Labour Market Ministers) as well as internal governance mechanisms between jurisdictions. Nevertheless, obligations for provinces to report and evaluate the various programmes delivered with federal or provincial funds seem insufficient and might lead to limited transparency and co-ordination. Programmes are mostly monitored and evaluated on an accounting classification basis. The content of the employment services is not really assessed, while reporting from P/Ts mostly relies on the funding origin of the programmes: those available for EI eligible unemployed (and funded through LMDAs) and those available to all unemployed but mostly targeted at the non-EI eligible and the most disadvantaged unemployed (funded through former LMAs and now CJF). Again, this results in a *system*-oriented monitoring rather than a *client*-oriented one that would for example try to identify what programme works best for whom regardless of EI eligibility.

CEIC (2014) points out some of the limitations of the employment system in Ontario. MTCU monitors the performance of local employment providers through gross outcome measures such as enrolment, gross job placement rates and spending targets by programme. But further improvements are required to enter the black box of the delivery system of employment services and its operational aspects and implement a solid evaluation methodology (including randomised experiments). Many EO providers are social welfare charities committed to helping their clients lowering – *a priori* – the risk of "free riders", but evaluation of net impacts of the programmes and services delivered to help jobseekers find a job are lacking. The quality of job placements is not reported and MTCU does not identify, neither best practices among EO sub-contractors nor inefficient practice [see DEEWR (2012), in the case of Jobs Services Australia]. Therefore, EO providers seem to focus more on serving disadvantaged unemployed and may thus be lacking apt re-employment assistance to displaced workers with stable work histories (CEIC, 2014).

In contrast with the situation in Ontario, *Emploi-Québec* local employment offices are staffed by civil servants who perform basic case management and provide core job-search assistance. These offices also make use of sub-contractors to deliver more intensive services (e.g. some types of training and specialised services to specific hard-to-place groups). MESS provides overall management and strategic orientation while leaving considerable autonomy to regional units of *Emploi-Québec* to determine how to tailor ALMPs to local needs. Despite this decentralisation, MESS appears to do a better job of monitoring the effectiveness of the ALMP services offered than MTCU in Ontario. Indeed, *Emploi-Québec* is quite unique among provincial public employment services in conducting rigorous evaluations of its services, including those provided by sub-contractors. Evaluations indicate that *Emploi-Québec* has obtained quite positive results from many of its ALMPs (CEIC, 2014).

Main OECD recommendations

The following recommendations, developed further in OECD (2010), still apply:

Implement "one-stop-shop" local agencies, gathering under the same roof the delivery of EI benefit and of employment services

The delivery of EI benefit by Service Canada and of employment services by either a network of providers like in Ontario, or an institution closer to a PES like *Emploi-Québec* may i) be misguiding for the unemployed in navigating the system; ii) dissociate the receipt of EI benefit from its conditionality of active job-search; and iii) lead to a poor activation system by inadequate job-search monitoring. From the point of view of a displaced worker, *Emploi-Québec* probably represents an easier system to navigate than *Employment Ontario*, since there is essentially only one entry door (i.e. the local public employment office). By contrast, entering the system in Ontario requires the displaced worker to locate an *Employment Ontario* sub-contractor and, in a larger community, to choose between a considerable number of them.[3] On the other hand, Service Canada is never co-located with *Emploi-Québec*, whereas it is sometimes co-located with *Employment Ontario* providers. These "one-stop-shops" would provide both income support and re-employment support, and should hold the responsibility for job-search monitoring and sanctions in the case of non-compliance.

Improve co-ordination between jurisdictions and between P/Ts

The complexity of the relationships between the federal and the P/T governments leads to challenging co-ordination in the implementation and delivery of employment services in Canada. Decentralisation of these programmes to P/Ts enables higher flexibility in the implementation and programmes better tailored to local needs, but at the sacrifice of uniformity of treatment. The fact that the federal government bears the cost of EI cash benefits potentially mutes the incentive of the P/T governments to operate their ALMPs so as to minimise benefit dependency and thus potentially makes it difficult to activate EI recipients, including displaced workers, or promote other national objectives, such as fostering greater migration from labour surplus to labour shortage provinces. However, this division of responsibilities appears to be deeply entrenched in the Canadian federalism. The OECD recommends promoting a *client*-oriented perspective for employment services rather than the existing *system*-oriented one. This would require improving the co-ordination between federal and provincial governments in the implementation of employment services, focusing on the unemployed bottom-to-top perspective rather than the existing top-to-bottom circuit derived from the financing and monitoring processes.

Conclusion

Canada is characterised by a deeply rooted institutional setting combining a federal jurisdiction with 13 provincial and territorial jurisdictions. Income support and employment services are designed and implemented by a variety of actors and re-employment support is segmented between EI and non-EI recipients. Moreover, the Canadian institutional setting is *system*-oriented rather than *client*-oriented, leading to uneasy navigation for displaced workers through this multi-layered institutional system providing re-employment support. Many of the changes discussed in Chapters 3 to 5 will be difficult to achieve without institutional changes. The OECD recommends implementing a "one-stop-shop" philosophy, gathering under the same roof the delivery of EI benefit and of employment services and improving the co-ordination between jurisdictions and between P/Ts.

Notes

1. Indeed, since the completion of signing LMDAs with all P/Ts in 2010, the Government of Canada only delivers Labour Market Partnership and Research & Innovation, while all other EBSM-similar programming is delivered by P/Ts.

2. To help job seekers find the appropriate service provider, MTCU has implemented an online portal, the Employment Ontario Self-Service, allowing potential clients to pre-screen and begin the application process for EO programmes and services. Information is also available on MTCU's website about services offered through EO, access to the service provider website and contact information. The EO call centre can also refer the client.
3. The structure of the systems in Ontario and Quebec are quite different. In Ontario, EO is meant to be a one-window approach to services that are offered through multiple sites. Having multiple EO service delivery sites, in large community, aims at increasing accessibility for those requiring support, rather than requiring people to travel long distances to one office.

References

CEIC (2014), "EI monitoring and assessment report 2012/13", Canada Employment Insurance Commission, Employment and Social Development Canada, March, http://www12.hrsdc.gc.ca/servlet/sgpp-pmps-pub?lang=eng&curjsp=p.5bd.2t.1.3ls@-eng.jsp&curactn=dwnld&pid=7982&did=1.

DEEWR – Department of Education, Employment and Workplace Relations (2012), "Good practice in Job Services Australia", DEEWR, Canberra, https://docs.employment.gov.au/system/files/doc/other/good_practice_in_job_services_australia.pdf.

OECD (2014), *Employment and Skills Strategies in Canada*, OECD Reviews on Local Job Creation, OECD Publishing, Paris, http://dx.doi.org/10.1787/9789264209374-en.

OECD (2010), *Sickness, Disability and Work: Breaking the Barriers: Canada: Opportunities for Collaboration*, OECD Publishing, Paris, http://dx.doi.org/10.1787/9789264090422-en.

Chapter 3

Preventing excessive displacements and early intervention policies in Canada

This chapter describes and assesses the most important programmes that take effect before workers are dismissed. Measures to prevent excessive job displacements are discussed first, including measures to anticipate restructuring or future changes in the labour market; the rules governing hiring and firing of workers; and the use of Short-Time Work schemes. The chapter then discusses the role of private and public early interventions that provide workers who will be displaced with an early start at finding a suitable new job. Overall provincial governments provide sound re-employment support to workers affected by mass layoffs that is tailored to this group's specific needs as soon as they are laid-off. This assistance plays a useful role but needs to be reinforced so as to start the adjustment process earlier for workers receiving advance notice or a large severance payment and to reach workers affected by small-scale displacements.

Employers' labour requirements vary continually as sales fluctuate and production technologies and work organisational practices evolve, but many of these changes can be accommodated through internal adjustments, rather than hiring and firing. For example, employees may be retained during a business downturn by temporarily reducing their hours of work or assigning them to non-production activities (e.g. training or maintenance work). Even when a firm's labour requirements have permanently declined for a certain type of worker, it may be possible to retrain those workers and transfer them to other parts of the firm. However, not all jobs can or should be saved, in which case timely, well-targeted and effective adjustment assistance can be provided to assist workers whose dismissal cannot be avoided to get an early start at finding new jobs. These types of preventive and anticipatory adjustment support are attractive to the extent that they can reduce the incidence of displacement and its adverse consequences for workers without undermining the dynamic efficiency of the economy.

Compared with other OECD countries, Canadian employers have few legislative or regulatory restrictions on changing the level of employment within their firms. This makes Canadian workers potentially more vulnerable to facing job loss whilst creating fewer incentives for employers to try alternative solutions to layoffs, although the empirical analysis in Chapter 1 does not indicate that the displacement rate in Canada is especially high compared with other OECD countries. As a consequence, a large part of the government's efforts consist of providing adjustment support to workers who are threatened with job loss or have been given layoff notices. This is typically achieved by using the rapid response concept, with the public employment service working closely with the employer, unions and other stakeholders to bring adjustment assistance to the affected workers. The challenge for policy is to extend adjustment assistance to individual dismissals and improve the effectiveness of these early intervention services where they exist.

Prevention and limitation of worker displacement

Early anticipation of employment and skills needs

Restructuring is a permanent feature of OECD labour markets affecting firms and their workers. Mechanisms anticipating change, such as forecasting of economic and labour market trends and forward-looking management of skills and jobs can potentially prevent some mass layoffs and plant closures in the first place, whilst improving the way firms adapt to change. These measures could range from national-level schemes in conjunction with other actors such as the social partners, academics and experts, through to regional, sectoral and company level.

In Canada, schemes to anticipate and address changes in the labour market are well-developed. These measures were further boosted by provincial authorities during the global financial crisis (see Box 3.1). The *Labour Market Partnership* (LMP) programme is an important federal initiative which enables employers, social partners and communities, by providing them with funds, to proactively develop plans and strategies for dealing with labour force issues and meeting human resource requirements. The measure falls under the umbrella of programmes provided through *Employment Benefits and Support Measures* (funded by Part II of the Employment Act), and though financed federally, it is administered and delivered by provincial authorities at the regional and local level. In 2012-13, the LMP measures accounted for CAD 156 million, representing 7.7% of the total expenditure under Part II of the Employment Insurance Act. To be eligible, applicants must form partnerships with other stakeholders and contribute financially towards the project costs. Funds are limited to CAD 500 000 per annum per project for a maximum duration of three years and are awarded through a call for proposal process. Although agreements formed under the LMP may vary from one province to another, funding is only available for activities addressing one or more of the following three areas:

- Improving capacity for dealing with human resource requirements including identification of trends and emerging issues such as skills gaps, training requirements and barriers to hiring and retaining.
- Assisting work force adjustments, including the work of employer/employee adjustment committees in times of downsizing and plant closures.
- Local economic development which may include research activities supporting a group of employers to access new markets and thus stimulating new job opportunities.

By way of example, in Ontario, the LMP programme is administered by the Ministry of Training, Colleges and Universities (MTCU). The ministry provides funding to 26 local workforce development boards across the province which are organised under an umbrella organisation entitled Workforce Planning Ontario. The mandate of the local boards is to identify workforce issues at the community level and provide solutions by engaging stakeholders and service partners. Activities undertaken by local boards to assist labour market adjustment include: i) producing labour market reports and profiles; ii) hosting career fairs and community events; iii) hosting websites and portals to job-search boards; and iv) disseminating information about education and training programmes in their regions and communities.

Box 3.1. Special measures to monitor labour market developments during the economic crisis in Quebec

Special initiatives to monitor developments in the labour market, financial markets and economic activity in specific industries were implemented in Quebec following the onset of the global financial crisis. Since 2008, members of the *Commission des partenaires du marché du travail* (CPMT) – a formal collaborative body that has a key role in terms of investment and training decisions on skills development with key market players – have organised monthly meetings to monitor the labour market situation. From the fall of 2010, as the Quebec labour market situation improved, these meetings have devoted more effort to the examination of structural issues and long-term issues such as dealing with long-term unemployment, job prospects for older workers and job quality, while maintaining the monitoring indicators of the labour market on a monthly basis.

These regular meetings led to the development of the *Pacte pour l'emploi Plus,* which offers a wide range of measures to meet labour market challenges, and the *Soutien aux entreprises à risque de ralentissement économique* (SERRÉ) programme, which offers training to workers during the economic downturn (see below).

Source: OECD questionnaire on policies for displaced workers.

The LMP programme creates opportunities to foster forward-looking policy making which may prevent and delay restructuring and provides a good platform for collaboration between different stakeholders that have an important role to play in managing restructuring. In addition, such governance structures which connect employment, training, and economic development stakeholders at the local level may be particularly useful in a context where co-ordination between ministries is relatively weak with siloes in the policy development process (OECD, 2014).

Legal provisions to limit dismissals are relatively limited compared to other OECD countries

Employment protection legislation (EPL) refers to the rules and procedures governing the dismissal of individuals or groups. It is important that these rules be designed so as to minimise the adjustment costs associated with maintaining a dynamic labour market that continuously reallocates labour towards its most valuable uses. This is a difficult challenge since ample evidence shows that overly strict hiring and firing rules can reduce job flows, reduce labour productivity, encourage labour market duality and thus hinder economic growth (Martin and Scarpetta, 2012; and OECD, 2013). Nonetheless, there is a role for EPL provisions that encourage employers to consider economically justified alternatives to permanent layoffs and, when some workers need to be displaced, require employers to facilitate the early provision of support services for these workers so as to smooth their transition to finding new jobs. For instance, employer-provided advance notice of planned layoffs can assist in implementing proactive measures, such as early re-employment services offered by the Public Employment Service (PES), or simply allow workers an early start on searching for a new job.

Advance notice and severance pay

In Canada, each of the ten provinces have their own Employment Standards Acts (ESAs) which set out *minimum* conditions and regulations relating to layoffs, such as provisions on advance notice, severance payments and consultation requirements. Under the ESA, employers are required to give notice of termination to employees that have completed at least three months of employment unless the employer can prove "just cause" (legal cause to dismiss an employee without notice of termination or termination pay).[1] The notice period increases with tenure in most provinces from a minimum of one week to a maximum of eight weeks for workers with tenure of eight years or more in Ontario and British Colombia and ten years or more in Quebec and Alberta. Federally regulated employees have the right to receive a minimum of two weeks' notice period. As in a number of other OECD countries, termination pay can be given in lieu of notice.[2]

Only the federal and Ontario jurisdictions have statutory severance pay provisions. Workers with at least one year of tenure in the federal jurisdiction are entitled to two days per year of service (with a minimum of five days). In Ontario, workers who have completed at least five years of service are entitled to one week per year of service, up to a maximum of 26 weeks.[3] However, in all provinces and territories (P/Ts) and in the federal jurisdiction, workers covered by collective agreements can receive far more generous severance packages. For instance, federally regulated employers provided permanently laid-off employees with on average eight days of wages per year of service in 2004. In large enterprises (100 and more employees), average severance pay was 11 days of wages per year of service (Venn, 2009).

Additional provisions for collective dismissals

The law grants additional protection in the case of collective dismissal. The definition of collective dismissals varies from one jurisdiction to another and whether a termination is a group termination under the ESA depends on five factors including: i) number of employees terminated; ii) type of employee; iii) length of time over which terminations occur;

iv) whether terminations are counted business-wide or by facility; and v) whether any exceptions apply.[4] Unlike the provisions for individual dismissals, the amount of notice given is determined by the number of employees dismissed rather than their length of employment. Accordingly, the extended notice period can range from a minimum of four to a maximum of 18 weeks (Table 3.1). For instance in Ontario, an employer must give eight weeks' notice if the employment of 50 to 199 employees is to be terminated, 12 weeks' in the case of 200 to 499 employees, and 16 weeks' notice for 500 or more employees. In all jurisdictions, except for Prince Edward Island, employers must also notify their respective labour authorities about collective dismissals, and in some jurisdictions, a copy of the notice must be given to employee representatives.[5]

Table 3.1. **Mandatory notice requirements for mass dismissal, by province**

Province	Time over which termination occurs	Number of employees terminated	Duration of notice	Recipient of notice
Federal	4-week period	50 or more	16 weeks	• Minister of Labour • Individual employees not represented by union • Certified association representing the employees
Alberta	4 weeks	50 or more	4 weeks	• Minister of Employment
British Columbia[a]	2-month period	50-100 101-300 Over 300	8 weeks 12 weeks 16 weeks	• Minister of Labour and Citizens' Services • Each terminated employee • Certified association representing the employees
Manitoba	4-week period	50-100 101-300 Over 300	10 weeks 14 weeks 18 weeks	• Minister of Labour • Certified association representing the employees • Individual employees not represented by union
New Brunswick	4-week period	10 or more, if they represent 25% of employer's workforce	6 weeks	• Minister of Post-Secondary Education, Training and Labour • Bargaining agent • Affected employees
Newfoundland and Labrador	4-week period	50-199 200-499 500 or more	8 weeks 12 weeks 16 weeks	• Minister of Environment and Labour • Each terminated employee
Northwest Territories/Nunavut	4-week period	25-49 50-99 100-299 300 or more	4 weeks 8 weeks 12 weeks 16 weeks	• Employment Standards Officer • Certified association representing the employees
Nova Scotia	4 weeks	10-99 100-299 300 or more	8 weeks 12 weeks 16 weeks	• Minister of Labour • Each affected employee
Ontario[b]	4 weeks	50-199 200-499 500 or more	8 weeks 12 weeks 16 weeks	• Director of Employment Standards (Ministry of Labour) • Affected employee
Prince Edward Island	No collective dismissal provision			

Table 3.1. **Mandatory notice requirements for mass dismissal, by province** *(cont.)*

Province	Time over which termination occurs	Number of employees terminated	Duration of notice	Recipient of notice
Quebec	2 months	10-99 100-299 300 or more	8 weeks 12 weeks 16 weeks	• Minister of Employment and Social Solidarity, with copy to: - Labour Standards Commission - Certified association representing the employees
Saskatchewan	4 weeks	10-49 50-99 100 or more	4 weeks 8 weeks 12 weeks	• Minister of Labour • Each terminated employee • Certified association representing the employees
Yukon	4 weeks	25-49 50-99 100-299 300 or more	4 weeks 8 weeks 12 weeks	• Director of Employment Standards

a) British Columbia's notice requirements are in addition to the amount of notice required for individual terminations.

b) Generally, Ontario's mass termination rules apply where the employment of 50 or more employees at an establishment is being terminated in the same four-week period. The group termination provisions do not apply when termination affects 10% or less of the number of employees who have been employed for at least three months and the terminations are not due to a closure of the business.

Source: See HR Insider (2009), "Layoffs, terminations & restructuring your workforce: Avoiding the cost of non-compliance", http://hrinsider.ca/specialreports/Layoffs%20Terminations%20&%20Restructuring%20Your%20Workforce%20-%20white%20paper%2060%20page.pdf; and *OECD Employment Protection Database*, 2013 update, www.oecd.org/employment/emp/oecdindicatorsofemploymentprotection.htm.

Unlike some other OECD countries, such as Japan, where employers are mandated to "justify" their decision and provide information on the range of measures taken to avoid redundancies (e.g. reduction of working time, early retirement, relocation of displaced workers in other establishments of the employer), by and large, Canadian employers are not required to consult with unions or staff representatives on any anticipated collective redundancies (apart from giving notice in some provinces). A few jurisdictions however do require employers to form a committee (usually called an adjustment committee or joint planning or reclassification assistance committee which has employer and employee representatives) to determine whether terminations can be avoided.[6] If the committee agrees that there are no realistic alternatives and that termination is necessary, it must establish methods for helping employees whose contracts are terminated to obtain other employment. In Quebec, for instance, employers who are considering closing plants or engaging in mass layoffs are required to set up a *Comité de consultation*, where management can consult with their unions and other stakeholders about possible alternatives to limit layoffs. Such consultation may also occur on the employer's own initiative or under collective agreement provisions.

The above described rules are only the minimum required by law; collective bargaining agreements and other contracts may contain additional notice requirements and severance payment provisions in the case of collective dismissals, albeit evidence suggests that only a few may actually do so. According to Ministry of Labour Quebec (2013), among the 1 800 collective agreements deposited in 2012, only 16% provide additional provision of notice period for collective dismissals, and 25% of salaried employees are covered by a collective agreement regulating severance in cases of collective dismissals.

Figure 3.1, Panel A, compares the strictness of employment protection against individual dismissal for workers with permanent employment contracts (i.e. open-ended as opposed to temporary contracts) across OECD countries in 2013.[7] According to this measure, Canada has one of the least stringent requirements. Panel B of Figure 3.1 provides cross-country comparisons of the additional requirements imposed on employers when implementing collective dismissals involving a significant number of workers. This type of regulation is somewhat stricter in Canada, placing it just above the average level of strictness for OECD countries. The overall EPL strictness for permanent workers against individual or collective dismissals is reported in Panel C of Figure 2.1. Canada is rated as being well below the OECD average.

EPL enforcement also matters. Data from Employment Insurance Coverage Survey (EICS) demonstrates that on average only half of displaced workers laid-off between 2000 and 2010 reported receiving any notice at all prior to their job loss. Out of those who received formal notice, this was: one to two weeks for the majority (42%); less than one week for around 24%; and more than five weeks for only around 8% (Figure 3.2). These patterns suggest that employer non-compliance with advance notification requirements could be quite high. Unfortunately, the EICS data do not indicate which workers received termination pay in lieu of legally required notification.

Relatively weak requirements for advance notice and possibly high non-compliance with these regulations could jeopardise the availability of timely support to workers and their re-employment prospect. For example, employer-provided advance notice of planned layoffs can give workers a head start in searching for a new job, as well as being a pre-requisite for implementing additional proactive measures. Research in the United States has shown that displaced workers receiving advance notice spend less time unemployed than workers laid-off without any advance warning (Nord and Ting, 1991 and 1992; and Swaim and Podgursky, 1990). There is also some indication of a positive effect on post-displacement wages for workers who have received advance notification (Rhum, 1994).

Figure 3.1. **Protection of permanent workers against individual and collective dismissal**

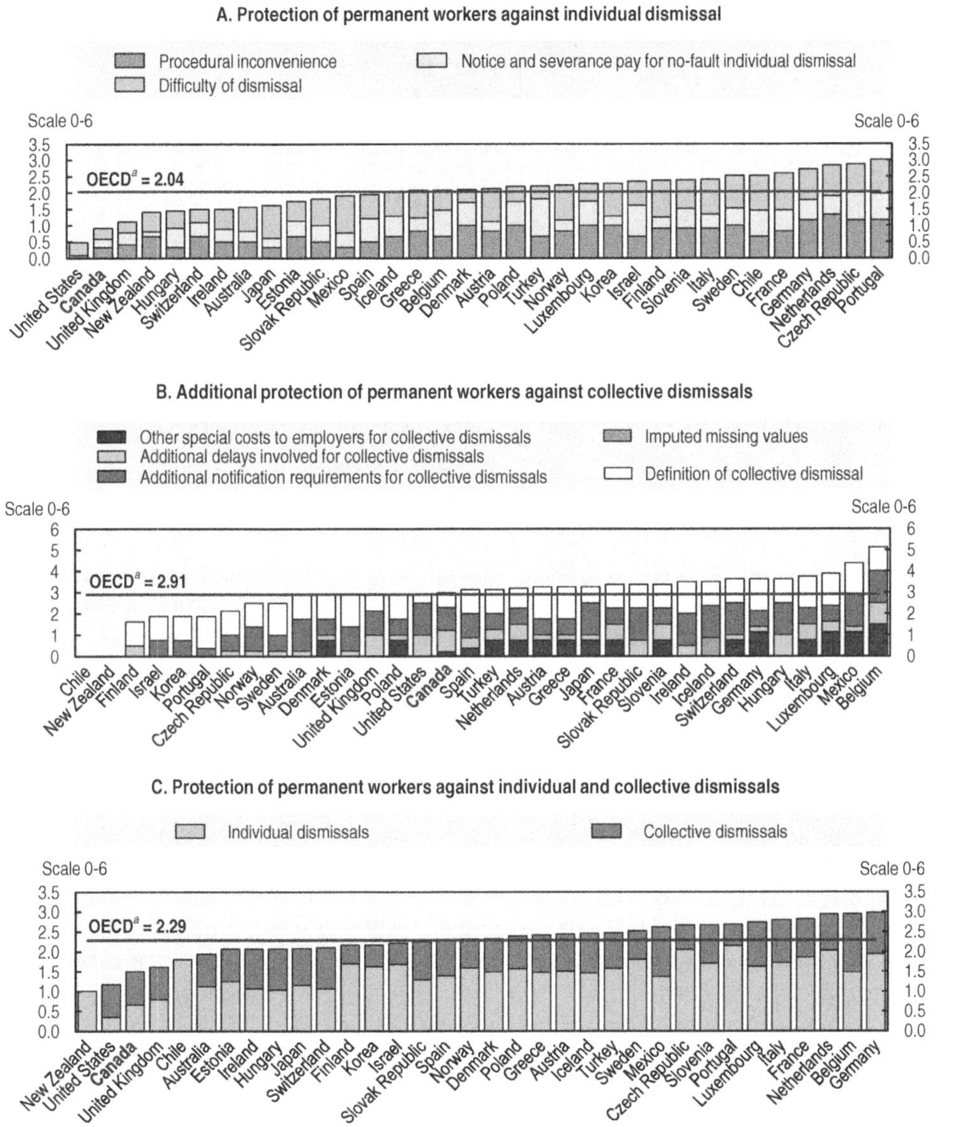

Note: The figure presents the contribution of different sub-components to the indicators for employment protection. The height of the bar represents the value of the indicator.

a) Unweighted average of the respective indicator shown in each panel for the 34 OECD countries.

Source: OECD Employment Protection Database, 2013 update, http://dx.doi.org/10.1787/lfs-epl-data-en.

StatLink http://dx.doi.org/10.1787/888933238716

Figure 3.2. **Worker-reported advance notice among displaced workers**

Share of displaced workers who received advance notice of dismissal, 2000-10

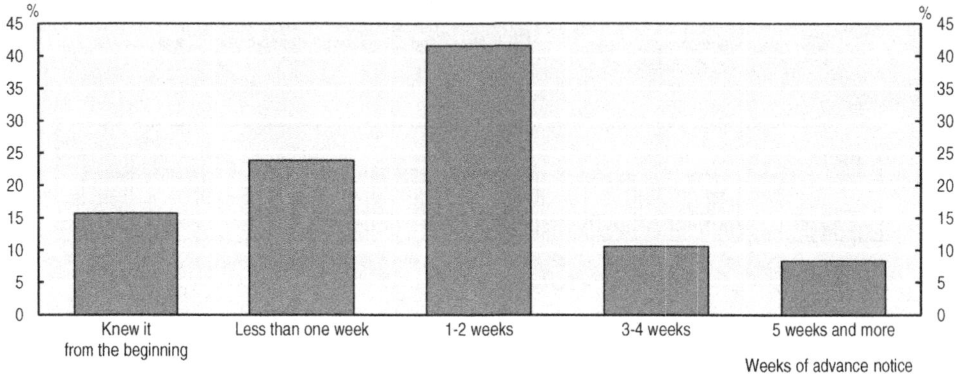

Source: OECD calculations based on data from the Employment Insurance Coverage Survey (EICS).

StatLink http://dx.doi.org/10.1787/888933238728

Figure 3.3 displays the cross-country association between EPL strictness for permanent workers and three measures of total labour turnover which plausibly could be affected by EPL: flows in and out of unemployment and the incidence of long-term unemployment. Both theoretical arguments and empirical research have shown that strict EPL is likely to reduce the propensity for permanent workers to be displaced into unemployment, but it also tends to dampen hiring rates so that unemployed persons take longer to move back into jobs (see the literature review in OECD, 2013, Chapter 2). These figures are suggestive of such a tendency, since unemployment inflows and outflows both tend to be lower in countries with stricter EPL, whereas the incidence of long-term unemployment tends to be higher and vice versa.[8] As expected given the low level of EPL strictness, Canada is among countries with highest flows into unemployment. Although this makes Canadian workers more vulnerable to experiencing job loss, they are also in a better position to find jobs quickly and are less likely to experience long-term unemployment compared with their counterparts in other OECD countries.

Overall, the design of EPL in Canada appears to be well suited to encourage the early provision of adjustment assistance to displaced workers in the case of a mass layoff or plant closing, while also granting employers flexibility to reduce staffing when necessary. However, this assistance is less likely to be available to workers affected by an individual layoff suggesting that there is potential for strengthening certain components of employment protection to promote successful adjustment of displaced workers by providing them with faster access to public and private re-employment services.

Figure 3.3. Simple correlations between EPL for permanent workers, labour market dynamics and the incidence of long-term unemployment

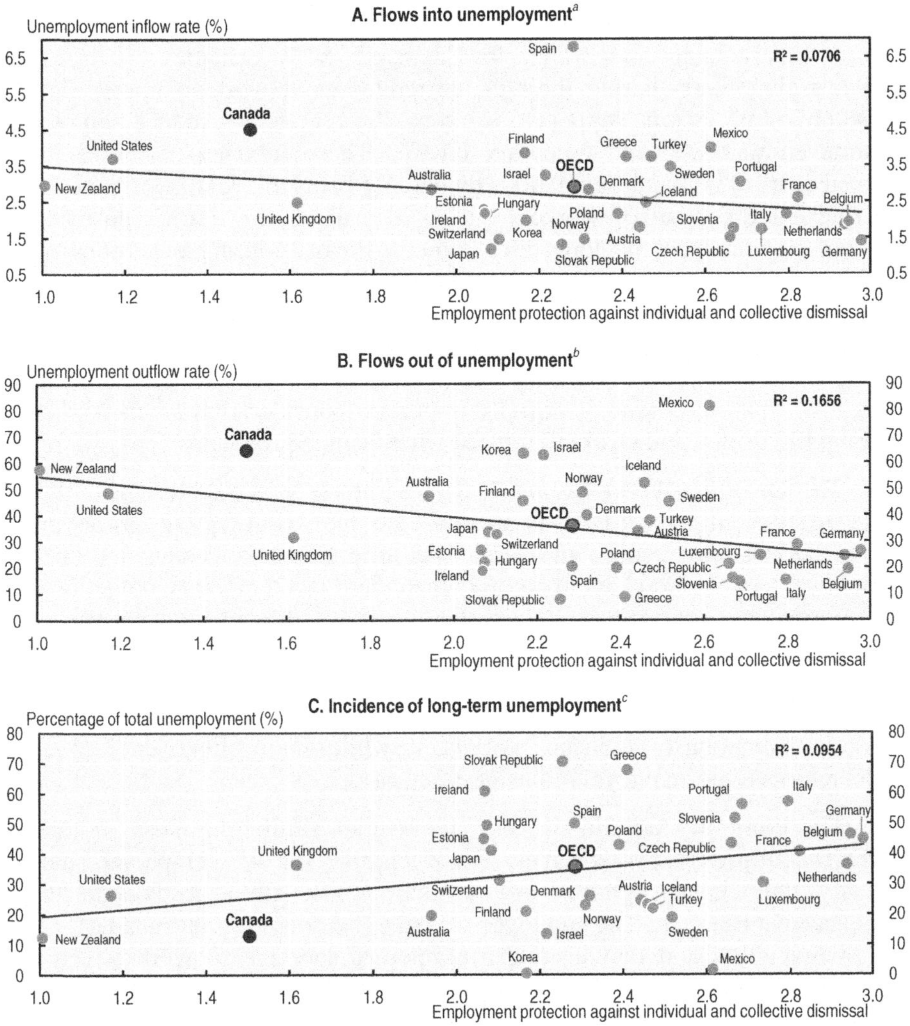

Note: EPL: Employment protection legislation.

a) The *unemployment inflow rate* is defined as the ratio of the number of unemployed who have been unemployed for less than one month to the number of employed one quarter earlier.

b) The *unemployment outflow rate* is defined as 1 *minus* the ratio of the number of unemployed who have been unemployed for more than a month to the total number of unemployed one quarter earlier.

c) Number of long-term unemployed (12 months or more) as a percentage of total unemployment.

Source: OECD calculations based on national labour force surveys; and *OECD Employment Protection Database*, 2013 update, http://dx.doi.org/10.1787/lfs-epl-data-en.

StatLink *http://dx.doi.org/10.1787/888933238739*

Work-Sharing programme plays an important role in preventing layoffs but there is scope to improve take-up and cost-effectiveness

Short-Time Work (STW) schemes are intended to preserve viable jobs at firms experiencing temporarily low demand. STW schemes do this by encouraging work-sharing through the reduction of working hours, while also providing income support to workers whose hours are reduced due to a shortened workweek or temporary layoffs. These schemes can lower the social costs of demand fluctuations by helping firms to avoid layoffs, i.e. the permanent dismissal of workers during a business downturn whose jobs would be viable in the long-run. Avoiding layoffs during recessions has potential benefits for both employers and workers. For the employer, work-sharing may be a means of retaining valued employees during a temporary downturn. Workers who are laid-off may take jobs elsewhere, meaning that any investments the firm has made in these workers' job skills are lost. This may be an especially important consideration when workers are highly skilled and costly to replace when demand rebounds.

The Canadian *Work-Sharing* (WS) programme was established in 1977 and reactivated in 1981-82 in response to the economic recession and continued as an ongoing measure. The programme is designed to help employers and workers avoid layoffs when there is a temporary reduction in the normal level of business activity that is a result of factors that are beyond the control of the employer. The WS programme is federally run and administered through Service Canada and provides income support to workers eligible for Employment Insurance (EI) benefits and who agree to work a temporarily reduced workweek while their employer recovers (i.e. returns to normal level of business activity).[9]

The eligibility criteria for WS are overall similar to those in other OECD countries' STW schemes. To be eligible for WS, employers must satisfy four main eligibility criteria that aim to limit deadweight and displacement effects. The employers must: i) be operating in Canada for at least two years and demonstrate a temporary shortage of work which is beyond their control; ii) demonstrate that a projected reduction in work activity will average between a minimum of 10% and a maximum of 60%; iii) implement a recovery plan designed to return the work unit to normal staffing levels and hours of work by the end of the agreement; and iv) have the consent of the union (if applicable) and employees. The employer must commit to maintain all existing employee benefits during the period of the WS agreement and be willing to fulfil the record keeping and reporting requirements of WS.

Canada's WS scheme is funded through the Employment Insurance (EI) Operating Account to which employers make financial contributions.

However, in contrast to many other OECD countries, employers do not bear any direct costs relating to the number of workers using the scheme. The WS programme is rather restrictive concerning the range of the reductions in working time that can be subsidised. The duration of WS agreements is for a minimum period of 26 consecutive weeks with a possible extension of up to 12 weeks to a maximum of 38 weeks.

Between 2009 and 2011, the Canadian Government introduced a number of temporary measures to make WS significantly more accessible to a greater number of firms and their employees during the recession that followed the global financial crisis. These modifications included:

- An extension of the duration of agreements: In Budget 2009, the duration of the WS agreements was raised by an additional 14 weeks to a maximum duration of 52 weeks. In recognition of continuing economic uncertainty, Budget 2010 extended the temporary changes by allowing employers with existing or recently terminated WS agreements to apply for an extension of an additional 26 weeks, rising the maximum duration of WS agreement to 78 weeks.
- Ease of eligibility requirements: Requirements of the recovery plan were changed so that employers only needed to have a plan to remain viable over the course of the WS agreement.[10]
- Removing the cooling-off period: Employers that have had their WS agreements expire could re-apply and enter into a new agreement involving the same group of the employees immediately after the end of a preceding WS agreement.
- Making the programme more flexible and efficient for employers: Under Budget 2011, policy adjustments included a simplified recovery plan, more flexible utilisation rules and technical amendments to reduce administrative burden.

Despite these changes, the increase in the WS take-up rate during the 2008-09 recession was amongst the lowest in the OECD, peaking at 0.4% of all employees in the Q4 2009 (Hijzen and Martin, 2013). This is only about one-tenth as large as peak enrolment figures in Germany and Japan. It is not immediately clear why the take-up was so much lower in Canada, given that the parameters of Work-Sharing roughly resemble those in other countries where take-up was much higher.[11] One partial explanation is that Canada was less affected by the 2008-09 global recession, but this cannot explain the full difference.[12] Another partial explanation is likely to be the fact that the WS programme does not include workers who experienced temporary layoffs, whereas STW schemes in many countries also encompass temporary layoffs.

How effective is the Work-Sharing programme in preserving jobs? Overall, there is substantial evidence that work-sharing programmes can avoid layoffs during economic downturns. Pooling evidence from 20 OECD countries, Hijzen and Martin (2013) concludes that STW programmes significantly reduced layoffs by increasing per capita reductions in working hours during the 2008-09 recession. In Canada, the WS programme is an important counter-cyclical measure, as seen in Figure 3.4: the number of WS claims rose to a high of 120 000 during the early 1990 recession, and then fell to approximately 50 000 per year during the economic expansion of the late 1990s and mid-2000s, but rose again in 2009-10 in the midst of the global financial crisis. Estimates also show that the Canadian WS scheme averted 35 thousand layoffs during 2009-10, more than seven times the estimated number prior and post-recession HRSDC (2013). However, this estimate is based on translating the number of unworked hours that were compensated by WS into worker equivalents and thus takes no account of possible deadweight and displacement effects.[13] Deadweight occurs when STW subsidies are paid for jobs that employers would have retained even in the absence of the subsidy, implying that this spending is a pure transfer which does not limit total job losses. Displacement occurs when STW schemes preserve jobs that are not viable without the subsidy, even after business conditions recover. In this case, a temporary subsidy delays, rather that averts, layoffs while a permanent subsidy would lock workers in low productivity jobs and thus represent a barrier to job creation by firms with the potential to grow.

Figure 3.4. **Work-Sharing programme is an important counter-cyclical measure**

Thousands

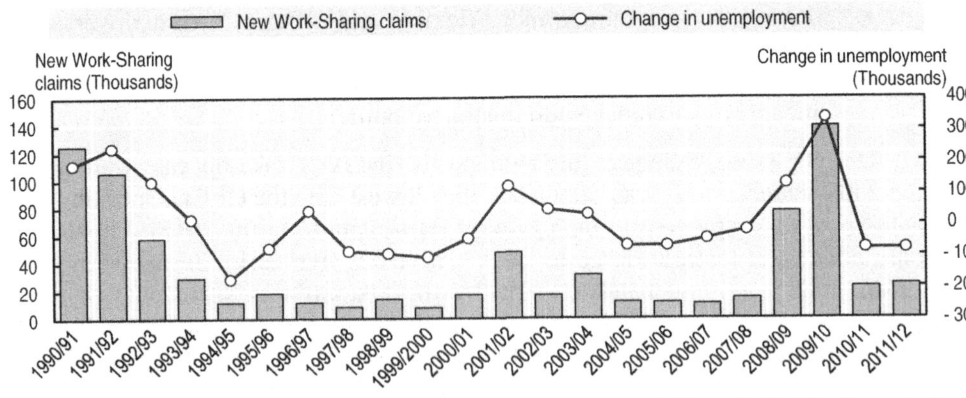

Source: HRSDC (2013), "Usage of the Work-Sharing program: 1990/91 to 2011/12", Strategic Policy and Research, Version 1.0, HRSDC, Evaluation Directorate; and *OECD Short-Term Labour Market Statistics Database*, www.oecd.org/statistics/.

StatLink http://dx.doi.org/10.1787/888933238743

The estimated employment effects in Hijzen and Venn (2011) suggests that deadweight could have been as high as one-third on average for the countries studied. While there are few estimates of the jobs lost once workers have exited these programmes, in Canada it has been estimated that, between 1991 and 2002, half of all the workers whose jobs had been preserved as a result of the programme were eventually laid off after they left the WS scheme (HRDC, 2004).

By and large, the WS scheme appears to be well-designed to play a useful role in preserving viable jobs during downturns, although it would be useful to probe further why it appears to have played a much smaller role in the 2008-09 recession than similar schemes in other OECD countries. It would also be worthwhile considering additional steps to increase the cost-effectiveness of WS. There are several approaches that can mitigate deadweight and displacement costs by ensuring that only firms experiencing problems resulting from temporary decreases in demand will wish to participate. One approach is to make firms bear a part of the wage costs for the hours not worked (like in France, Hungary and Japan) or to pay full wages for an initial period of short-time work (like in Norway and Switzerland). Another approach is to require firms to repay all or part of the subsidy if the employee is laid off after the programme ends. In this respect, the Dutch part-time unemployment scheme (*Deelitjid WW*) goes the furthest by requiring companies to repay half of the part-time unemployment benefits paid to their employees if the employee is laid off in the three months following their participation in the scheme (OECD, 2009). It should be noted, however, that all of these measures are likely to discourage take-up and thus would not necessarily enhance overall programme effectiveness.

As is the case for regular EI, there is a risk that the WS scheme could inadvertently subsidise jobs in declining industries (e.g. forestry and manufacturing), maintaining economically non-viable jobs and interfering in the restructuring process in some parts of Canada. Figure 3.5 shows an index of the annual participation in WS in proportion of the employment at the national level and in the provinces of Quebec and Ontario. The proportion of WS claims in the Province of Quebec has been systematically higher than for the national average every year since 1990. The variation in programme usage across provinces is probably due in considerable part to differences in the industrial composition of employment. Quebec also has a separate programme *Aménagement et réduction du temps de travail* (ARTT) which partly supplements the Work-Sharing programme. However, the ARTT is largely designed to manage permanent downward adjustments in average working hours for the purpose of encouraging additional hiring and thus increasing the level of employment (Box 3.2).

Box 3.2. **Additional Short-Time Work scheme in Quebec**

In addition to the federal Work-Sharing programme, Quebec has since 1966 a provincial programme allowing employers to reorganise and reduce working time (*Aménagement et réduction du temps de travail* – ARTT): employees agree with their employer to reduce their working hours for a given period of time, in order to avoid layoffs in the firm and/or hire job seekers. ARTT is a Short-Time Work measure negotiated within a firm's *comité de concertation* for one year, renewable twice.

This measure, financed by the *Fond de développement du marché du travail* and implemented by *Emploi-Québec* is accessible to all firms in Quebec, but mostly targets medium and large firms. *Emploi-Québec* contributes to ARTT plans by paying the company financial incentives: the usual financial contribution amounts to 50% of eligible expenditures of an ARTT plan, up to a maximum annual contribution of CAD 6 000 for each "full-time equivalent" (FTE) job that has been preserved through other workers' working-time reduction. Several ways of reducing working time are allowed in the ARTT programme, including reduction of weekly working time; working part time; job sharing; reduction of overtime; compensatory leave; unpaid leave; sabbatical leave with deferred treatment; accumulation of leave; progressive retirement; study leave; parental leave and early retirement.

Source: OECD questionnaire on policies for displaced workers; and Emploi-Québec (2011), "Concertation pour l'emploi : Aménagement et réduction du temps de travail (CT)", Guide des mesures et des services d'emploi, http://emploiquebec.gouv.qc.ca/guide_mesures_services/05_Mesures_progr_Emploi_Quebec/05_6_Concertation_pour_emploi/03_CPE_ARTT.pdf.

Figure 3.5. **Work-Sharing index, fiscal years 1990/91 to 2011/12**

Annual participation in Work-Sharing in proportion of the employment level compared with the annual Canadian proportion

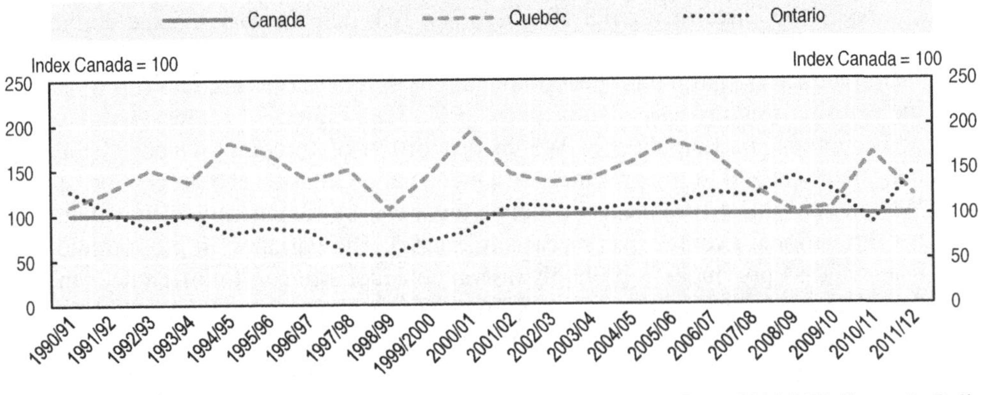

Source: HRSDC (2013), "Usage of the Work-Sharing Program: 1990/91 to 2011/12", Strategic Policy and Research, Version 1.0, HRSDC, Evaluation Directorate.

StatLink http://dx.doi.org/10.1787/888933238753

Training to upgrade skills during cyclical downturns

Investing in skills and training is increasingly becoming an important component of labour market policies to counter cyclical pressures on the labour market. Among other potential benefits, these policies can: i) retrain workers during periods of slow business activity so to make them more productive once the economy recovers, and ii) help provide a pathway back into employment for those who have lost their jobs. During the 2008-09 recession, a number of OECD countries provided training and retraining measures in combination with Short-Time Work schemes. Unlike in some countries where training was compulsory, employers in Canada were not required to provide training in order to qualify for the Work-Sharing programme.[14] Despite the potential benefits associated with training activities, some evidence suggests that training often is not appropriate or cannot easily be organised. Evaluation results from an earlier programme (*Work Sharing While Learning*) implemented in Canada in 2002, in which employers were responsible for all training costs, and employees had access to Employment Insurance benefits for up to one year while attending employer-funded training, highlighted several shortcomings. For instance the cost of training is a major inhibiting factor; companies undergoing major restructuring while reducing production lacked funds to pay for training; the programme also incorrectly assumed that major restructuring requires training for employees, but this was not necessarily the case and most training was done informally and on-the-job. There were also significant difficulties in scheduling non-work-based training to coincide with WS days off-the-job due to frequent, unpredictable variation in production and workforce utilisation. Workers, especially those who are not likely to face layoffs by reason of seniority, were unwilling to accept a drop in income if they were not compensated with increased time off, and instead were required to attend training (HRSDC, 2005).

Even though in Canada, the WS programme as it is implemented did not offer compulsory training, special training measures were offered to employed workers through provincial public training support schemes. For example, in Quebec, a special temporary programme, *Soutien aux entreprises à risque de ralentissement économique* (SERRÉ), was established between 2008 and 2010 to support firms to upgrade skills of their employees threatened with layoff during the economic downturn.[15] The programme funded both through employer contributions and the Ministry of Employment offered two types of training: basic training, including literacy, French and mathematics; and training in other related activities of the company.[16] Employers could receive a grant of up to CAD 100 000, including travel and subsistence expenses, educational materials of their employees participating in the training and salaries of the trainer. Although the programme could be combined with the WS scheme, this was not a prerequisite. A survey among firms participating in the programme (MESS, 2010) shows extremely high satisfaction rates both for the employers and the employees. Employers perceived the programme to have improved: i) worker's skills (96%), motivation (89%), versatility (86%)

and the work environment (84%); and ii) the quality of products or services (83%), the reduction of errors and wastes (84%) and the competitiveness of the company (82%). Of those employees who participated in the programme, around 94% were kept in employment after the end of the programme, of which 28% stayed in their jobs with reduced working-time arrangements (MESS, 2010).

Dismissals and early intervention services to smooth the transition to new jobs

The role of early intervention services (*transition services* or *rapid response services* in Canada) including job-search assistance and career counselling, becomes critical in the context where the dominant form of involuntary downward employment adjustment is layoffs into unemployment. While there is a strong rationale for intervening as soon as workers are given advance notice, there are also likely to be costs that need to be factored into the choice early intervention. For instance, providing intensive support to workers who are temporary laid-off can be costly as many of them revert back to their previous jobs. There are also potential concerns relating to deadweight costs as some of these workers may find jobs in any case without the intervention. In what follows, examples of adjustment support from Ontario and Quebec are discussed in further detail.

Early intervention measures to help dismissed workers to find new jobs are given a high priority

Access to support and counselling early on before actual layoff occurs is given a high priority by Canadian authorities to minimise the negative effects of restructuring. There are several different ways in which transition services are organised, delivered, funded and provided to displaced workers. Typically, arrangements will require a joint effort of employers, public employment services and social partners. Sometimes requirements to offer services are mandated by law but often, this goes beyond legislative requirements, or is achieved through collective agreements at national, sectorial, regional or company level.

Employers who intend to proceed with collective dismissals in the federal jurisdiction and three provinces including British Columbia, Manitoba, and Quebec are compelled by law to establish a joint committee to develop an adjustment programme aimed at minimising the number and impact of job losses and assisting affected workers in finding new employment. In other provinces, regulations do not automatically require a joint planning committee but authorise the government to order the employer to form one at any time to provide special services to assist both displaced workers and communities adapting to labour market changes.

In Ontario, the *Rapid Re-employment and Training Service* (RRTS) provides an immediate response to large-scale layoffs with the objective of connecting individuals with Employment Ontario (EO) services to help them regain employment. As part of the response process, it assesses the *level* and *type* of support required which means that every RRTS response is tailored to each layoff situation. The response begins when the Ministry of Labour receives the notice of termination for 50 or more workers. This information is then passed on to Ontario's Ministry of Training, Colleges and Universities (MTCU), responsible for initiating the RRTS process. Under the RRTS, MTCU endeavours to react within an hour of an announcement concerning permanent facility closures or substantial layoff situations by contacting the employer, the union, Employment Ontario service provider(s) and other stakeholders to begin organising adjustment assistance for the affected workers. Depending on the severity of the layoff and the capacity of the local employment service provider, the type of services offered may vary from providing information sessions and raising awareness to setting-up a so-called "Action centre," where displaced workers can access job-search assistance, financial counselling and personal counselling to deal with the stress of job loss (see Box 3.3). Where the ministry is aware of closures through the media, MTCU is also proactive in reaching out to those organisations in advance of the receipt of termination notices.

The Ministry of Employment and Social Solidarity (MESS) in Quebec also places high priority in providing prompt, accessible and tailored adjustment assistance to workers affected by firm closing and other mass layoffs. When MESS is informed of a pending mass layoff which concerns 50 or more workers, it contacts the employer, the union and other stakeholders, to set up a reclassification assistance committee (*Comité d'aide au reclassement* – CAR), quite similar to Action centres in Ontario. In contrast to Ontario however, employers by law should contribute 50% of the cost of the CAR budget or offer at least equivalent assistance to the affected workers directly if they choose to opt out.[17] Anecdotal evidence suggests that larger firms with well-developed human resources departments often prefer this approach, believing that they are better able to tailor the assistance offered to their departing employees' needs. The stakeholders agree on a president, that is, a professional consultant who is recruited to administer the CAR, and a convenient site for it to use. The president then develops a plan for offering tailored re-employment assistance to the workers who are to be displaced and hires staff as needed. The CAR can then function for up to two years. Displaced workers still requiring assistance when the CAR dissolves are referred to *Emploi-Québec*. A "reclassification plan" is developed for each dismissed worker and includes a combination of tailored services to help workers find a new job as quickly as possible. When the number of redundant workers is insufficient to justify the setup of a CAR, these workers are either informed by *Emploi-Québec* of the re-employment services they can receive in a local employment centre, or can be referred to a reclassification committee (*Comité d'aide au reclassement à entrées continues* – CREC) (see below for more details).

Box 3.3. **Ontario's Rapid Re-employment and Training Service: How does it work?**

A three-tiered response may be taken depending on the severity of the layoff and the capacity of the local employment service provider(s):

Tier 1: If local re-employment services have sufficient capacity to assist the affected workers, then the RRTS is limited to delivering information sessions and raising awareness of the different employment services available to the workers who will lose their jobs. These sessions may take place at Service Canada or by arranging EO service providers to go on-site or extend their hours of operation so that affected workers can use services before layoffs occur. Anecdotal evidence suggests that around 90% of the layoffs are dealt with using Tier 1 service, but these tend to be the layoffs affecting relatively few workers.

Tier 2: In a situation where EO service providers do not have sufficient capacity to meet demand, additional services can be arranged. Typically, this includes short-term training for affected workers; supplementing employment services with adjustment funding to provide outreach to affected workers or use of the *Adjustment Advisory Programme* (AAP) to establish an Action centre to deal with large scale closures. Through these Action centres, displaced workers can access: i) job-search assistance; ii) financial counselling and personal counselling to deal with the stress of job loss; iii) individual and group needs assessment; iv) vocational and educational counselling, and v) referral to EO programmes including the *Second Career* (SC) programme. Every laid-off worker develops an action plan within 15 days of his or her initial assessment and will have access to customised training, skills upgrading, job placement and relocation services. In general, Action centres should not operate for more than a year.

Tier 3: When adjustment situations have an adverse impact on the local economy or the community, a larger and a broader inter-ministry approach is taken. A local adjustment committee is established and led by an independent chair, to co-ordinate the implementation of the Service Action Plan. This plan is put in place within 30 days of the initial response and outlines the roles of the service providers in the community who will be delivering the services. A key component of the process is the development of a multi-disciplinary Rapid Response team, which is formed at the local or regional level to provide timely, focused and integrated training and employment solutions to affected workers and communities.

Source: OECD questionnaire on policies for displaced workers.

Undoubtedly, both of the models avoid the delays that could arise if the government waited for displaced workers to find their own way to Service Canada or the provincial and territorial employment services, while also allowing services to be tailored to the group's particular needs. There are no rigorous evaluations of the two programmes, but according to an evaluation of a labour adjustment programme in Greater Hamilton (in Province of Ontario) that served smaller groups of displaced workers from a number of workplaces during the global financial crisis and provided similar services to that of the Action centre concluded that among the 652 clients that came for support, 50% found jobs since first coming to the centre (Klassen and Fraser 2011).

Results from similar rapid response programmes from other countries confirm the potential benefits emerging from these schemes. For example, in Hungary, the re-employment assistance committee (akin to rapid response in Ontario) that was first used during 1994 and 1998, to help with 60 enterprise layoffs (including heavy and light industry, public administration and the army) led to a dramatic reduction in the time it took workers to find new jobs. Project statistics show that assistance cut in half the time it took workers to find new jobs – from 265 days to 130. This reduction provided considerable financial savings to the government for UI payments and other social services (Hansen, 2009). At the same time, participation in job counselling and training provided through such programmes also promoted better worker morale and reduced negative effects caused by the downsizing process (Tzafrir et al., 2006).

Delivering early intervention services effectively remains a challenge

Despite the various benefits associated with early intervention, various factors including lack of incentives for both employers and workers can undermine the effectiveness of the above described measures. One major concern is the *timing* of such interventions. Though the rapid response services are expressly intended to intervene early in the process, many of the activities under both the RRTS in Ontario and the CAR in Quebec are deferred until the workers are actually laid-off. The main rationale for this delay is that going beyond basic informational meetings during the notice period, for example by offering re-employment services, could disrupt production and hence discourage employers from co-operating with the public employment service by notifying them of impending layoffs and working with them to provide adjustment assistance to retrenched workers. Indeed, in Quebec, during 2008-09, nearly 60% of the layoff notifications were received later than the mandated provisions, potentially delaying access to even basic adjustment services whilst workers still have a job.

Public employment services may also face challenges as they sometimes become reluctant to intervene early because some announced layoffs never occur due to unexpected improvements in conditions, causing government authorities to be wary of spending too much money and time on workers who may end up staying in their current jobs. Finally, the extent to which early intervention services can be effective in linking displaced workers quickly with the labour market may also depend on the requirement on individuals to engage with such services. Currently participation in Action centres and CAR for example is on a voluntary basis.

Early intervention is also likely to be ineffective for workers that are laid off several times from the same firm for a certain period of time with a scheduled date for potential reintegration, known as "mise à pied" in Quebec. In industries where wages are relatively high (e.g. due to high tenure or strong unions) and workers have very specific skills that are of little interest to other employers, these not-yet completely displaced workers have little or no incentive to accept or even search for another job, until the plant definitively closes. Similarly, in Ontario, an employer may put an employee on a temporary layoff without specifying a date on which the employee will be recalled to work. Even in these very uncertain situations, displaced workers may overestimate their chances to be reintegrated and may not look for other employment opportunities as their attachment to the firm and their previous work environment remain high. Early notification is likely to have very little effect in this case, as workers continue to hope to be recalled as long as the firm remains open.

Providing better incentives to various actors including employers, employees and the PES may help to address some of these challenges. Sanctions for non-compliance of the legislation concerning advance notice of mass layoffs are used as one way to improve employer incentives to co-operate with public authorities early on. In Quebec, employers can be fined up to CAD 1 500 for each week of the delay in sending notice of dismissals. Nevertheless, enforcement of such sanctions is often problematic as it is often difficult to determine the cause of non-compliance. In some cases, delays in notifications occur because employers have paid compensation in lieu of notice or that collective redundancies were driven by unforeseen events which leaves employers with very little time to notify the authorities. Moreover, sanctions are not applicable to so-called "run-away firms" that simply close without warning, walking away from their obligations to provide advance notice and to work with labour market authorities leaving workers they displaced without any early reintegration measures.

While the use of sanctions might be difficult, strengthening individual obligations may improve the effectiveness of early intervention services. There is no evidence on the take-up rates of rapid response services but displaced workers in receipt of severance payments could have fewer incentives to seek such support. This is particularly problematic since these workers are also at risk of not receiving any job-search assistance and training via public employment services until they receive Employment Insurance benefits. The delay to re-employment support can be up to two years for those in receipt of very large severance packages hurting re-employment prospects of especially older workers (see Chapter 1 for more details). Similarly, workers that are laid-off temporarily may also have little incentive to utilise these services early on as they wait to be recalled at some point during their unemployment spell.

Introducing obligations may in this case ensure that the most vulnerable individuals do not fall through the cracks. In order to minimise unemployment duration and facilitate early contact with employment services, several countries have resorted to extending obligations to workers dismissed regardless of the availability of rapid response services. For example, in Switzerland, as part of the required job-search efforts, unemployed workers also need to give proof of job-search activities between dismissal notification and the first interview at the PES to receive unemployment benefits (Duell et al., 2010). A similar preventative approach was adopted in Germany as part of the Hartz reforms, where workers are obliged to register as jobseekers three months before their job ends or, for those with shorter notice, within three days after receiving notice of dismissal (Mosley, 2010). This registration obligation allows the PES to make referrals to vacancies before the first unemployment benefit payment.

Recent measures in France, using a tripartite approach, have gone further in addressing incentives for employers, employee and the PES to better facilitate early reintegration measures through the *Contrat de sécurisation professionnelle* (Box 3.4). This could be an interesting approach also for Canada.

Box 3.4. **Incentives and disincentives effects of the French *Contrat de sécurisation professionnelle* (CSP)**

In 2011, France implemented[1] a tailored programme called *Contrat de sécurisation professionnelle* (CSP – Career Path Security Contract) to improve incentives for the employer, the affected employees and PES to better facilitate the use of early transition services. Whatever their tenure, all workers dismissed for economic reason (individually or collectively) from a firm with less than 1 000 employees or filing for bankruptcy,[2] are entitled to enter the programme.

This programme lasts a maximum of 12 months and includes a range of measures such as job-search assistance, intensive counselling, individual interviews with a specific caseworker, skills evaluation, access to training and follow-up support during the entire programme to improve re-employment prospects. The costs of this programme is shared by the PES, the employer and the former employee, providing incentives for all actors to facilitate better co-operation and potentially improve the take-up of the programme.

Employers

Under the programme, employers have to offer the CSP to the workers they plan to dismiss before the actual dismissal takes place. In the case of non-compliance, the employer must pay the French PES *Pôle emploi* a fine equivalent to two months of gross salary which is increased to three months if the displaced worker agrees to a CSP after being informed by the PES.

Box 3.4. **Incentives and disincentives effects of the French *Contrat de sécurisation professionnelle* (CSP)** *(cont.)*

Displaced workers

Displaced workers participate in the cost of CSP by allocating their severance pay to the PES (up to maximum of 3 months of gross salaries) and accepting to waive the notice period.[3] They also accept to waive their training rights acquired in their previous job (*Droit individuel à la formation* – DIF).[4] These sums are instead used to finance the CSP. The worker has 21 days to make a decision during which his/her contract cannot be terminated. In case of acceptance, the contract ends after the 21-day period without any additional notice period. This enables the PES to have a very early access to displaced workers and to be able to work quickly on their re-employment or retraining prospects. In case of refusal of the CSP, the employer and employee follow the usual economic dismissal procedure (with notice period). In addition, displaced workers participating in the CSP, with at least one year of tenure, are entitled to a higher unemployment benefit than other unemployed individuals (approximately the same amount as their previous net wage). The CSP also offers wage insurance for displaced workers finding a job which pays less than 85% of their earnings in the previous job (the so-called *Indemnité différentielle de reclassement* – IDR).

Public employment services

In turn, the PES contributes by providing much more intensive and close follow-up, e.g. one interview per week in the first phase of the programme (which lasts for one month) and at least one per month in the remaining 11 months of the programme. Additional assistance is also provided during the first three months of a new job. Caseworkers are exclusively working with displaced workers and therefore have a better knowledge of their specific needs and issues. The higher unemployment benefit is also partly covered by the PES.

According to a recent evaluation, around 54% of displaced workers who participated in the programme between 2009 and 2011 obtained employment upon its completion (compared to re-employment rate of 44% in Canada during the same period, as seen Chapter 1). Both the severe downturn of the French labour market conditions at that time and the very high replacement rate of the CSP-specific unemployment benefit may explain the somewhat low re-employment rates. Displaced unemployed are likely to have fewer incentives to take-up a job despite the existence of the wage insurance scheme (IDR) as the latter does not cover the entire wage loss contrary to the unemployment benefits under the CSP.

---

1. A similar programme (*Contrat de transition professionnelle)* was already experimented since 2006 in some territories.
2. Workers dismissed for economic reason from firms with more than 1 000 employees are entitled to a *congé de reclassement*, very similar to the CAR in Quebec or the Action centres in Ontario.
3. Severance package is paid to the employee depending on his tenure, as for any economic dismissal.
4. By law, every employee can acquire from his or her employer "credit hours" of 20 hours of training per year, which can be cumulated over six years (so up to a maximum of 120 hours). The initiative to use this right to training belongs to the employee, but the implementation of the DIF requires the consent of the employer on the choice of the training. DIF has since been reformed with the creation in 2015 of the "personal training account" (*Compte personnel de formation*).

Source: Dares-Pôle emploi (2013), "L'accompagnement renforcé des demandeurs d'emploi : Évaluation du recours aux opérateurs privés par Pôle emploi de 2009 à 2011", *Synthèse.Éval'*, No.°03, January; and website of the Ministère du Travail, de l'Emploi, de la Formation professionnelle et du Dialogue social, http://travail-emploi.gouv.fr/informations-pratiques,89/les-fiches-pratiques-du-droit-du,91/accompagnement-des-mutations,593/le-contrat-de-securisation,13990.html.

Not all displaced workers benefit from early intervention services

While workers affected by mass dismissals typically will receive some kind of rapid response intervention, as described above, many displaced workers will only receive re-employment support from the core active labour market programmes in their provinces or territories which are often not tailored to the needs of displaced workers. In addition, where there are no legal provisions to provide adjustment support, some large employers may do so in good faith, but this is often problematic for small to medium enterprises due to financial constraints. Quebec is the only province providing specialised adjustment assistance to workers affected by individual and small scale displacements. These workers can enrol in *Comités d'aide au reclassement à entrées continues* (CREC) which are open to all displaced workers from different firms and provide services similar to those provided by a CAR. CRECs meet the needs of regions: i) facing multiple redundancies in small and medium firms (therefore not reaching the 50-displaced workers threshold); and/or ii) that do not have enough PES staff to cope with the sudden and massive influx of displaced workers in a local employment centre. To ensure sufficient capacity is available, *Emploi-Québec* outsources these CREC outplacement services to specialised external resources.

A permanent scheme such as CREC has many advantages. First, it can meet the distinct needs of displaced workers that are often not met in public employment services as they are typically targeted to assist very disadvantaged groups such as the long-term unemployed. Indeed, displaced workers in both Ontario and Quebec are likely to receive limited job counselling except for some groups of displaced workers who may receive support via the *Targeted Initiative for Older Workers* (a federal-provincial cost-shared initiative) or the *Second Career programme* (SC) offered by the Province of Ontario (see Chapter 5 for more details). Even when displaced workers may not require such intensive support, the PES may not be adequate e.g. having suitable vacancies for highly skilled displaced workers. Second, the CREC model could be more conducive to delivering services such as "peer" support because of familiarity and shared experience between staff and clients. Third, CREC are a useful tool in the case when the company is bankrupt; has already left the area without notice (the so-called "runaway-firms"); or refuses to participate in the setting up of a reclassification assistance committee. Finally, the take-up of support could be better in a dedicated service rather than the PES which may have some stigma attached to it.

In the context of the very low protection of permanent workers against individual dismissals in Canada and relatively weak provisions to assist these workers into new jobs after job loss, there may be a case for extending the CREC model more widely in Canada. A more permanent service such as the CREC could be financed by employers paying a fee based on their labour costs as done in Sweden, where so-called Job Security Councils, operating in parallel to the PES, play a vital role in the restructuring process by providing continuous and tailored services to displaced workers (Box 3.5). The size of such a service that runs along the PES would also need to be considered carefully since it may suffer from erratic flows i.e. large inflows in time of economic crisis or big industrial shifts. One solution would be to establish only a small number of offices which may serve populations of more than one employer or region. Indeed, during the global financial crisis, labour Action centres were established in the Province of Ontario (Greater Hamilton) to serve smaller groups of displaced workers from a number of workplaces throughout the community who would not qualify to start their own Action centre.[18]

Box 3.5. **Job Security Councils in Sweden**

Job Security Councils were first developed in the 1970s against the backdrop of the deteriorating economic conditions in Sweden in the late 1960s and the massive job loss of white-collar workers in the wake of the oil crisis in 1973. The PES was not regarded by employers as providing sufficient support for white-collar workers to find new jobs (Diedrich and Bergström, 2006). The councils are based on collective agreements between social partners in a sector or occupational field, such as white-collar workers in the private sector. Job Security Councils are actively involved in the process of restructuring and provide advice and consultation to employers and trade unions at an early stage in the process. They also provide transition services and guidance to workers who are made redundant.

The councils' activities are financed through employer contributions fixed as a percentage of their total payroll. The contribution level is determined as part of the collective agreement (currently 0.3% of payroll). As such, the council operates as a form of insurance, distributing the risk and costs of restructuring among its members, which allows access for workers in small and medium enterprises (European Commission, 2010).

Job Security Councils themselves claim that around 90% of their participants found a solution within nine months: 78% found new employment, 8% started a new business and 6% chose to start longer duration education.

Source: Diedrich, A. and O. Bergström (2006), "The job security councils in Sweden", School of Business, Economics, and Law, Göteborg University and Institute of Management of Innovation and Technology (IMIT) report, www.imit.se/pdf/reports/2007_145.pdf; and European Commission (2010), "27 National seminars on anticipating and managing restructuring", EU Synthesis Report, International Training Centre of the ILO, Turin.

Conclusion

Compared with other OECD countries, Canadian employers face relatively few legislative restrictions on reducing employment within their firms. This may make Canadian workers more vulnerable to experiencing job loss than their counterparts in other countries, but it also results in a flexible labour market in which most unemployed persons can find another job relatively quickly. In the context of relatively unrestrictive employment protection rules, the Work-Sharing scheme can provide a useful incentive for employers confronting a temporary reduction in business activity to retain valuable employees by temporarily reducing working hours.

Canada places considerable emphasis on early intervention measures to facilitate worker's transition to new jobs. Advance notice in Canada is usually combined with adjustment assistance to workers affected by mass layoffs. At least in the cases of Ontario and Quebec, the provinces intervene rapidly once they are notified of a plant closure or a mass layoff. Both provinces make use of the rapid response concept with the public employment service working closely with the employer, unions and other stakeholders to begin offering adjustment assistance to the affected workers before they become unemployed. This model avoids the delays that could arise if the government waited for displaced workers to find their own way to Service Canada or the provincial and territorial employment services, while also allowing services to be tailored to each group's particular needs.

Provinces can react quickly in case of mass layoffs when employers are co-operative, but co-operation is not always forthcoming and the services offered before the layoff occurs can be quite limited. A number of steps can be taken following the examples of other OECD countries to address the lacking incentives of all actors to foster greater co-operation among employers, employees and the public employment services and to ensure more effective delivery of early intervention measures. For instance, in order to connect potential displaced workers with job-search and counselling support early on, mandatary registration with the PES during the dismissal period should be considered.

While workers affected by mass dismissals typically will benefit from a rapid response intervention, at least in the two provinces analysed here, many displaced workers do not benefit from such measures and thus rely on re-employment support from the core active labour market programmes in their local area. This can be problematic if it leads to a significant delay in the initiation of adjustment assistance or the services offered by the PES are not geared to meet the needs of displaced workers. The CREC in Quebec is an interesting attempt to extend the rapid response model to reach workers displaced by individual or small scale layoffs. Another approach is to assure that the core labour market programmes provide suitable income and re-employment support to all displaced workers who need them. The subsequent chapters assess these programmes according to how well they meet the adjustment assistance needs of displaced workers.

Notes

1. Employees must have completed a minimum period of service of 30 days in Manitoba and of six months in New Brunswick, Prince Edward Island and Yukon.

2. Termination pay is a lump-sum payment equal to the *regular wage* for a *regular workweek* that an employee would otherwise have been entitled to during the written notice period. It is not a substitute for severance payments.

3. In Ontario, an employer who severs an employment relationship with an employee is required to pay severance pay if the employer has a payroll of USD 2.5 million or more, or the employer is severing the employment of 50 or more employees over a six-month period because all or part of the business is being permanently discontinued.

4. For example in Quebec, collective redundancies are defined as either the termination of employment for ten or more employees in the same establishment over a period of two consecutive months; or the temporary layoffs of at least ten employees for six months or more.

5. A notice of group termination of employment must specify the name of the employer; the location at which the termination takes place; the nature of the industry; the date or dates on which the employer intends to terminate the employment of any one or more employees; the estimated number of employees in each occupational classification whose employment will be terminated; the reason for the termination of employment; and the name of any trade union certified to represent any employee in the group of employees whose employment is to be terminated or recognised by the employer as a bargaining agent for any such employees.

6. Employers, under the federal jurisdiction, are also required to setup an adjustment programme. If the committee is not able to agree on an adjustment programme, either part can apply to the Minister of Labour for the appointment of an arbitrator, to settle outstanding issues.

7. This overall stringency indicator of the regulation of individual dismissals for workers on permanent contracts is obtained as the simple average of the three sub-component indicators for: i) procedural inconveniences related to the provision of advance notice; ii) duration of notice and amount of severance pay; and iii) difficulty of dismissal. For further details about the construction of the OECD indicators, see OECD (2013), Chapter 2.

8. The correlation of EPL strictness with unemployment inflows and outflows are -0.27 and -0.41 respectively, while the correlation with the incidence of long-term unemployment rate is 0.31. All correlations are significant at a 5% level.

9. In addition to being responsive to the needs of the economy, the Canadian WS programme includes special measures that may be used to assist employers who are experiencing a temporary shortage of work due to disasters and states of emergency

10. At the end of 2012, the WS programme reverted to operating under the previous rules of agreement durations and provided a simplified recovery plan for employers. HRSDC continues every month to closely monitor the economic situation related to WS so as to identify any new developments or departures from current trends that may indicate the need to offer additional temporary measures.

11. Hijzen and Venn (2011) compares STW schemes in 24 OECD countries, showing that most other OECD countries have adopted eligibility rules that are similar to those in Canada.

12. The peak to trough decline in GDP was only about half as large in Canada as in Germany and Japan, but the increase in the take-up rate was only about one-tenth as large.

13. One factor increasing the total number of hours subsidised by WS is that the global recession and the temporary increase in the maximum allowable duration of WS benefits had a major impact on extending the duration of WS schemes: the average duration of receipt of WS benefits ranged from a minimum of 15.8 weeks in 2004-05 to a maximum of 39.4 weeks in 2008-09 (HRSDC, 2013).

14. The Czech Republic, Hungary, the Netherlands and Portugal introduced a requirement that workers participate in training during their idle hours (OECD, 2010).

15. The SERRÉ programme was extended for two more years (2010-12) in the specific area of Montréal, becoming the so-called SEMER programme (*Soutien aux entreprises de la métropole pour l'emploi et la relance*).

16. Quebec is the only province in Canada where employers are legislated to allot 1% of their total payroll towards employee training.

17. In Ontario, the percentage of rapid response intervention costs shared may vary, but an equal split of the costs between employer, union and province is most common.

18. The Action centre was set up in partnership with the United Way of Burlington and Greater Hamilton, the Ministry of Training, Colleges, and Universities (MTCU), and the Social Planning and Research Council of Hamilton.

References

Dares-Pôle emploi (2013), "L'accompagnement renforcé des demandeurs d'emploi : Évaluation du recours aux opérateurs privés par Pôle emploi de 2009 à 2011", *Synthèse.Éval'*, No. 03, January.

Diedrich, A. and O. Bergström (2006), "The job security councils in Sweden", School of Business, Economics, and Law, Göteborg University and Institute of Management of Innovation and Technology (IMIT) report, http://www.imit.se/pdf/reports/2007_145.pdf.

Duell, N., P. Tergeist, U. Bazant and S. Cimper (2010), "Activation Policies in Switzerland", *OECD Social, Employment and Migration Working Papers*, No. 112, OECD Publishing, Paris, http://dx.doi.org/10.1787/5km4hd7r28f6-en.

Emploi-Québec (2011), "Concertation pour l'emploi : Aménagement et réduction du temps de travail (CT)", Guide des mesures et des services d'emploi, http://emploiquebec.gouv.qc.ca/guide_mesures_services/05_Mesures_progr_Emploi_Quebec/05_6_Concertation_pour_emploi/03_CPE_ARTT.pdf.

European Commission (2010), "27 National seminars on anticipating and managing restructuring", EU Synthesis Report, International Training Centre of the ILO, Turin.

Hansen, G.B. (2009), *A Guide to Worker Displacement: Some Tools for Reducing the Impact on Workers, Communities and Enterprises*, Skills and Employability Department, ILO, Geneva.

Hijzen, A. and S. Martin (2013), "The role of Short-Time Work schemes during the global financial crisis and early recovery: A cross-country analysis", *IZA Discussion Papers*, No. 7291, Institute for the Study of Labor, March, Bonn, http://ftp.iza.org/dp7291.pdf.

Hijzen, A. and D. Venn (2011), "The role of Short-Time Work schemes during the 2008-09 Recession", *OECD Social, Employment and Migration Working Papers*, No. 115, OECD Publishing, Paris, http://dx.doi.org/10.1787/5kgkd0bbwvxp-en.

HR Insider (2009) "Layoffs, terminations & restructuring your workforce: Avoiding the cost of non-compliance", http://hrinsider.ca/specialreports/Layoffs%20Terminations%20&%20Restructuring%20Your%20Workforce%20-%20white%20paper%2060%20page.pdf.

HRDC – Human Resources Development Canada (2004), "Evaluation of the Work-Sharing programme", Final Report, February.

HRSDC – Human Resources and Skills Development Canada (2013), "Usage of the Work-Sharing Program: 1990/91 to 2011/12", Strategic Policy and Research Branch, Version 1.0, Evaluation Directorate, mimeo, January.

HRSDC (2005), "Summative evaluation of Work Sharing While Learning and Increased Referrals to Training", Final Report, EI Evaluation, Audit and Evaluation Directorate, Strategic Policy and Planning Branch, HRSDC, April.

Klassen, C. and M. Fraser (2011), "Supporting laid off workers in Hamilton: The value of Employment Training at the Hamilton Jobs Action centre", Final Report, Social Planning and Research Council of Hamilton, May.

Martin, J.P. and S. Scarpetta (2012), "Setting it right: Employment protection, labour reallocation and productivity", *De Economist*, Vol. 160, No. 2, pp 89-116, June, http://link.springer.com/article/10.1007/s10645-011-9177-2.

MESS – Ministère de l'Emploi et de la Solidarité sociale (2010), "Évaluation des effets du programme de soutien aux entreprises à risque de ralentissement économique (Serré): Les effets bruts", MESS, Direction de l'évaluation, May.

Ministry of Labour Quebec (2013), "Portrait statistique des conventions collectives analysées au Québec en 2012", Direction de l'information sur le travail, September.

Mosley, H. (2010), "Reform of placement services – Peer Review on 'Systematic preventive integration approach (Support) for jobseekers and unemployed'", Mutual Learning Programme: Host Country Discussion Paper – Germany, in consortium with GHK Consulting Ltd and CERGE-EI, 10 September.

Nord, S. and Y. Ting (1991), "The impact of advance notice of plant closings on earnings and the probability of unemployment", *Industrial and Labor Relations Review*, Vol. 44, No. 4, July, pp. 681-691.

OECD (2014), *Employment and Skills Strategies in Canada*, OECD Reviews on Local Job Creation, OECD Publishing. Paris, http://dx.doi.org/10.1787/9789264209374-en.

OECD (2013), *OECD Employment Outlook 2013*, OECD Publishing, Paris, http://dx.doi.org/10.1787/empl_outlook-2013-en.

OECD (2010), "Moving beyond the jobs crisis", in *OECD Employment Outlook 2010*, OECD Publishing, Paris, http://dx.doi.org/10.1787/empl_outlook-2010-en.

OECD (2009), "The jobs crisis: What are the implications for employment and social policy?", in *OECD Employment Outlook 2009*, OECD Publishing, Paris, http://dx.doi.org/10.1787/empl_outlook-2009-en.

Rhum, C. (1994), "Advance notice, job search, and postdisplacement earnings", *Journal of Labor Economics*, Vol. 12, No. 1, January, pp. 1-28.

Swaim, P. and M. Podgursky (1990), "Advance notice and job search: The value of an early start", *Journal of Human Resources*, Spring, Vol. 25, No. 2, pp. 147-178.

Tzafrir, S., R. Mano-Negrin, G.H. Harel and D. Rom-Nagy (2006), "Downsizing and the impact of job counselling and retraining on effective employee responses", *Career Development International*, Vol. 11, No. 2, pp. 125-144.

Venn, D. (2009), "Legislation, collective bargaining and enforcement: Updating the OECD employment protection indicators", *OECD Social, Employment and Migration Working Papers*, No. 89, http://dx.doi.org/10.1787/223334316804.

Database references

Employment Insurance Coverage Survey (EICS), Statistics Canada http://www23.statcan.gc.ca/imdb/p2SV.pl?Function=getSurvey&SDDS=4428.

OECD Employment Protection Database, 2013 update, http://dx.doi.org/10.1787/lfs-epl-data-en.

OECD Short-term Labour Market Statistics Database, www.oecd.org/statistics/.

Chapter 4

Access to and adequacy of income support for displaced workers in Canada

Income loss is one of the major costs borne by workers following job displacement. How to compensate displaced workers whilst improving their transition back into employment is one of the most critical challenges facing policy makers. In Canada, most displaced workers with stable work histories have relatively good access to income support through Employment Insurance (EI) whilst they look for new jobs. However, the severance payment provisions and the relatively short duration of EI benefit entitlements result in delayed coverage and re-employment support among older and long-tenured displaced workers, precisely the group who suffer the greatest barriers in returning to the labour market and income losses post displacement. A major challenge is to expedite re-employment support to workers in receipt of severance payments and boost incomes for older long-tenured workers whilst ensuring adequate incentives for them to find new jobs.

The statistical data for Israel are supplied by and under the responsibility of the relevant Israeli authorities. The use of such data by the OECD is without prejudice to the status of the Golan Heights, East Jerusalem and Israeli settlements in the West Bank under the terms of international law.

Among other costs, displacement comes with substantial earning losses. Since displaced workers bear a disproportionate share of the costs associated with structural economic and policy changes that benefit most individuals, it makes good sense for "winners" to adequately compensate the "losers". Public policies such as unemployment insurance and other income support benefits play an important role to cushion income losses borne by these workers while out of work. In some cases, they may also receive severance payments from their employers. Wage Insurance has received considerable attention as an additional form of compensation that is targeted at large earning losses which persist even after displaced workers find new jobs, but there is little experience with operating such schemes.

The Canadian Employment Insurance system has a number of unique features. Notably unemployment benefit eligibility, entitlement and payment level are determined in part by the local unemployment rate in 61 economic regions. The way in which severance payments interact with eligibility to Employment Insurance is also unusual as such payments delay access to income and employment support for displaced workers. This is of particular concern for older and long-tenured workers; even though severance payments can provide a substitute for EI, the delay in accessing active labour market programmes can potentially damage their re-employment prospects. At the same time, income adequacy is a major issue for long-tenured Canadian workers who typically experience greater income losses even when they have found new jobs.

Sources for income support for displaced workers

Employment Insurance

The main programme providing temporary income support for displaced workers is Employment Insurance (EI). The programme is largely administered and delivered by the federal Department of Employment and Social Development Canada (ESDC) and funded by mandatory contributions of employees and employers.[1] The programme also pays for active labour market programmes through Labour Market Development Agreements (LMDAs) with the Canadian provinces and territories (see Chapters 2 and 5 for more details).

As in most other OECD countries, to qualify for the unemployment benefit, known as EI *Regular benefit*, a worker must be involuntary unemployed; available for and actively seeking employment; and have completed a minimum period of contributions. However, there are a number of unique and key features to the Canadian EI system. First, in contrast to many other OECD countries, eligibility for benefits is based on the total number of hours worked, rather than on days, weeks, months worked or the amount of paid contributions. Second, eligibility, duration and benefit level in each of the 61 economic regions are determined on the basis of regional unemployment rates (see discussion below). Finally, no benefits are paid for a transitional period of two weeks, the longest waiting period in the OECD.[2] In combination, these features arguably make the EI system more generous for part-year seasonal workers than in other OECD countries (Gray and Sweetman, 2001; and Gray and McDonald, 2010); less generous for long-tenured workers; and very restrictive for people with very short unemployment spells (van Audenrode et al., 2005).

The impact of local labour market conditions on EI entitlements has important implications for displaced workers. Under the so-called Variable Entrance Requirement (VER), the number of hours required to qualify may vary between 420 and 700 hours in the preceding 52-week *qualifying period* depending on the average regional unemployment rate over the preceding three months.[3] For instance, a minimum of 420 hours (around 12 weeks full-time) of work is required in areas of high unemployment (over 13%) and 700 hours (20 weeks of full-time employment) in areas of low unemployment (6% or lower).[4]

Likewise, the maximum number of weeks of benefit entitlement increases with the unemployment rate in a region and the amount of insurable hours accumulated. The maximum EI benefit period ranges from 14 weeks to 45 weeks, usually over a period of 52 weeks: 14-36 weeks in regions with the lowest levels of unemployment (6% or lower), and 32-45 weeks in regions with the highest level of unemployment (above 13%).

During the global financial crisis, regular EI benefit entitlements were extended by five extra weeks to 19 to 50 weeks, depending on the number of insurable hours in the qualifying period and the unemployment rate in the region. Similarly, the duration of EI was increased significantly (up to 20 additional weeks) for long-tenured workers with an active claim between 2009 and 2010.[5]

The EI benefit payment rate is set at 55% of average weekly insurable earnings. Eligible earnings are capped at Maximum Insurable Earnings (MIE) which in 2015 was set to CAD 49 500 (level corresponding to the average weekly wage in 2014) resulting in a maximum gross benefit of CAD 524 per week.[6] However, as mentioned above, the benefit level is also influenced by the regional unemployment rate. Since 2013, claimant's average weekly earnings are calculated by taking the total earnings during the best weeks, i.e. weeks in which claimants earned the highest salary in the qualifying period. The "best" weeks, otherwise known as the "minimum divisor," ranges from 14 to 22 weeks, depending on the regional unemployment rate.[7]

Severance payments and their impact on Employment Insurance eligibility

Severance payments can be an important part of the compensation workers receive for displacement, especially for older and long-tenured workers who bear some of the largest earning losses. These payments may also encourage employers to internalise some of the social costs or negative externalities resulting from redundancies. Nevertheless, excessive severance awards may impede efficiency-enhancing mobility, as discussed in Chapter 3. An important issue that has received less attention is the way severance payments affect EI eligibility and how that can interfere with the way unemployment insurance and active labour market programmes operate for displaced workers.

Eligibility to EI for displaced workers is interlinked with severance payments, which are considered as income from employment and, as a result, may delay eligibility to EI or even reduce it in some cases. Essentially, in the Canadian system, severance payments like in a few other OECD countries, initially substitute for EI benefits (Table 4.1). The resulting delay in can be substantial. For the purpose of calculating the additional waiting period, lump-sum severance payments are considered as a series of wage payments, with each weekly payment corresponding to the individual's weekly earnings prior to job loss. For example, a worker receiving severance pay equivalent to six weeks of earnings will only qualify for regular EI benefits eight weeks after layoff (including the two-week standard waiting period).

The maximum combined duration of severance pay and EI is set at 104 weeks. This has two major implications: first, it implies that benefits will be cut short if the combined duration would exceed 104 weeks. Specifically, workers with severance payments of more than 57 weeks can expect to see a reduction to their EI entitlements assuming they qualify for the maximum 45-week EI benefit. Beyond this threshold, each extra week of severance pay means one week less of potential EI entitlements.[8] Second, a worker receiving a large severance package equivalent to 102-week pay or more would have her or his EI benefit eliminated altogether.

It is difficult to determine how many workers exceed the 57-week threshold. The federally mandated severance pay is modest, consisting of two days of a person's wage for every year of service. In Ontario, the legally mandated amount of compensation is higher, at one week of severance pay for each year of service up to a maximum of 26 weeks, still well below the 57-week threshold. However, workers covered by collective agreements can receive much more generous severance packages than what is required in the Employment Standards Act (Venn, 2009).[9] Further evidence from court rulings suggest that employers may be required to provide 50 or more weeks of severance pay in lieu of notice to long-serving rank-and-file workers, and 80 or more weeks to those higher in the corporate hierarchy (Arthurs, 2006). This suggests that these rules in particular reduce EI entitlements for long-tenured workers as they are more likely to be receiving long severance payments. Data from the Employment Insurance Coverage Survey show that around half of all displaced workers report to have received severance payment at some point after their job loss (Figure 4.1). At 53% the share of long-tenured displaced workers in receipt of severance payment is slightly higher.

Figure 4.1. **Displaced workers are more likely to receive severance or termination payments following dismissals**

Percentage of workers reporting receipt of severance pay or any other employer-provided payment when the job ended, 2000-10

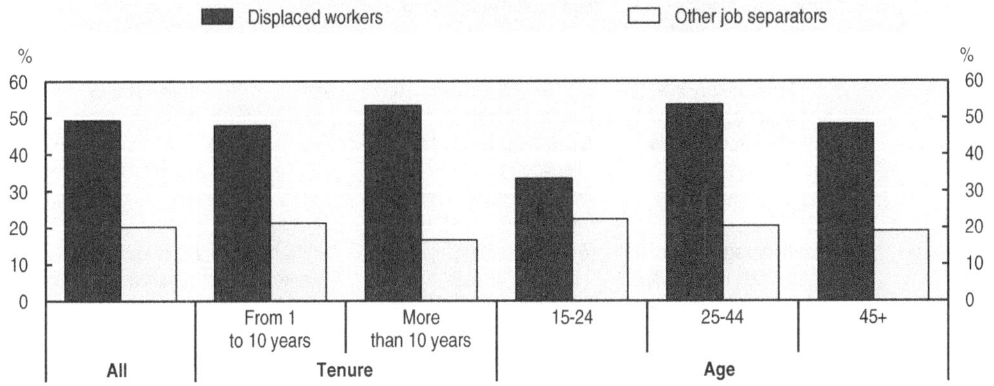

Note: Includes severance pay or pay instead of vacation, pension pay-out, early retirement package, wages instead of notice, sick-leave credits or payments for unused sick benefits and any other payments received when the job ended.

Source: OECD calculations based on data from the Employment Insurance Coverage Survey (EICS).

StatLink http://dx.doi.org/10.1787/888933238760

Although severance payments can be considered as an additional form of "compensation" for displaced workers for their job loss, arguably their function is akin to that of employment insurance schemes i.e. providing income support to unemployed workers. Thus, while receiving severance payments in lieu of EI can be considered to be reasonable from an income-needs perspective of workers, one major concern related to extended unemployment periods without regular EI benefit entitlement is that it can leave jobseekers without effective re-employment support during a long period of unemployment. Jobseekers without EI benefit entitlement qualify for only basic job-search assistance and have limited access to related active labour market programmes. Even then, participation is not mandatory and is difficult or impossible to monitor and enforce unless it is tied to benefit payments.

Table 4.1. **Characteristics of severance pay schemes in selected OECD countries**

	Legal base and eligibility conditions	Amount in statutory law	Collective bargaining coverage rate[a]	Interaction with UI entitlement
Australia	Federal statutory law and provisions in collective agreements	Min: tenure ≥ 1 year and < 2 year = 4 weeks Max: tenure ≥ 9 years and < 10 years = 16 weeks Tenure ≥10 years = 12 weeks	45% (2007)	Waiting period for UB is increased by number of (wage) weeks received in severance pay
Austria[b]	Statutory law: Access to individual accounts only if tenure over 3 years. Otherwise account carried over to next employer	Amount depends on the capital accrued in the fund, investment income earned and capital guaranteed	99% (2010)	None
Canada	Federal statutory law and provisions in collective agreements	Min: tenure < 1 year = 0, tenure ≥ 1 year and < 3 years = 5 days after which tenure ≥ 3 years = 2 days for each year of tenure	29% (2012)	Waiting period for UB is increased by number of (wage) days received in severance pay
Denmark[c]	Statutory requirement for white-collar workers and collective agreements only for blue-collar workers	White collars: Min: 1 month > 12-year tenure; 2 month > 15-year tenure; 3 months > 18-year tenure Blue collars: Min: 1 month > 3 years of service; 2 months > 6 years of service; 3 months > 8 years of service	85% for all workers (2007)	For blue-collar workers, the amount of severance pay is the difference between 85% of their monthly salary and the amount of their UB. Since initial replacement rates are most often above 85%, severance pay is rarely paid. In effect the amount of severance pay is reduced by the amount of unemployment benefit.
Finland	No severance pay	n.a.	90% (2008)	n.a.
France	Statutory law and provisions in collective agreements	Min: tenure ≥ 1 year. 2 months Max: tenure ≥ 20 years: 5.3 months	90% (2008)	Waiting period for UB is increased if severance pay exceeds legal minima, by a duration in days corresponding to the extra-amount in severance pay divided by previous daily wage (total waiting period capped at 75 days).

Table 4.1. **Characteristics of severance pay schemes in selected OECD countries** *(cont.)*

	Legal base and eligibility conditions	Amount in statutory law	Collective bargaining coverage rate	Interaction with UI entitlement
Germany	Statutory law: an employee working in a firm with at least ten employees who is dismissed on the basis of compelling operational reason is entitled to severance pay if he renounces to go to court	Half a month's pay per year of tenure	61% (2010)	None
Japan	No legal requirement. Provisions in collective agreements		16% (2008)	
Korea	No legal requirement. Provisions in collective agreements		10% (2008)	None
New Zealand[d]	No legal requirement in general but right to negotiate severance pay in case redundancy is due to outsourcing (note). Provisions in collective agreements		17% (2007)	None
Sweden	No legal requirement. General provisions established in collective agreements respectively for white collars aged over 40 and for blue collars aged over 40 and with 50 months of employment over the last 5 years	White collars: complements UI at a max of 70% of previous wage for a period of 6-18 months depending on age. Blue collars are entitled to a lump sum increasing with age	91% (2011)	Amount depends on UI for white collars
United States	No legal requirement. Provisions in collective agreements		13% (2011)	Waiting period for UB or reduction in the amount depending on the state

Note: UB: Unemployment benefit; n.a.: No severance payments for workers.

a) The collective bargaining coverage rate provides an indication of the proportion of the workforce potentially covered under these agreements and therefore likely to receive higher severance packages than the legislated ones.

b) *Austria*: Conditions refer to workers with contracts concluded after January 2003.

c) *Denmark:* Conditions are regulated by collective agreements per sector for blue-collar workers and by regulation for white-collar workers.

d) *New Zealand:* In case of restructuring, defined as outsourcing, the employee has the right to ask for transfer to the contractor. If refused, the worker can negotiate redundancy arrangements.

Source: OECD Employment Protection Database, 2013 update, http://dx.doi.org/10.1787/lfs-epl-data-en; *ILO Employment Protection Legislation Database*, http://www.ilo.org/dyn/eplex/termdisplay.severancePay?p_lang=en; *ICTWSS Database* for adjusted bargaining coverage rates; and Lindquist, G.S. and E. Wadensjö (2007), "Social and occupational security and labour market flexibility in Sweden: The case of unemployment compensation", *IZA Discussion Papers*, No. 2943, Institute for the Study of Labor, July, Bonn, http://ftp.iza.org/dp2943.pdf.

Benefit coverage among displaced workers

Overall, displaced workers have good access to Employment Insurance

The relatively low entrance requirements for unemployment benefit in Canada compared with other OECD countries make it relatively easy for displaced workers to receive EI. Data from SLID show that during 2000-10, around 62% of workers received regular EI benefit at *some* point during their unemployment spell in the first year following displacement (Figure 4.2). Therefore, almost two-thirds of displaced workers may qualify for the range of active labour market programmes (ALMPs) available only to EI claimants (see Chapter 2). This share is significantly higher than for workers who lost their job due to other reasons (end of temporary or fixed-term contracts) who may not have accumulated sufficient insured hours to qualify for EI.

Figure 4.2. **Displaced workers have good access to EI upon job loss**

Share of displaced workers and other job separators who ever received EI, before and after the global financial crisis, 2000-10

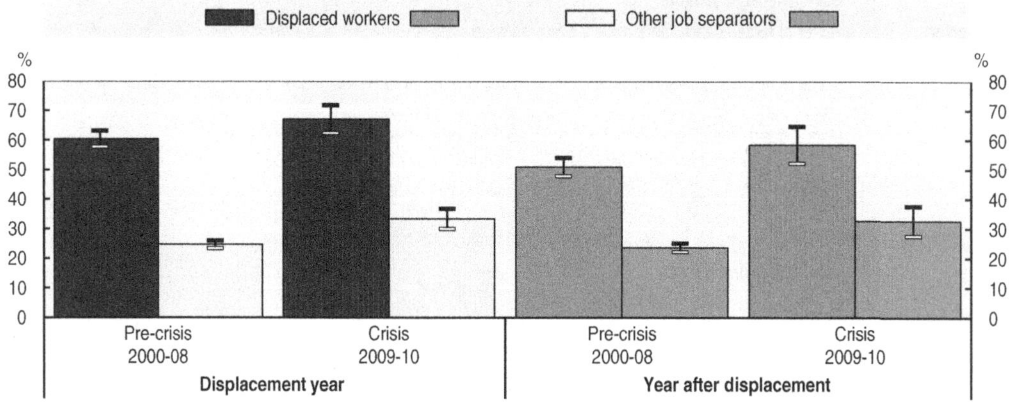

Note: The whisker symbol on the figure represents the 95% confidence interval.

Source: OECD calculations based on data from the Survey of Labour and Income Dynamics (SLID).

StatLink http://dx.doi.org/10.1787/888933238776

Following the onset of the economic downturn in 2008, benefit coverage increased for all recent job losers; by seven and nine percentage points, respectively for displaced workers and other job losers. This trend reflects the temporary EI extension of five weeks for all eligible workers and of up to 20 weeks for long-tenured workers. However, according to Mendelsohn and Medow (2010), overall benefit coverage in the most recent recession was much lower than in the earlier downturns of the 1980s and 1990s. This trend decrease is consistent with EI reforms in the 1990s, which introduced tighter eligibility requirements.[10]

Current coverage rates of those still not employed

Current EI coverage rates, i.e. the share of displaced workers not employed and receiving EI at the time of the survey, are an alternative measure of coverage, which can also be used to assess the firmness of the safety net. In addition, an assessment of the adequacy of the EI system needs to take into account the impact of severance payments which represent an important alternative source of income for many displaced workers.

Figure 4.3 presents i) EI coverage rates at the time of the survey, and ii) the proportion of displaced workers not receiving EI because of severance payments. Data from the Employment Insurance Coverage Survey (EICS) – see Box 4.1 – show that during 2000-10, about 61% of the workers who were displaced and still not employed were receiving regular EI at the time of the survey. Again, this coverage rate is significantly higher than for workers who lost their job in the same period for reasons other than displacement and for all non-employed. The overall pool of non-employed includes more disadvantaged individuals who may not have worked for a long time as well as jobseekers looking for their first job.

Figure 4.3. **Current EI coverage rates among displaced workers are much higher than for other groups of non-employed workers**

Percentage of non-employed workers currently receiving EI by reason of non-employment, 2000-10

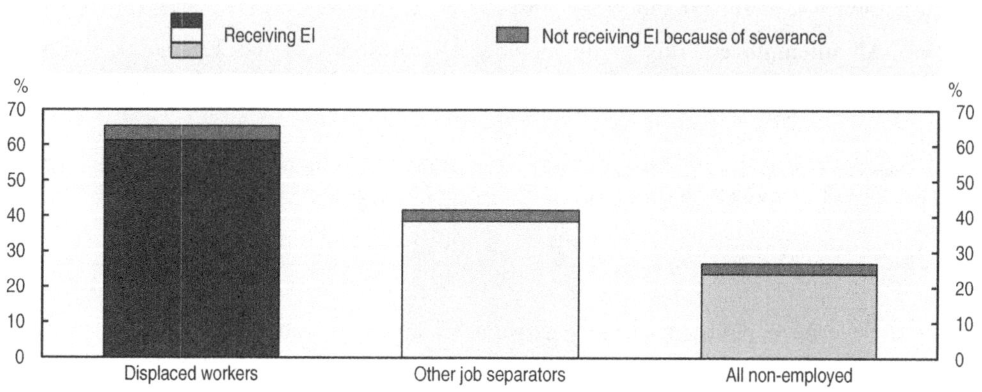

Note: EI: Employment Insurance.

Source: OECD calculations based on data from the Employment Insurance Coverage Survey (EICS).

StatLink http://dx.doi.org/10.1787/888933238786

Box 4.1. **Employment Insurance Coverage Survey**

The Employment Insurance Coverage Survey (EICS) is built on a sub-sample of the Labour Force Survey (LFS) collected four times every year. It focuses on five groups (or types) of persons who are potential employment insurance recipients: i) Persons who were unemployed during the reference week; ii) Persons employed part-time during the reference week; iii) Persons not in the labour force during the reference week; iv) Persons employed full-time during the reference week who started their current job during the previous three months; and v) Mothers of infant's under age one working during the reference week.

For the purpose of the calculations presented in this chapter, the sample is restricted to persons who were unemployed during the reference week *and* those not in the labour force. The main reason for including those not in the labour force in the sample is that a sizeable proportion (around one-quarter) of displaced workers falls into this category.

As described in Chapter 1, displaced workers are defined as workers who lost their jobs due to economic reasons or business conditions (e.g. company went out of business). Only salaried employees with tenure of 13 months or more, having worked within the last two years, are considered. Job loss due to reasons of pregnancy, family responsibilities, retirement and school attendance is excluded from the sample.

Where relevant, outcomes for displaced workers are compared with the following two groups:

- **Other job separators**: This includes workers who are unemployed or not in the labour force due to the end of a seasonal job, a temporary job, fixed-term or contract (non-seasonal) work or a casual job;
- **All unemployed**: This group includes all categories of job separations (with no tenure restrictions) as well as long-term unemployed and labour force entrants (and re-entrants).

Source: Statistics Canada (2011), "Microdata user guide: Employment Insurance Coverage Survey 2011", Special Surveys Division, Statistics Canada, http://odesi1.scholarsportal.info/documentation/EICS/2011/eics2011gid.pdf.

Severance payments reduce current EI coverage rates regardless of the reason for job loss as these payments are treated as income from employment in the Canadian system. The impact of such payments becomes more pronounced when looking at particular age, tenure and education groups (Figure 4.4). Lower EI coverage rates among older, long-tenured displaced non-employed and those with tertiary education due to severance pay entitlements may not be problematic from an income perspective. However, delayed EI entitlement is by far the biggest barrier to receiving re-employment support among older and long-tenured displaced unemployed who already struggle in finding their way back to the labour market.

Figure 4.4. **The impact of severance pay on EI coverage rates varies by age and tenure**

Percentage of displaced workers currently receiving EI by gender, age, tenure and education, 2000-10

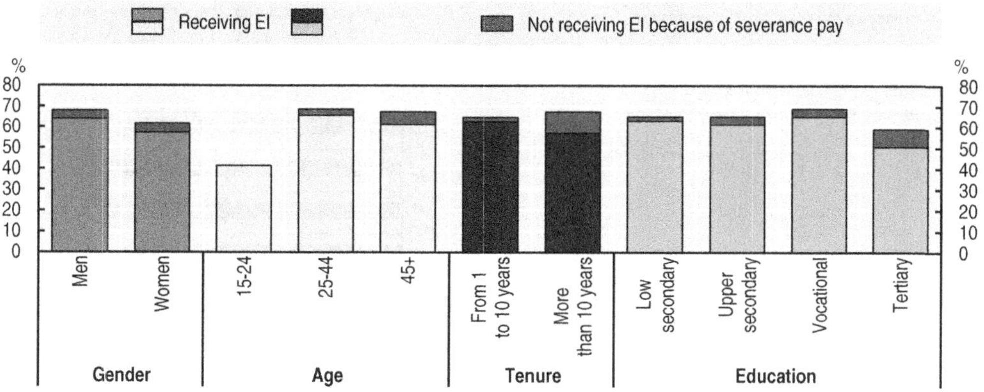

Note: EI: Employment Insurance; *Tenure* is defined for paid employees at last job only.

Source: OECD calculations based on data from the Employment Insurance Coverage Survey (EICS).

StatLink http://dx.doi.org/10.1787/888933238797

EI coverage rates by province

The EI system is designed to offer more extensive protection to workers living in high unemployment areas than those living elsewhere. Current EI coverage rates do, in fact, vary substantially across regions (Figure 4.5, Panel A). In general, coverage rates are significantly higher in provinces with high unemployment. However, this pattern is somewhat weaker for displaced workers with at least one year of tenure, who have higher coverage rates regardless of where they live due to more stable employment histories (Figure 4.5, Panel B).

Figure 4.5. **Coverage rates vary substantially by region**

Percentages, 2000-10

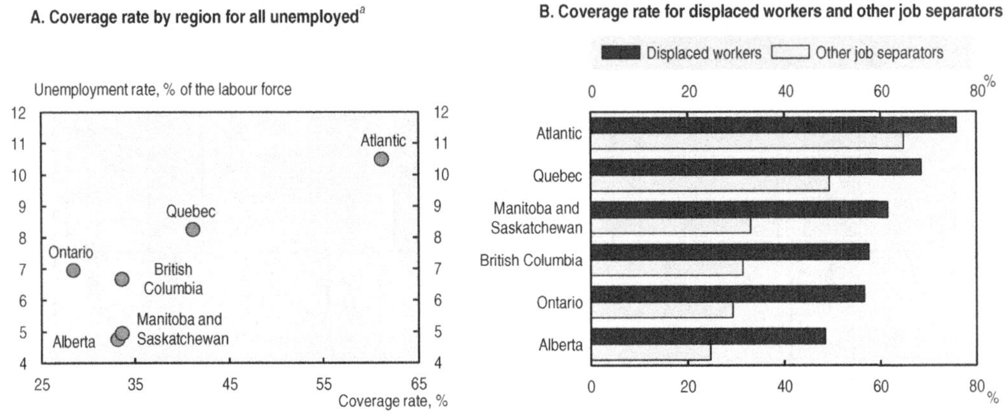

Note: Atlantic region is made up of Nova Scotia, New Brunswick, Newfoundland and Labrador and Prince Edward Island.

a) *All unemployed* includes all categories of job separations (with no tenure restrictions) as well as long-term unemployed and labour force entrants (and re-entrants).

Source: OECD calculations based on data from the Employment Insurance Coverage Survey (EICS).

StatLink http://dx.doi.org/10.1787/888933238807

Employment Insurance benefit levels are adequate for those who receive them, but durations are short

Figure 4.6 provides a cross-country comparison of the net replacement rates (NRR) of unemployment benefits on the basis of the OECD tax-benefit model and averaging across two earnings levels and four stylised family situations. NRRs in Canada are somewhat higher during the first year of unemployment than the OECD average (58% versus 54%). But at around ten months, benefit durations are shorter than in other OECD countries and, as a result, average NRRs are low when assessed over longer spells of unemployment. This implies a relatively less generous treatment of the long-term unemployed compared with many other OECD countries. The five-year NRR is 29% on average across OECD countries, but only 25% in Canada. Calculations reported in Figure 4.6 are for those with lower to average earnings prior to unemployment. As in most other countries, those with higher earnings, including longer-tenured workers, have significantly lower NRRs as benefit calculations are subject to an earnings ceiling.

Figure 4.6. **Net replacement rates of unemployment benefits in OECD countries**

Net benefit relative to net income by duration of unemployment (percentages), 2012[a]

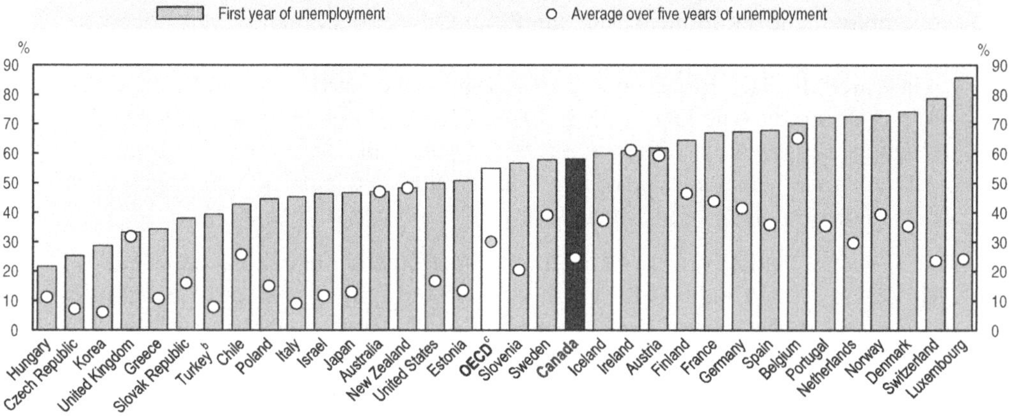

Note: APW: Average production worker; AW: Average worker.

a) Net replacement rate is the ratio of net income while out of work to net income while in work. Calculations consider cash incomes (excluding, for instance, employer contributions to health or pension insurance for workers and in-kind transfers for the unemployed) as well as income taxes and mandatory social security contributions paid by employees. To focus on the role of unemployment benefits, they assume that no social assistance or housing-related benefits are available as income top-ups for low-income families. Family benefits are included in the calculation. Any entitlement to severance payments is also not accounted for. Net replacement rates are calculated for a prime-age worker (aged 40) with a "long" and uninterrupted employment record. They are averages over 12 months, four different stylised family types (single- and two-earner couples, with and without children) and two earnings levels (67% and 100% of average full-time wages). Due to benefit ceilings, net replacement rates are lower for individuals with above-average earnings.

b) AW value is not available. Calculations are based on APW.

c) Unweighted averages of the 33 OECD countries shown in the chart above.

Source: OECD Tax-Benefit Models, www.oecd.org/els/social/workincentives.

StatLink http://dx.doi.org/10.1787/888933238816

To what extent did the generosity of EI change during the global financial crisis? Previous analysis highlighted that Canada was one of the very few OECD countries where the generosity of EI rose modestly during the crisis through a combination of automatic extension tied to rising unemployment rates, and additional discretionary extensions on a temporary basis (OECD, 2011). The NRR averaged over the first two years of unemployment increased from 32% in 2007 to 39% in 2009. Even then, these NRRs remained well below the majority of the OECD countries for which data is available.

The relatively low long-term replacement rates in Canada are an effective way to minimise disincentives arising from more generous payments which may erode the willingness to work and thereby increase unemployment duration. At the same time, concerns about poverty need to be considered, especially for disadvantaged groups such as older workers who are displaced; because this group has particular difficulties in reintegrating into the labour market (see Chapter 1). Additional evidence for example suggests that older workers (55 years and older) have the highest entitlement exhaustion rate, which is likely attributable to the challenges they face in securing new employment following a job loss (CEIC, 2014).

Poverty statistics are not available specifically for displaced workers. However, related indicators can shed some light on the extent of economic hardship for this group. Data from EICS 2000-10 show that around one in four displaced workers struggle to make ends need: they report that household income is insufficient to meet expenses and that cuts in expenses had to be made (Table 4.2). A significant proportion also reports to receive financial assistance from and to do odd jobs for friends and relatives. In contrast, displaced workers who receive severance pay do better than those receiving EI or neither.

Table 4.2. **Displaced workers with EI are at a greater risk of falling into economic hardship**

Percentage of displaced workers who are currently not employed, 2000-10

	Receiving EI	Not receiving EI nor severance pay	Not receiving EI, received a severance package
Sufficiency of household income to meet day-to-day expenses (Met most or all of regular expenses and financial commitment)	74.8	77.7	87.1
Increased reliance on credit (Yes)	33.4	28.0	17.8
Cut expenses to make up for shortfall in income (Yes)	23.1	19.0	11.1
Received some financial assistance from friends or relatives (Yes)	12.5	14.3	4.9
Got a job, started a business or did odd jobs (for friends or relatives) (Yes)	15.6	13.9	4.2

Note: EI: Employment Insurance.

Source: OECD calculations based on data from the Employment Insurance Coverage Survey (EICS).

StatLink http://dx.doi.org/10.1787/888933238977

Overall, displaced workers in receipt of EI show greater signs of financial distress than their counterparts who neither receive EI nor severance pay. For the latter group, wages or earnings of the spouse and income from investments make up the biggest source of funds used to meet household expenses (Figure 4.7). These results suggest that while EI is moderately well targeted on displaced workers with the greatest need for income support, it is not generous enough to fully meet their needs.

Figure 4.7. **Main sources of funds to meet household expenses among displaced workers**

Percentages, 2000-10

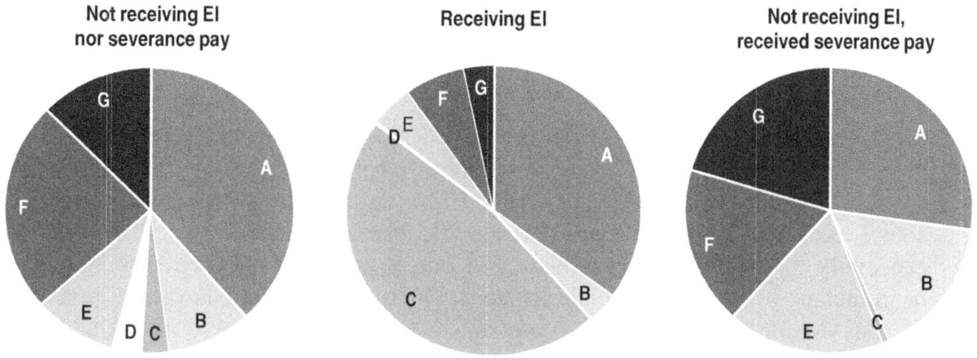

A. Wages or self-employment earnings of spouse/partner/family member
B. Own wages or self-employment income
C. Employment Insurance (EI)
D. Social assistance
E. Pensions, disability insurance, workers' compensation
F. Income from investments, interest, dividends, rentals or saving
G. Other

Source: OECD calculations based on data from the Employment Insurance Coverage Survey (EICS).

StatLink http://dx.doi.org/10.1787/888933238828

Access to social assistance is limited

If displaced workers do not qualify for EI or do not find employment before the end of the maximum benefit payment period, they may need to rely on alternative sources of income support, such as social assistance. In Canada, social assistance is a "needs-tested" benefit administered by the provinces and territories, which set their own rules and payment rates. Generally, eligibility is subject to income and assets tests which take into account housing costs and the size of the household. If there is a budgetary deficit (i.e. non-exempted income is below the cost of basic needs), the household qualifies for social assistance. The total payment amount consists of a basic personal allowance, a shelter allowance to assist in the payment of (total actual) housing costs and, in some provinces, allowances for regularly-recurring approved special needs. For example, in Ontario, eligible individuals with no dependants on Ontario Works[11] (income and employment assistance for people who are in temporary financial need) may receive a combined basic needs allowance and a maximum shelter allowance of CAD 656 per month for a single-person household (effective from October 2014). This payment increases based on the presence of a spouse, the number of members in the household and the number of children in the household.[12] Benefits are paid as long as there is a need (i.e. as long as household assets are within allowable limits and non-exempt income is insufficient to cover basic needs or approved special needs) and provided that all other administrative requirements are met, for example job-search and training requirements for employable clients.[13] Non-compliance can lead to penalties ranging from a specified reduction in benefits to a full withdrawal of benefits, for a prescribed period of time.

As shown in Figure 4.7, very few displaced workers not covered by EI or severance pay receive social assistance benefits suggesting that social assistance is a less effective backstop to EI for displaced workers. Accessing social assistance may also present specific challenges for older workers, especially those close to retirement. For one, many displaced workers may be reluctant to apply to social assistance in the first place due to stigma reasons. Second, although social assistance might provide some immediate financial security, it threatens their income security during retirement since eligibility conditions imply that individuals must deplete most of their liquefiable assets such as cash, retirement savings plans and other investments. While younger displaced workers may have more time to recover their financial losses before they enter their retirement years, older workers are forced to use up resources they were encouraged to accumulate for their retirement (LeBlanc and McMullin, 1997).

Similarly, access to disability benefits for displaced workers is also restricted. While in many OECD countries, older workers who exhaust or do not qualify for EI or social assistance, often end up on "last-resort" disability benefit providing an alternative source of income, such transitions from unemployment and social assistance to disability have been limited in Canada due to strict eligibility criteria (Finnie et al., 2011). This resonates with the findings shown in Panel A of Figure 1.12 (Chapter 1) which illustrate that few displaced workers are sick and disabled. However, closing off of this source of income support makes it all the more essential to assure that displaced workers have adequate access to more appropriate forms of income support which can prevent them from falling into poverty, as discussed below.

Income protection in the case of bankruptcy was increased during the recession

A separate non-contributory federal scheme was set up in 2008 – the Wage Earner Protection Program (WEPP) – to give dismissed workers greater protection in the case of bankruptcy of their employer. The programme provides partial recovery of unpaid wages, vacation pay in the case of bankruptcy that accrued during the six-month period preceding their employer's bankruptcy or receivership. WEPP coverage was expanded in 2009 to provide compensation for unpaid severance and termination pay. A second expansion in 2011 extended the programme to cover employees who lose their jobs when their employer's attempt at restructuring takes longer than six months and is subsequently unsuccessful. Eligible workers can receive up to four times the maximum weekly insurable earnings as defined in the Employment Insurance Act (CAD 3 646 in 2013). This programme provides an important form of relief to displaced workers affected by bankruptcies; between July 2008 and March 2013, over 58 000 WEPP claimants have received more than CAD 133 million overall. However, difficulties and delays have arisen when firms close without a formal declaration of bankruptcy (so-called "walk away firms").

Adequacy of income support for older and long-tenured displaced workers

Post-displacement adjustment can be particularly difficult for older and long-tenured workers with firm-specific skills and little or no previous experience with job transitions: they face greater difficulties in re-entering the labour market and significant financial losses when subsequently re-employed in low-paying jobs (as seen in Chapter 1). The above analysis raises several issues about the current setup and design of the EI system and its ability to adequately compensate older and long-tenured displaced workers whilst facilitating their return to the labour market. The rest of this chapter discusses a number of policy options to minimise adverse consequences of displacement of older and long-tenured workers.

Extending benefit duration while maintaining incentives to work

Chapter 1 showed that only about one in two displaced workers are re-employed within one year, raising the possibility for a considerable number of displaced workers to exhaust their entitlement to EI benefits while still being unemployed. This raises the question whether longer payment periods should be allowed for displaced workers who are particularly at-risk of long-term unemployment, such as older displaced workers. Currently, the maximum duration of EI benefit entitlement is relatively short compared to the limits specified for unemployment benefit schemes in other OECD countries (Figure 4.8).[14]

Figure 4.8. **Unemployment benefits in Canada are paid for a relatively short period**

Maximum duration of unemployment benefit payments in months, selected OECD countries, 2012[a, b]

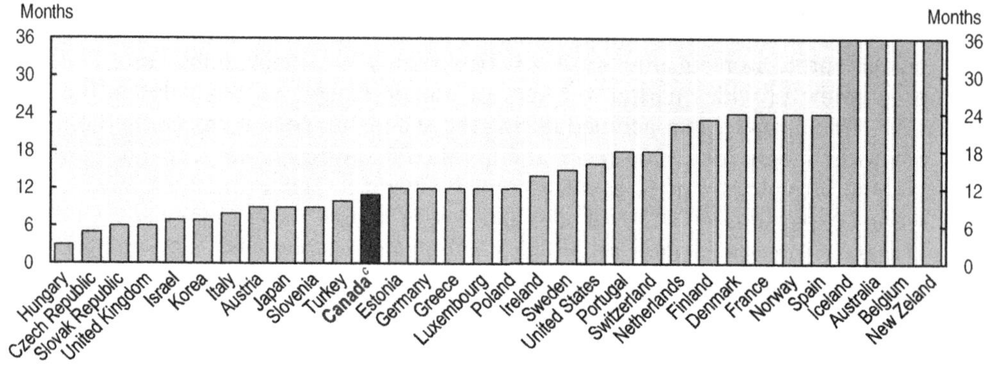

a) Maximum benefit durations for a 40-year-old displaced worker with 22 years of contributions (continuous employment since age 18).

b) No duration limit, for Australia, Belgium and New Zealand.

c) The maximum duration of Employment Insurance payments in Canada depends on the unemployment rate in the relevant EI region. The 11-month duration shown corresponds to the unemployment rate of 9% in Ontario in July 2012. The duration of Unemployment Insurance Benefits in the United States varies with state rules and unemployment rates. The 16-month duration shown reflects the situation in Michigan in July 2012.

Source: OECD Tax-Benefit Models, www.oecd.org/els/social/workincentives.

StatLink http://dx.doi.org/10.1787/888933238831

Canadian expert groups on older workers and on unemployment support have made a series of recommendations to tackle these issues, including: i) longer benefit duration, and ii) higher benefit levels for older workers (HRSDC, 2008; and Mowat, 2011). In addition, they propose to unifying entrance requirement and duration of Employment Insurance across regions in order to make EI more equitable for all groups (see Box 4.2 for more details). Indeed, in many OECD countries, unemployment benefit provisions are more generous for older workers as benefit amounts and/or durations are linked to age or contribution histories.[15] However, across European countries, the general trend has been to abolish age-specific clauses and cut back very generous unemployment benefits which merely bridge periods without a job until the worker becomes eligible for a pension and incur high fiscal costs.

Box 4.2. Unifying entrance requirement and duration of Employment Insurance (EI) across regions

The variation in EI eligibility and entitlement rules with regional unemployment rates means that displaced workers with similar work histories face different rules and can be entitled to different levels of public income support simply because they live in different regions. These differences have led some to advocate a unified EI system in which conditions for benefit eligibility and duration are the same for all workers. Yet, the potentially offsetting advantages of modifying access and generosity accordingly to the labour market are should also be acknowledged. For instance, the lower job-finding rates in slack labour markets imply longer expected durations of unemployment at any given level of job-search intensity. Extending benefit durations might therefore help to ensure that unemployment compensation systems: i) continue to facilitate a reasonable match between jobseeker and vacancies; and ii) provide adequate income support during the jobless spell. Particularly in the context of sharp cyclical downturns, *automatic* adjustments may prove to be an attractive option since they minimise the risk that modifications come at the wrong time (e.g. before unemployment increases), are distorted by political considerations (e.g. there may be a temptation to raise benefit levels for newly unemployed, rather than extending durations for those with weak job prospects), or remain in place for too long (Immervoll, 2012).

A fundamental problem, however, is that the local unemployment rate is a poor proxy of an unemployed worker's chances of regaining employment and a poor basis for allocating EI benefits (Bishop and Burleton, 2009). For one, the backward-looking average unemployment rate does not capture the direction of unemployment or provide an accurate status of current labour market conditions. In other words, EI rules are adjusted with a lag whereby workers living in areas of rising unemployment are likely to face more stringent eligibility rules to EI even though they may experience difficulty in findings jobs. The recent economic downturn provides a good illustration of this. Areas hit hardest by the recession such as Ontario had the strictest eligibility requirements because it entered the recession with relatively low unemployment rates. As a result, increases in EI beneficiaries in Ontario were smaller than other regions such as Alberta since the beginning of the recession (Leonard, 2009). This problem can also be illustrated by an alternative indicator such as the share of workers who are neither employed nor receiving EI following job loss but are potentially in need of income support. OECD calculations based on SLID show that at 20%, this share is the highest in Ontario even though Ontario has lower unemployment rates than some other provinces. A number of other indicators including changes in the number of hours worked, the job-to-vacancy ratio and the local unemployment rate, should be considered to better respond to the changes in labour market conditions (OECD, 2011).

Source: Bishop, G. and D. Burleton (2009), "Is Canada's Employment Insurance program adequate?", TD Economics, Special Report, 30 April, Toronto, www.td.com/document/PDF/economics/special/td-economics-special-gb0409-ei.pdf; and Immervoll, H. (2012), "Reforming the benefit system to 'make work pay': Options and priorities in a weak labour market", *IZA Policy Papers*, No. 50, Institute for the Study of Labor, November, Bonn, http://ftp.iza.org/pp50.pdf; Leonard, J. (2009), "Time to get real on EI reform", *Policy Options*, Institute of Research for Public Policy (IRPP), September, Montréal; and OECD (2011), "Income support for the unemployed: How well has the safety-net held up during the 'Great Recession'?", in *OECD Employment Outlook 2011*, OECD Publishing, Paris, http://dx.doi.org/10.1787/empl_outlook-2011-en.

In addition, ample evidence suggests that generous unemployment benefits risk weakening the job-search incentives of unemployed individuals. There is a broad consensus that while allowing unemployed more time to find more stable and better quality job matches, overly generous unemployment benefits tend to increase the duration of unemployment by reducing job-search intensity and the willingness to accept job offers (Caliendo et al., 2009; and Klerman, 2013). A comparison between the job-finding rates of displaced workers who received EI at some point since job loss and those who did not, illustrates this issue (Figure 4.9). Within the first year of job loss, re-employment rates are indeed lower for those receiving EI than those without, indicating that those with EI entitlement take longer to look for (or accept) jobs. However, this pattern reflects the combined impact of the disincentive effect of EI and entitlement effects (as unemployment is a condition for receiving EI benefits). One year after displacement, return-to-work rates increase for both groups, with and without EI, and the gap in re-employment rates narrows markedly. This pattern is consistent with benefit recipients increasing their search efforts as they approach and pass EI expiry.

Figure 4.9. **Re-employment rates of displaced workers vary with EI eligibility**

Percentage of displaced workers and other job separators re-employed within one and two years, by whether or not they are entitled to EI benefits, 2000-10

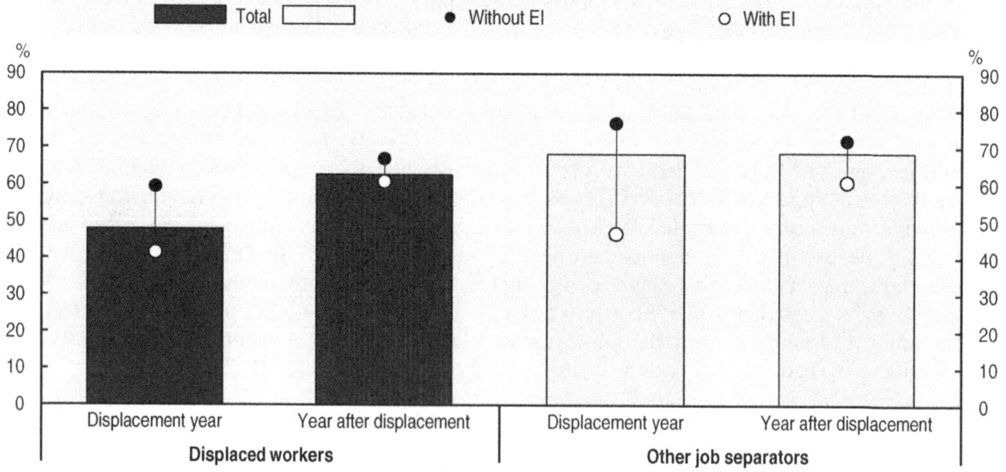

Note: EI: Employment Insurance.

Source: OECD calculations based on data from the Survey of Labour and Income Dynamics (SLID).

StatLink http://dx.doi.org/10.1787/888933238845

There is limited evidence of these issues and behaviours with a specific focus on older long-tenured displaced workers. Additional data from EICS on job-search behaviour and patterns using two different measures, *looking for work* and *the number of hours looked for work*, provides important insights:

- In general, unemployed displaced workers in receipt of EI at the survey date are more likely to look for a job than their counterparts without EI. This is consistent with EI rules that require availability of work and job-search requirements to qualify for regular benefits (Figure 4.10, Panel A). However, displaced workers with tenure of more than ten years receiving unemployment benefit are less likely to report that they are looking for work than workers with relatively shorter tenure. This suggests that disincentive or discouragement effects may be particularly strong for this group, possibly indicating a need for more intensive job-search assistance and monitoring (see Chapter 5).

- Older and long-tenured workers receiving unemployment benefit, whether unemployed due to economic or other reasons, spend slightly fewer hours looking for a job than their less tenured counterparts (Figure 4.10, Panel B). The lower job-search efforts among older and long-tenured unemployed could be explained by their lower motivation as they have relatively fewer years remaining in the labour market until retirement. Indeed, a large proportion of older unemployed displaced workers are pessimistic about their chances of finding an acceptable job in the next three months. Some 38% of the unemployed aged 45 and over felt that their chances of finding such a job were "not very good" – twice that for the unemployed aged 15-24. Similarly, up to 38% of displaced workers with long tenure report to have poor chances of finding employment (OECD calculations based on data from EICS).

- Finally, older and long-tenured workers, whether in receipt of severance pay or not, are less likely to report to look for a job than all other groups except displaced workers aged 15-24 years (Figure 4.10, Panel C). This is in line with evidence from other countries where severance payments have been shown to increase the duration of non-employment (Hijzen, 2011).

These findings indicate that any moves towards making EI more generous for older workers could come at the expense of longer unemployment duration especially under the current Canadian activation regime which remains relatively weak in comparison to many other OECD countries (see Chapter 5 for more details).

Figure 4.10. **Job-search behaviour of displaced workers varies with age and tenure**

Percentage of displaced workers reporting job search and average hours of job search, by selected population characteristics, 2000-10

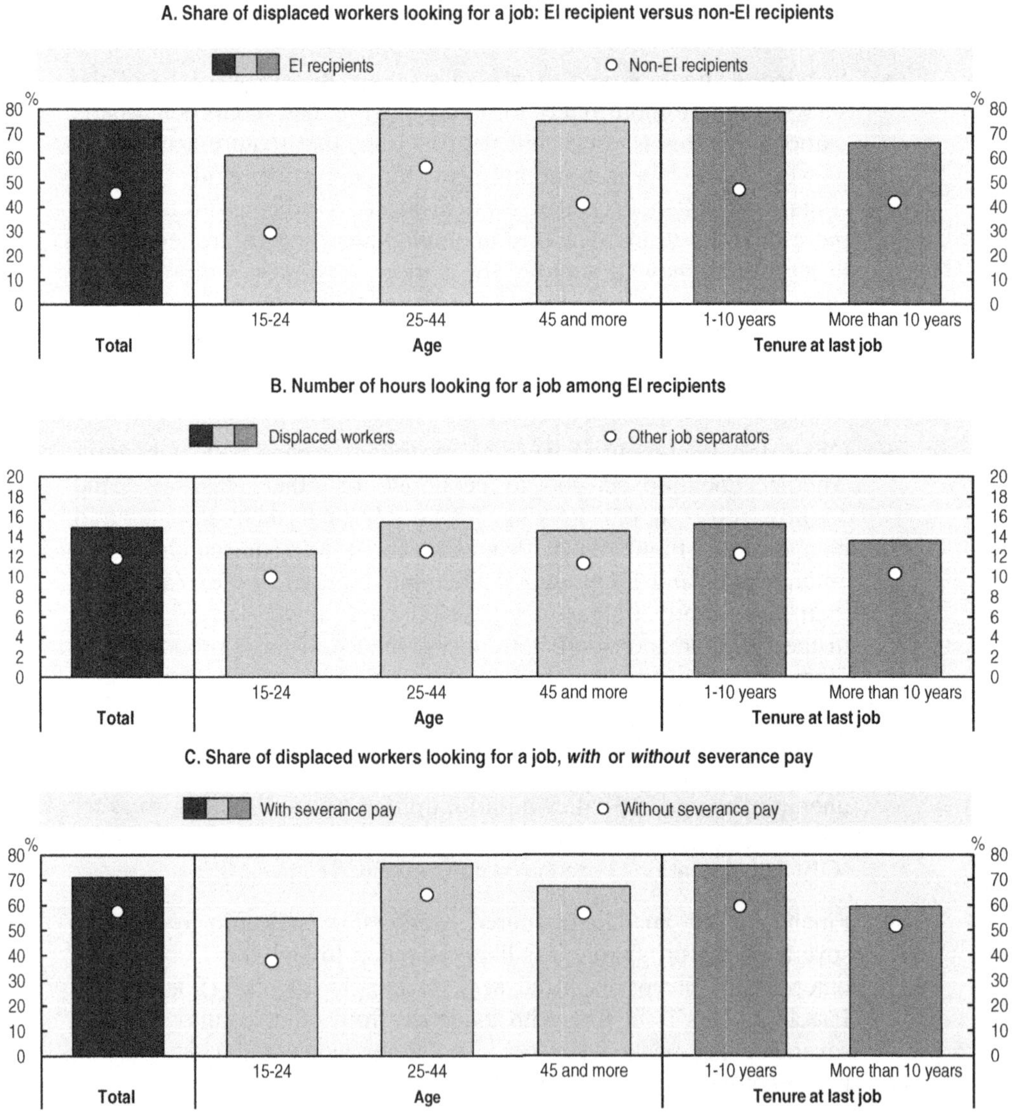

Note: EI: Employment Insurance.

Source: OECD calculations based on data from the Employment Insurance Coverage Survey (EICS).

StatLink http://dx.doi.org/10.1787/888933238857

Recent programmes such as the Career Transition Assistance (CTA) temporarily introduced during the economic crisis were attempts to overcome some of the challenges outlined above. The programme intended to provide additional income support to long-tenured displaced workers whilst offsetting disincentives effects arising from more generous benefits. The CTA had two components: extended duration of EI benefits to up to two years for eligible long-tenured displaced workers who participate in longer-term training (Extended Employment Insurance and Training Incentive – EEITI); and earlier access to EI regular benefits for displaced workers investing in their own training using all or part of their severance package (Severance Investment for Training Initiative – SITI). The latter in particular was a move in the right direction in tackling the adverse effects created by EI rules that delay effective employment support to displaced workers in receipt of severance payments potentially hurting their re-employment prospects.

These changes represented important steps in expanding coverage and allowing earlier re-employment support to those incurring the biggest losses due to displacement. However, the take-up of the scheme had been very low (ESDC, 2014a). This can be partly attributed to the fact that eligibility to both of the initiatives was conditional upon participation in training exclusively during the initial phase of the programme. According to the evaluation of the programme, many older displaced workers expressed a lack of need for training. Lack of awareness of the programme was another factor behind the low take-up. About half of survey respondents eligible for CTA said, approximately one year after their job loss, they were not aware of the initiative.

Against the relatively poor outcomes of CTA and the robust evidence on the disincentive effects created by generous unemployment benefits, an alternative policy response can be to extend unemployment benefit with a declining profile whereby net replacements rate fall with the duration of unemployment payments. For example, in Sweden unemployment benefit is paid at a net replacement rate of 80% in the first 200 days and falls to 70% on day 201 (until the maximum duration of 300 days) to maintain good work incentives over the unemployment spell. Similarly in the Czech Republic, the net replacement rate falls from 65% to 45% from five month onwards.

Longer unemployment benefit payments the level of which falls with the duration of unemployment, can be a useful policy tool where individual search behaviour is an important influence on the unemployment rate but income adequacy during unemployment is also a central policy consideration. The decline in benefit levels "later" increases search incentives for all unemployed workers "now", whereas the welfare losses associated with low levels of benefit "later" affect only a limited proportion of the same unemployed workers because many of them find work earlier, and never suffer from the lower levels of benefit (OECD, 2002).

Increasing the maximum length of time that long-tenured displaced workers can draw EI benefits would reflect the recognition of their potential adjustment difficulties, whilst the decline in payments over time can provide additional incentives for displaced workers to accept available jobs and return to work faster. Even then, any extensions of EI benefits should be accompanied by systematic monitoring of job-search and mandatory participation in active labour market programmes. Recent evaluation of the extension of EI for long-tenured workers during the global financial crisis highlighted that compared to a sample of similar claimants, long-tenured workers were least likely to search for employment during their unemployment spell, but when engaged in job-search, they had a higher number of hours spent per week and received greater number of interviews (ESDC, 2014b).

Finally, the relatively poor result of the Severance Investment for Training Initiative also calls for experimenting with alternative policy options to speed up access to adequate re-employment support for those in receipt of severance pay. As described in Chapter 3, some countries extend job-search obligations and re-employment assistance to workers during their notice period or at least as soon as they are laid off to reduce the period of joblessness by facilitating early contact with PES. This type of intervention potentially could fill the "gap" which some Canadian displaced workers experience in accessing support to find a new job whilst they are in receipt of severance payments and help to mitigate the disincentive effects created by such benefits.

Is wage insurance a useful supplement to unemployment benefits?

Wage insurance (WI) has been proposed as a supplement to unemployment insurance to compensate displaced workers for a part of the earning losses that sometimes persist long after they have become re-employed. Similarly to unemployment benefits, which offset a portion of the earnings losses due to post-displacement unemployment, wage insurance pays displaced workers who accept new jobs at lower wages an earnings subsidy that replaces a fraction of the difference between earnings on the old and the new job. Typically, it is proposed that this subsidy would be limited in duration (maybe one or two years) and also limited to certain groups who are particularly at risk of experiencing a permanent loss of earnings, such as older and long-tenured displaced workers and/or workers who become re-employed within a certain period (e.g. within six months after displacement).

Similar to EI, wage insurance raises a number of issues for policy makers, but there is much less experience to draw upon to guide policy choices. Proponents of WI argue that it can provide more equitable sharing of the gains from economic restructuring by reducing the adjustment costs faced by those who are hurt the most. It is also argued that wage insurance would improve incentives for speedy re-employment as unemployment benefits become less attractive relative to accepting a new job. A third potential benefit is that WI can diminish political opposition to efficiency-enhancing policies, such as trade liberalisation, by mitigating workers' anxieties about the job and earnings insecurities that can accompany economic restructuring (OECD, 2005). But WI also comes with potential problems. First, the cost could be very high unless subsidies are tightly targeted. Tight targeting, however, would be likely to create inequities between displaced workers re-employed at lower wages who receive the WI benefit and similar workers who do not. Second, it has also been argued that WI would be subject to large deadweight losses were benefits paid to displaced workers likely to find a new job relatively quickly even without the subsidy. To the extent WI speeds up re-employment, resulting shorter unemployment spells could come at the expense of shifting workers into low-quality jobs with low wages, little career structure and poor prospects for training and wage growth (Jones, 2009) or at the expense of more disadvantaged job seekers. Finally, there may be a risk of employers being able to offer lower wages than they would in the absence of such schemes.

A number of scholars including the Expert Panel on Older Workers have recommended pilot programmes to assess the viability and cost-effectiveness of wage insurance in the Canadian context (Riddell, 2011; and Jones, 2009). The testing of such a scheme in Canada is however not new. Earlier pilot schemes such as the Earnings Supplement Project (ESP) in the late 1990s were primarily designed with the intention to shorten unemployment duration and reduce unemployment benefit spending. Evaluations of the ESP however proved to be disappointing: the scheme failed to achieve its goal of speedy re-employment (see Box 4.3). Although providing income insurance was not the main objective of the ESP, it is important to bear in mind that WI schemes also intend to compensate displaced workers for part of their loss in life-time earnings potential; this goal can be achieved even if the speed of re-employment is not increased. In 2014, *Emploi-Québec* implemented a pilot project in five regions to assess whether the partial compensation of wage reduction helps to encourage long-tenured job losers to stay active longer in the labour market. The programme is well-targeted because only those aged 55 and over are eligible, minimising associated dead-weight costs. However, no evaluation is available at this stage.

Box 4.3. **Impact of earlier pilots of Wage Insurance (WI) in Canada**

The Earnings Supplement Project (ESP) was a test of whether a financial incentive can encourage unemployed people to return to work more quickly than they otherwise would. The primary goal was to shorten the re-employment process experienced by displaced workers.

The programme had the following features and conditions:

- Eligibility was limited to workers who experienced a permanent job separation after at least three years of continuous employment.
- The maximum job-search period was 26 weeks to be eligible for the earnings supplement and was measured from the time the supplement was offered to the worker.
- The maximum supplement eligibility period was 24 months. This period also began when the supplement offer was made at the start of the EI spell. Therefore, participants initially had the choice of trading off job-search time for supplement time, up to the maximum permissible job-search period.
- Beneficiaries who found full-time jobs within 26 weeks at wages inferior to their weekly insurable earnings were eligible for supplemental payments equal 75% of the earnings difference. A weekly maximum was set at CAD 250 and payments could be received for a maximum of two years.

The programme was tested on two groups comprising a total of 5 912 individuals in 1995 and 1996. Two separate randomised experiments were carried out targeting displaced workers and repeat users of unemployment benefits. Main findings are listed below:

- ESP was found to have a small (4.4 percentage points at peak) and short-lived impact on the re-employment of displaced workers.
- It was expected that the reduced job-search period and incentive to accept lower paid jobs would provoke a wage-suppressing effect, i.e. encourage acceptance of jobs with lower wages. In fact, the wages of ESP participants were 4.6% lower than those of the control group.
- The programme had almost no effect on the amount or duration of unemployment benefits received by the two groups.

Source: Bloom, H., S. Schwartz, S. Lui-Gurr, S-W. Lee, J. Peng and W. Bancroft (1999), "Testing a re-employment incentive for displaced workers: The Earnings Supplement Project", Social Research and Demonstration Corporation (SRDC), May, www.srdc.org/media/195754/testing.pdf.

A few other OECD countries such as the United States, France and Germany also use wage insurance schemes to cater income needs of displaced workers. Evidence on the impact of such schemes on re-employment rates is largely restricted to the United States. For instance, under the US Alternative Trade Adjustment Assistance programme (ATAA), eligible workers aged 50 and over could receive a payment of 50% of the difference between their new salary and their old salary for up to a maximum of USD 10 000 for a period of up to two years. To be eligible, older workers must have been certified that they were displaced from their jobs. A recent evaluation on the ATAA shows that the take-up has remained low and raises important issues related to the design and implementation of the programme. The report identifies that low-take up of the scheme can be attributed to: i) a complex administrative system; ii) strict eligibility criteria i.e. jobseekers were expected to find employment within 26 weeks which was difficult for older displaced workers who did not have any transferable skills; and iii) lack of outreach (D'Amico et al., 2012).

The absence of a clearly successful working model of WI illustrates that the first policy priority for assisting displaced workers facing the risk of permanently lower earnings should be to use ALMPs, retraining and re-location assistance to try to improve their access to better jobs (as discussed in Chapter 5). However, significant permanent earnings losses are likely to remain. Recent literature suggests that older workers who have been displaced from employment tend not to recover well in terms of their earnings when they re-enter the labour force. For example, a Statistics Canada 2008 survey found that almost half of the displaced older workers surveyed had at least 25% lower earnings in their new job (Pignal et al., 2010). The latest evaluation of the Targeted Initiative for Older Workers (TIOW) program found that participants experienced a decrease in earnings of only about 13 percentage points. The TIOW programme may have mitigated potentially more negative labour market impacts among programme participants as might have been the case in the absence of the programme (ESDC, 2014c). These evaluation results suggest that further experimentation with WI programmes merits serious consideration, even as further efforts are made to improve ALMPs for displaced workers.

Several different designs could be piloted at the same time, as was done with the ESP. In particular, it might be worthwhile to explore combinations of WI and special ALMPs targeted at older and long-tenured displaced workers. Such a package might help to increase take-up in view of the take-up problems both WI and CTA have encountered in the past, when used separately.[16] Evidence from other types of earnings supplement programmes shows that providing some additional services or supports such as participation in job-clubs in addition to financial incentives can significantly increase the proportion of the targeted clientele who will take advantage of the offer. This was indeed the case for the Self-Sufficiency Project (SSP) Plus[17] which offered earnings supplements to single parents who have been receiving social assistance for at least one year, on condition that, within one year of being selected for the programme, they leave welfare for full-time work (Greenwood and Voyer, 2000). Since most long-tenured displaced workers are likely not to have any recent job-search experience, providing intensive job-search assistance hand-in-hand with the offer of financial assistance on a post-displacement job might increase the number of displaced workers able to find jobs and help them find better jobs, which would reduce earnings losses and, therefore, the earnings supplements paid by the government.

If one or more WI pilots should be attempted, careful attention should also be given to the following design issues: i) *having a well-defined goal*: rapid re-entry into work force versus compensation for wage loss; ii) *eligibility and targeting*: workers facing biggest barriers to re-enter the labour market versus workers laid off in specific sectors; and iii) *generosity*: being large enough to induce the desired behavioural changes, but limiting deadweight loss in order to be affordable for the public purse. The design and target groups for the programme will differ according to the goals being pursued. Overall, the relative merit of introducing an earnings supplement programme for displaced workers should be evaluated against other types of interventions offered to this group.

Conclusion

The unemployment benefits offered by the EI system are relatively more generous for part-year seasonal workers than for older and long-tenured displaced workers. The latter enjoy relatively high benefit coverage upon job loss in contrast to workers who lose their jobs for reasons other than economic ones. But, at around ten months, benefit durations are shorter than in most other OECD countries and, as a result, average replacement rates are low when assessed over longer spells of unemployment. The shorter payment duration encourages more rapid re-employment and is probably adequate for most job losers in Canada, since long-term unemployment is relatively rare. However, the shorter payment duration also implies greater income insecurity for the subset of displaced workers who are at a higher risk of long-term unemployment, especially given the very strict eligibility criteria for other financial support such as social assistance. Thanks to the temporary increase in the duration of unemployment benefit payments, protection for unemployed workers increased during the global financial crisis.

Of particular concern in Canada is the adequacy of the EI system for older long-tenured workers. This group is particularly apt to exhaust their EI entitlement before they become re-employed if they access benefits immediately upon becoming unemployed (subject to the two-week waiting period). Some members of this group receive substantial severance-payments which create a different problem, namely, long delays in accessing EI benefits and hence also most types of re-employment services. The federal government took steps to improve generosity of EI for long-tenured displaced workers and provide them with more rapid access to benefits and retraining through the Career Transition Programme. The programme had good potential in providing greater income support whilst facilitating return to work, but it was introduced only as a temporary measure and struggled to attract participants.

A number of other policy options are also available, although they all pose difficult trade-offs. The first is to extend the duration of EI benefits but in combination with a payment rate that falls over time, thereby recognising the potential adjustment difficulties faced by older displaced workers, whilst providing additional incentives for them to accept available jobs and return to work faster. However, it is important that any expansion of EI entitlements is coupled with greater activation requirements given the disincentive effects such change may have on job-search behaviour of unemployed individuals. Moreover, like in some other OECD countries, job-search requirements during the dismissal period and mandatory registration with the PES should be considered to speed-up access to re-employment services and to encourage greater job-search efforts among workers who are in receipt of severance payments.

Finally, wage insurance programmes are increasingly proposed as a mechanism to compensate for a part of the persistent earnings losses faced by some displaced workers, particularly older and long-tenured workers. It would be worthwhile piloting some WI scheme (again), carefully bearing in mind that the goals of the programme should include a balance of labour supply incentives and compensation for an enduring loss of earnings potential, as well as drawing on lessons from previous pilots. Models that combine WI with targeted job-search assistance and retraining options appear particularly promising, since this combination could both reduce earnings losses and improve re-employment prospects while compensating some of the portion that remain. Such a combination has also proven to improve take-up rates of similar earnings supplement schemes in the past.

Notes

1. The employee contribution to EI is set at 1.78% of their earnings up to a ceiling of CAD 44 200, while the employer contribution is set at 2.49% (1.4 times the employee percentage) of earnings up to the same limit.

2. The *OECD Tax-Benefit Models*, available through www.oecd.org/els/social/workincentives summarises the main entitlement rules for unemployment and related out-of-work benefits.

3. The exceptions are new and re-entrants to the labour market that require 910 hours of insurable employment in the preceding 52-week qualifying period, rather than the 420 to 700 hours required for other claimants.

4. The length of time one needs to work in order to qualify for benefits is one of the lowest in OECD countries (Venn, 2012).

5. According to EI rules, long-tenured worker is someone who has contributed at least 30% of the annual maximum EI premiums for at least seven out of 10 calendar years prior to the start of their claim; and has received no more than 35 weeks of regular EI benefits in the five years prior to the start of their claim.

6. Low-income families with children can, however, receive up to 80% of their average weekly insurable earnings with the Family Supplement.

7. Under the previous legislated method, low-earning weeks (including weeks without earnings) could have reduced claimants' benefit rates.

8. The 57-week threshold is reached by subtracting the two weeks of waiting period and 45 weeks of EI (assuming that displaced workers qualify for this) from the maximum combined duration of severance pay and EI of 104 weeks.

9. See also Chapter 3 for more details on severance payment rules in Canada.

10. In 1993, reforms to the EI programme made unemployed workers who refuse to accept suitable employment or who were fired "with cause" ineligible for EI benefits. In 1996, another series of reforms to the EI programme increased the amount of work that new and returning workers needed prior to job loss in order to qualify for EI benefits.

11. Ontario provides a second social assistance programme – Ontario Disability Support Program – which provides financial assistance and employment support to enable people with disabilities and their families.

12. A couple household with two children aged 0-17 can receive up to a maximum of CAD 1 124 per month.

13. The Province of British Columbia has established a limit on the length of time a client may receive benefits. Employable clients are limited to a cumulative 24 months of social assistance out of every 60 months.

14. The maximum duration of EI payments depends on the unemployment rate in the relevant EI region. The 11-month duration shown in Figure 4.8 corresponds to the unemployment rate of 9% in Ontario in July 2012.

15. In Germany, for example, older workers can receive up to 18 months of UI after 55 years and 24 months after age 58. Likewise, French unemployed older workers aged 60 and over are compensated for up to eight years, which is six years longer than the maximum standard unemployment duration. In Austria, recipients aged 40 and above can receive up to 39 weeks of benefits (after 312 weeks of work in ten years), while workers aged 50 and above are entitled to 52 weeks (after 468 weeks of work in the last 15 years).

16. This would require relaxing the rapid re-employment requirement tied to WI, i.e. to become rapid re-employment after being retrained.

17. In the SSP Plus sub-study, participants could receive help in preparing résumés, take part in a job-finding club, were given job leads and were assigned to job coaches. The effect on programme take-up was dramatic. Slightly more than half of those eligible for incentives plus services left welfare for full-time work within a year.

References

Arthurs, H.W. (2006), "Fairness at work – Federal labour standards for the 21st Century", Federal Labour Standards Review, Canada, http://www.labour.gc.ca/eng/standards_equity/st/pubs_st/fls/pdf/final_report.pdf.

Bishop, G. and D. Burleton (2009), "Is Canada's Employment Insurance program adequate?", TD Economics, Special Report, 30 April, Toronto, http://www.td.com/document/PDF/economics/special/td-economics-special-gb0409-ei.pdf.

Bloom, H., S. Schwartz, S. Lui-Gurr, S-W. Lee, J. Peng and W. Bancroft (1999), "Testing a re-employment incentive for displaced workers: The Earnings Supplement Project", Social Research and Demonstration Corporation (SRDC), May, http://www.srdc.org/media/195754/testing.pdf.

Caliendo, M., K. Tatsiramos and A. Uhlendorff (2009), "Benefit duration, unemployment duration and job match quality: A regression-discontinuity approach", *IZA Discussion Papers*, No. 4670, Institute for the Study of Labor, December, Bonn, http://ftp.iza.org/dp4670.pdf.

CEIC – Canada Employment and Insurance Commission (2014), *The 2012/13 EI Monitoring and Assessment Report*, Canada Employment Insurance Commission, Employment and Social Development Canada, March, www.esdc.gc.ca/en/reports/ei/monitoring2013/index.page.

D'Amico, R., C. Geckeler, D. Khemani, D. Kogan and M. Midling (2012), "The evaluation of the implementation of the trade and globalization adjustment assistance Act (TGAAA)", Final Report prepared as part of the evaluation of the Trade Adjustment Assistance program, Social Policy Research Associates (SPR), August.

ESDC – Employment and Social Development Canada (2014a), "Evaluation of the career transition assistance initiative", Final Report, Strategic Policy and Research Branch, March, http://www.esdc.gc.ca/eng/publications/evaluations/skills_and_employment/2014/ctai.shtml.

ESDC (2014b), "Evaluation of the extension of Employment Insurance Regular Benefits for long-tenured workers", Final Report, 11 August, http://www12.edsc.gc.ca/sgpe-pmps/p.5bd.2t.1.3ls@-eng.jsp?pid=8775.

ESDC (2014c), "Summative evaluation of the Targeted Initiative for Older Workers", Final Report, Strategic Policy and Research Branch, 5 May, www.esdc.gc.ca/eng/publications/evaluations/skills_and_employment/2014/tiow.shtml.

Finnie, R., D. Gray, I. Irvine and Y. Zhang (2011), "The income sources for long-term workers who exhaust employment insurance benefits", Mowat Centre Employment Insurance Task Force Background Paper, Mowat Centre for Policy Innovation, School of Public Policy and Governance, University of Toronto, http://www.mowateitaskforce.ca/sites/default/files/Finnie.pdf.

Gray, D. and J.T. McDonald (2010), "Seasonal employment in Canada: Its decline and its persistence", *Canadian Public Policy*, Vol. 36, No. 1, University of Toronto Press, pp. 1-27, March, www.jstor.org/stable/20695154.

Gray, D. and A. Sweetman (2001), "A typology analysis of the users of Canada's Unemployment Insurance system: Incidence and seasonality measures", in Schwartz, S. and A. Aydemir (eds.), "Essays on the repeat use of Unemployment Insurance", pp. 15-61, Social Research and Demonstration Corporation (SRDC), October, Ottawa, http://www.srdc.org/media/8874/ESP2-English.pdf.

Greenwood, J. and J.P. Voyer (2000), "Experimental evidence on the use of Earnings Supplements as a strategy to 'make work pay'", in *OECD Economic Studies*, Vol. 2000/II, No. 31, pp. 43-67, OECD Publishing, Paris, http://dx.doi.org/10.1787/eco_studies-v2000-2-en.

Hijzen, A. (2011), "The labour market effects of unemployment compensation in Brazil", *OECD Social, Employment and Migration Working Papers*, No. 119, OECD Publishing, Paris, http://dx.doi.org/10.1787/5kg0prkh67d0-en.

HRSDC – Human Resources and Social Development Canada (2008), "Supporting and engaging older workers in the new economy", Expert Panel on Older Workers, Ottawa, http://publications.gc.ca/collections/collection_2010/rhdcc-hrsdc/HS4-105-2008-eng.pdf.

Immervoll, H. (2012), "Reforming the benefit system to 'make work pay': Options and priorities in a weak labour market", *IZA Policy Papers*, No. 50, Institute for the Study of Labor, November, Bonn, http://ftp.iza.org/pp50.pdf.

Jones, S.R.G. (2009), "Older workers in the new economy: The role of Wage Insurance and the rethinking of Employment Insurance", *Canadian Public Policy*, Vol. 35, No. 4, University of Toronto Press, pp. 499-511, December, www.jstor.org/stable/27759562.

Klerman, J.A. (2013), "Unemployment insurance in the early 21st Century", Abt Associates Thought Leadership White Paper, January.

LeBlanc, L.S. and J.A. McMullin (1997), "Falling through the cracks: Addressing the needs of individuals between employment and retirement", *Canadian Public Policy*, Vol. 23, No. 3, University of Toronto Press, pp. 289-304, September, www.jstor.org/stable/3551573.

Leonard, J. (2009), "Time to get real on EI reform", *Policy Options*, Institute of Research for Public Policy (IRPP), September, Montréal.

Lindquist, G.S. and E. Wadensjö (2007), "Social and occupational security and labour market flexibility in Sweden: The case of unemployment compensation", *IZA Discussion Papers*, No. 2943, Institute for the Study of Labor, July, Bonn, http://ftp.iza.org/dp2943.pdf.

Mendelsohn, M. and J. Medow (2010), "Help wanted: How well did the EI program respond during recent recessions?" Mowat Centre for Policy Innovation, Mowat Note, School of Public Policy & Governance, University of Toronto, September, http://mowatcentre.ca/wp-content/uploads/publications/10_help_wanted.pdf.

Mowat (2011), "Making it work: Final recommendations of the Mowat Centre, Employment Insurance task force", Final Report, Mowat Centre for Policy Innovation, School of Public Policy & Governance, University of Toronto, www.mowateitaskforce.ca/sites/default/files/MakingItWork-online.pdf.

OECD (2011), "Income support for the unemployed: How well has the safety-net held up during the 'Great Recession'?", in *OECD Employment Outlook 2011*, OECD Publishing, Paris, http://dx.doi.org/10.1787/empl_outlook-2011-en.

OECD (2005), "Trade-adjustment costs in OECD labour markets: A mountain or a molehill?", in *OECD Employment Outlook 2005*, OECD Publishing, Paris, pp. 23-72, http://dx.doi.org/10.1787/empl_outlook-2005-en.

OECD (2002), "The ins and outs of long-term unemployment? in *OECD Employment Outlook 2002*, OECD Publishing, Paris, pp. 187-243, http://dx.doi.org/10.1787/empl_outlook-2002-6-en.

Pignal, J., S. Arrowsmith and A. Ness (2010), "First results from the Survey of Older Workers, 2008", Research Paper, Special Surveys Division, Statistics Canada, Catalogue No. 89-646-X, November, Ottawa, http://odesi1.scholarsportal.info/documentation/PHIRN/SOW/89-646-x2010001-eng.pdf.

Riddell, W.C. (2011), "Unemployment compensation and adjustment assistance for displaced workers: Policy option for Canada", Mowat Centre Employment Insurance Task Force Background Paper, Mowat Centre for Policy Innovation, School of Public Policy and Governance, University of Toronto, www.mowateitaskforce.ca/sites/default/files/Riddell.pdf.

Statistics Canada (2011), "Microdata user guide: Employment Insurance Coverage Survey 2011", Special Surveys Division, Statistics Canada, http://odesi1.scholarsportal.info/documentation/EICS/2011/eics2011gid.pdf.

van Audenrode, M., A-A. Fournier, N. Havet and J. Royer (2005), "Employment Insurance in Canada and international comparisons", Groupe d'analyse, 10 March, Montréal, http://web.hec.ca/scse/articles/Fournier.pdf.

Venn, D. (2012), "Eligibility criteria for unemployment benefits: Quantitative indicators for OECD and EU countries", *OECD Social, Employment and Migration Working Papers*, No. 131, OECD Publishing, Paris, http://dx.doi.org/10.1787/5k9h43kgkvr4-en.

Venn, D. (2009), "Legislation, collective bargaining and enforcement: Updating the OECD employment protection indicators", OECD Social, Employment and Migration Working Papers, No. 89, OECD Publishing, Paris, http://dx.doi.org/10.1787/223334316804.

Database references

Employment Insurance Coverage Survey (EICS), Statistics Canada http://www23.statcan.gc.ca/imdb/p2SV.pl?Function=getSurvey&SDDS=4428.

ICTWSS, Database on Institutional Characteristics of Trade Unions, Wage Setting, http://www.uva-aias.net/208.

ILO Employment Protection Legislation Database, www.ilo.org/dyn/eplex/termdisplay.severancePay?p_lang=en.

OECD Employment Protection Database, 2013 update, http://dx.doi.org/10.1787/lfs-epl-data-en.

OECD Tax-Benefit Models, www.oecd.org/els/social/workincentives.

Survey of Labour and Income Dynamics (SLID), confidential data, Statistics Canada, http://www23.statcan.gc.ca/imdb/p2SV.pl?Function=getSurvey&SDDS=3889.

Chapter 5

Re-employment support for displaced workers in Canada

This chapter describes the main active labour market programmes available to help displaced workers get back to work quickly as well as retrain, when necessary. Canada primarily relies on general job-search assistance and skills development programmes to assist displaced workers and these services appear to be well suited to assist the majority of displaced workers to find suitable jobs quickly. However, a substantial number of displaced workers require more intensive job-search assistance and relatively few appear to receive it via general employment services. Canada also implements several targeted measures for older and long-tenured displaced workers that provide more intensive adjustment assistance tailored to the needs of these groups. These programmes are promising but currently reach only a small share of displaced workers and are not well established as permanent programmes.

Policies to avoid unnecessary redundancies play a limited role in Canada (Chapter 3). Instead most of the emphasis is placed on income support (Chapter 4) and adjustment assistance programmes following displacement, which are the focus of this chapter. These include several measures specifically targeted on older and long-tenured displaced workers. This chapter assesses how effectively the Canadian labour market programmes, both mainstream and targeted, manage to foster the rapid re-employment of displaced workers into suitable jobs.

Employment service needs of displaced workers

How do displaced workers look for jobs in Canada and how do employers recruit?

Job-search methods do not differ between displaced workers and other job separators. Among displaced workers who looked for a job during the reference week, 43% declared as their primary source for finding a job that they contacted employers directly (either by sending a CV, visiting or calling an employer, or having a job interview, Figure 5.1) and this proportion is even higher for young displaced workers (64%).

The second most common job-search method for displaced workers is via internet access or kiosk (18%). This is well in line with the Public Employment Service (PES) strategy of job-matching which heavily relies on internet and mobile phone devices such as the Job Bank and Connecting Canadians with Available Jobs (see below). For displaced workers in particular, job search via internet is strongly positively correlated with education and declines with tenure, illustrating the need to target additional job-search assistance towards low-qualified as well as long-tenured displaced workers, in order to teach them how to look for a job online. Displaced workers have longer employment spells than other job separators and, for some of them, have not searched for a job for a very long time. They therefore need to catch up on recent recruitment methods.[1] Other frequent job-search methods include job advertisements (15%) and networking with community, friends and others (14%). Less than 10% of displaced workers use public or private employment agencies to find jobs and even fewer contacts are made with unions to look for a job.

MESS (2013) analyses the recruitment techniques of Quebec *employers*. Three quarters of employers rely on individual interviews and 62% on the CVs of job applicants, which is in line with the main service supports provided to the unemployed by the PES. By contrast, employers rarely use tests, whether of job-performance, personality or aptitude. Employers rely instead on school grades and skills certifications to assess the skills and competencies of displaced workers.

Figure 5.1. **Direct employer contact is the most frequent job-search method for all unemployed Canadians**

Job-search methods of respondents who declared having looked for work during the reference week (percentages), 2000-10

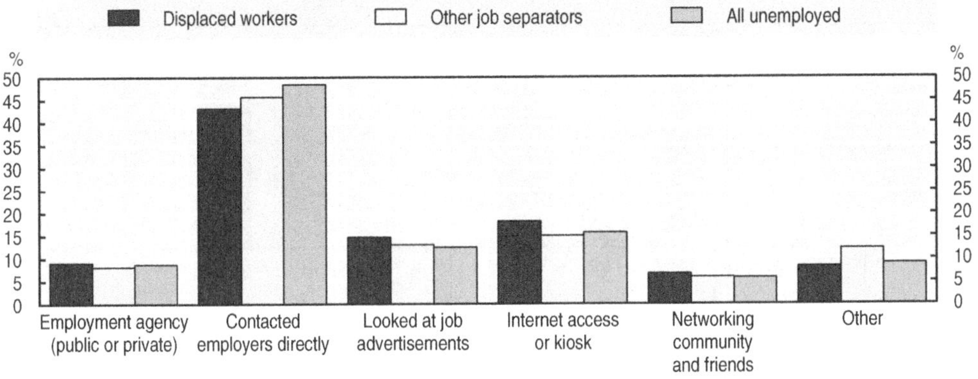

Note: Information available only for the unemployed and persons not in the labour force but receiving regular Employment Insurance (EI), who looked for work during the reference week.

Source: OECD calculations using data from the Employment Insurance Coverage Survey (EICS).

StatLink http://dx.doi.org/10.1787/888933238866

How intensively do displaced workers look for jobs in Canada?

The incidence of job search is higher for displaced workers.[2] More than three displaced workers out of four (76%) declare having searched for a job during the reference week, as compared to only 63% of workers who lost their job for other reasons (Figure 5.2). For both groups, the incidence of job search increases with educational attainment and decreases with tenure. Young displaced workers are less likely to search for a job.

On average, displaced workers and other job separators are less likely to report that they have looked for a job than other unemployed people. The latter group includes new entrants to the labour market as well as a disadvantaged group of unemployed. These two groups are likely to have limited resources, e.g. they may have either not qualified for Employment Insurance (EI) at all (new entrants) or have exhausted their EI entitlements (the long-term unemployed) and thus are more motivated to look for a job than any other group of job separators. Conversely, those unemployed who lost their jobs as temporary or seasonal worker are the least likely to report job search. In this regard, the new strengthened activation measures targeting seasonal workers go in the right direction.

Figure 5.2. **Displaced workers search for jobs more regularly than other jobseekers**

Incidence of job search for displaced workers and other job separators (percentages), 2000-10

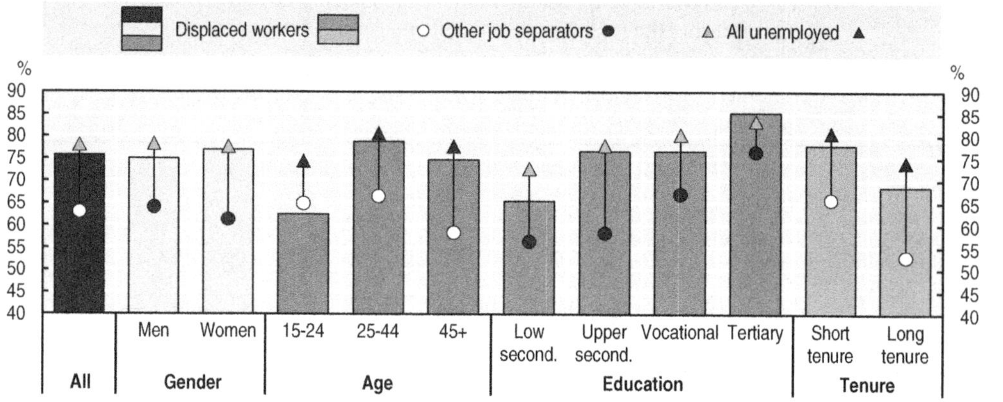

Note: Second.: Secondary. Information available only for the unemployed and persons not in the labour force but receiving regular Employment Insurance (EI).

Source: OECD calculations using data from the Employment Insurance Coverage Survey (EICS).

StatLink *http://dx.doi.org/10.1787/888933238870*

Displaced workers look for jobs much more intensively than workers who lose their job for other reasons. Displaced workers spend an average of 12.3 hours per week looking for work, in comparison with 9.3 hours spent by workers who lost their jobs for other reasons and 9.5 hours for the stock of all unemployed (Figure 5.3, Panel A). This difference largely results from the lower proportion of displaced workers who spend less than four hours looking for work (15%) compared with other job separators (25%, Figure 5.3, Panel B).

Figure 5.3. **Displaced workers invest more time in looking for a job**

Respondents who declared having looked for a job during reference week, 2000-10

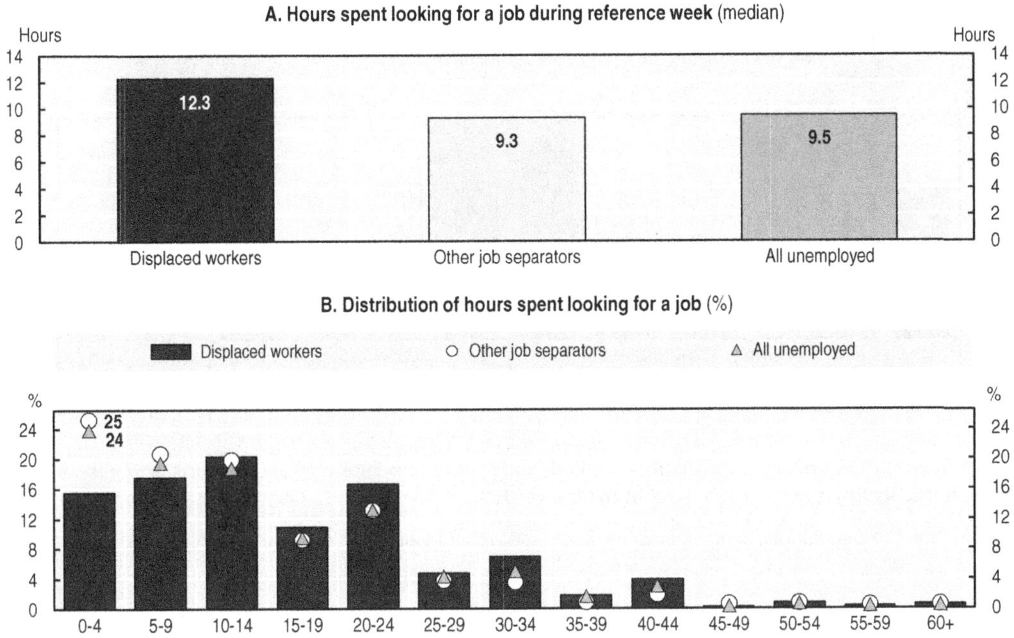

Note: Information available only for the unemployed and persons not in the labour force but receiving regular Employment Insurance (EI), who looked for a job during the reference week.

Source: OECD calculations using data from the Employment Insurance Coverage Survey (EICS).

StatLink *http://dx.doi.org/10.1787/888933238888*

Displaced workers are rather pessimistic about their chances of finding a job

A significant proportion of older and long-tenured displaced workers are pessimistic about their chances of finding a job soon. Around 36% of displaced workers with long tenure felt their chances were "not very good," compared to 28% of those with short-tenure (Figure 5.4). Similarly, around a third of the displaced workers with low education reported to have not very good chances of finding an acceptable job compared with a quarter of those with tertiary education. This suggests that low job-search effort may reflect discouragement or objectively poor job-search prospects, pointing towards the importance of combining the monitoring of job-search efforts with counselling services intended to improve the prospects of finding suitable jobs.

Figure 5.4. **Older displaced workers are quite pessimistic about their job prospects**

Chances of finding an acceptable job in the next three months are declared "not very good" (percentages), 2000-10

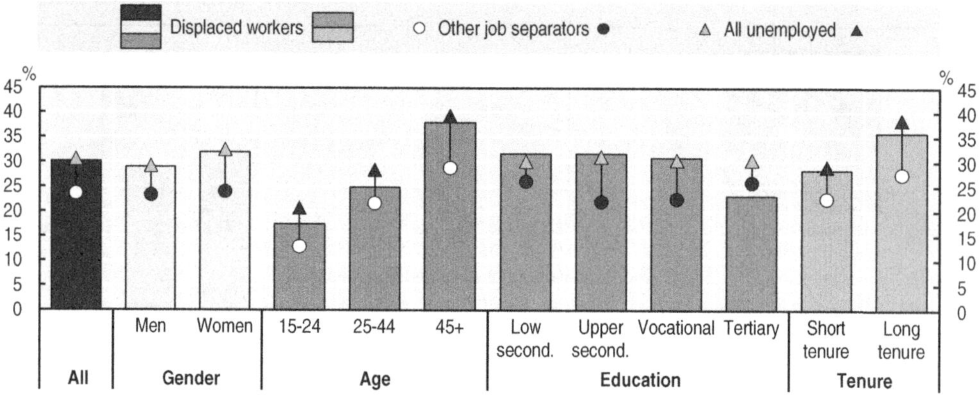

Note: Second.: Secondary. Information available only for the unemployed and persons not in the labour force but receiving regular Employment Insurance (EI).

Source: OECD calculations using data from the Employment Insurance Coverage Survey (EICS).

StatLink *http://dx.doi.org/10.1787/888933238898*

What kind of labour market programmes do displaced workers feel they need?

When unemployed respondents assessed their chances of finding an acceptable job in the next three months as "not very good," the EICS asked what help they would need most in finding one. Among all displaced workers (except those aged 15-24 years old), "skills training" was the most frequent response (Figure 5.5, Panel A). Chapter 1 showed that displaced workers are more likely to have worked in a declining industry and occupation and to have relatively little formal education, and therefore perceive a need to change their skills in order to find a new job.

Displaced workers felt they are in need of skills training more often than other unemployed persons (20% vs. 15%, see Figure 5.5, Panel A). The perceived need for training is particularly high for female and older displaced workers (Figure 5.5, Panel B). Around one displaced worker out of eight felt a need for more academic education, and the same proportion a need for help in their job search.

Figure 5.5. **Displaced workers more often express a need for skills training**

Measures needed to help the unemployed find a job (percentages), 2000-10

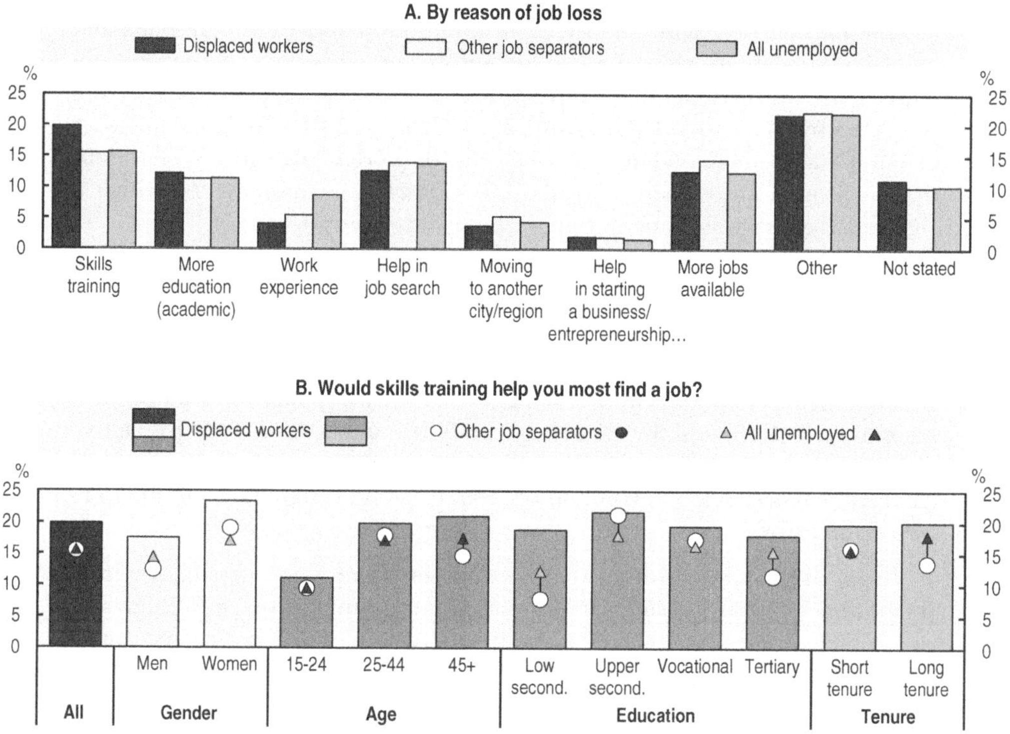

Note: Second.: Secondary. Information available only for the unemployed and persons not in the labour force but receiving regular Employment Insurance (EI).

Source: OECD calculations using data from the Employment Insurance Coverage Survey (EICS).

StatLink http://dx.doi.org/10.1787/888933238907

The Canadian activation strategy

Labour market expenditure in Canada focused on training during the crisis and moved towards an employer-driven approach

Labour market expenditure is low compared to other countries

During the recession following the Global Financial Crisis (GFC), spending on labour market programmes represented an important component of crisis fiscal stimulus packages in most countries. According to ILO (2014), based on a survey of 65 advanced, emerging and developing economies, 11.7% of crisis response stimulus measures in advanced economies and 5.1% in emerging economies were devoted to active labour market programmes. In the case of Canada, emphasis was put on helping the automobile industry with almost CAD 13.7 billion spent through loans and other instruments to support General Motors and Chrysler. The department of Finance estimated that approximately 52 000 Canadian jobs were protected by this support (Government of Canada, 2010). To a much lesser extent Canada increased its expenditures on certain categories of labour market programmes, such as skills development and training for which a significant effort was made during the crisis (see below).

Compared with other OECD countries, expenditure on labour market programmes is relatively low in Canada. In 2012, it amounted to 0.83% of GDP compared with 1.58% on average in the OECD, placing Canada in the 18th position among OECD countries, and at the 22nd position considering expenditures per unemployed (Figure 5.6). Canada's total expenditure per unemployed decreased by 24% between 2002 and 2012 (-34% for active programmes and -18% for passive programmes) even if part of this decrease can be attributed to the devolution of labour market programmes to the P/Ts (see Chapter 2).

Less than a third of total expenditure on labour market programmes (29%) was allocated to active programmes, placing Canada in the 26th position among OECD countries. Among these active measures, Canada reduced by 45% its federal spending per unemployed in PES and administration[3] between 2002 and 2012 (Figure 5.7, Panel A). This important cut in federal expenditures for placement and related services for the unemployed (including face-to-face interviews with a caseworker) requires P/Ts to adapt their employment service delivery and funding to answer structural adjustments. Active measures strongly rely on training in Canada (Figure 5.7, Panel B) while employment incentives only represent a small share (3%). In comparison, the United States, with similar expenditures on actives measures, dedicated almost 8% to employment incentives, and Northern European countries like Denmark or Finland, around 20% of their (much higher) expenditures on active measures. There is room for an increase in spending on active measures in Canada, in order to strengthen placement services and intensify interviews with caseworkers for displaced workers, especially the older long-tenured ones, a population that has been identified in this review as facing important barriers to re-employment (see Chapter 1).

Figure 5.6. **Labour market spending in Canada is low compared with many other OECD countries**

Public expenditure on active and passive labour market programmes in OECD countries, 2002 and 2012[a] (spending per unemployed, as a percentage of GDP per capita)

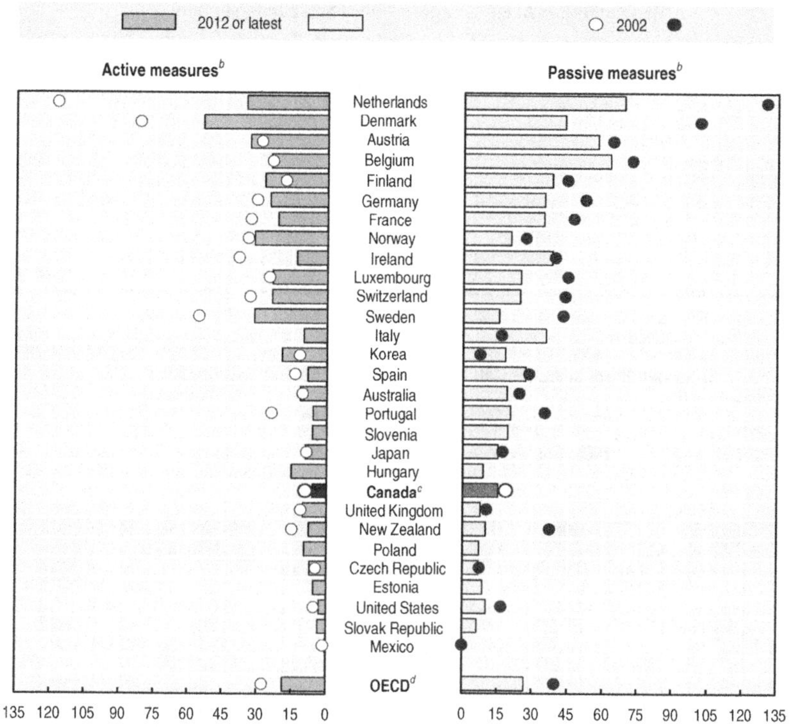

Note: GDP: Gross domestic product. Countries are ranked in decreasing order of the total of both active and passive measures in 2012. P/Ts: Provinces/Territories. Data refer to fiscal years for Australia, Canada, Japan, New Zealand, the United Kingdom and the United States.

a) Data refer to 2011 for Estonia, Luxembourg, Poland and Spain. Data refer to fiscal years 2010/11 for Australia and 2009/10 for the United Kingdom.

b) *Active measures* refer to Categories 1 to 7, *Passive measures* to Categories 8 and 9 of the *OECD/Eurostat Labour Market Programme Database*. For more details about the categories, see Grubb and Puymoyen (2008).

c) Data include federal expenditure on programmes implemented by the P/Ts, but do not generally include the provinces' additional or complementary funding of these programmes.

d) Unweighted averages for countries where both active and passive measures are shown for 2002 and 2012, i.e. except Estonia, Hungary, Italy, Poland, the Slovak Republic and Slovenia.

Source: OECD/Eurostat Labour Market Programme Database, http://dx.doi.org/10.1787/data-00312-en, *OECD Population and Labour Force Dataset*, a subset of the *Annual Labour Force Statistics* (ALFS) *Database*, http://dotstat.oecd.org/Index.aspx?DataSetCode=ALFS_POP_LABOUR; and Grubb, D. and A. Puymoyen (2008), "Long time series for public expenditure on labour market programmes", *OECD Social, Employment and Migration Working Papers*, No. 73, OECD Publishing, Paris, http://dx.doi.org/10.1787/230128514343.

StatLink *http://dx.doi.org/10.1787/888933238918*

Figure 5.7. **The decline in labour market spending in Canada partly reflects the devolution of responsibilities**

Public expenditure per unemployed, as a percentage of GDP per capita (Panels A and B) and percentages (Panel B), by category of spending, 2002 and 2012[a]

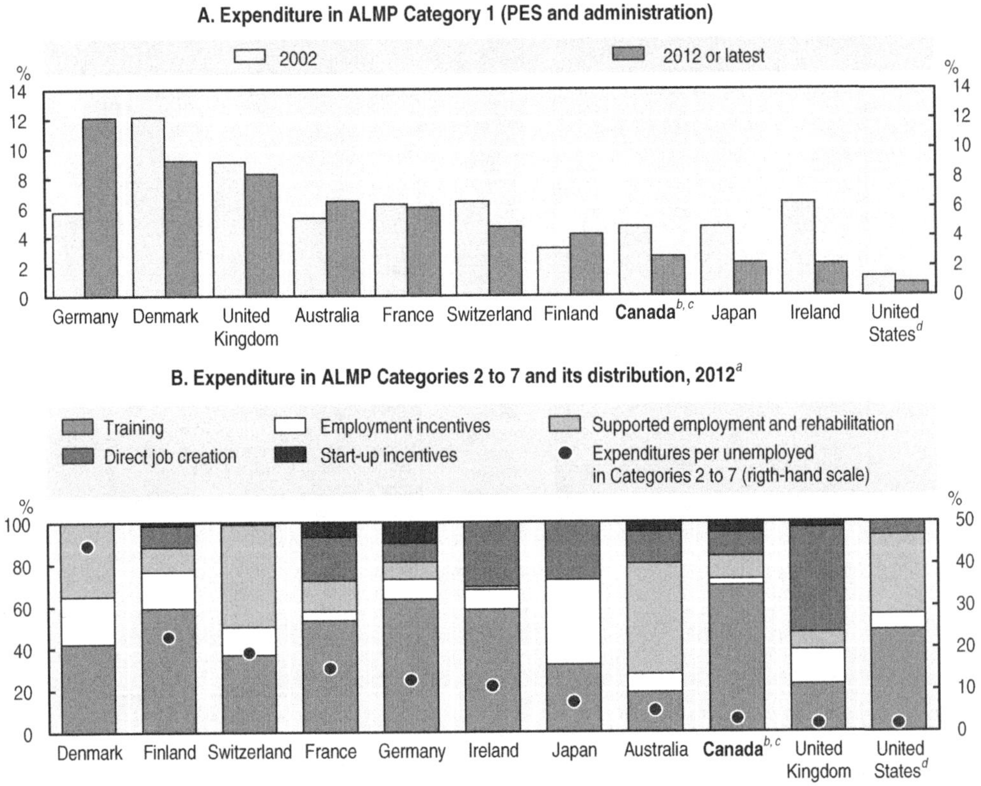

Note: ALMP: Active labour market programme; GDP: Gross domestic product; PES: Public Employment Service. P/Ts: Provinces/Territories. Countries are ranked in decreasing order of expenditure on PES and administration (in Panel A), and in decreasing order of expenditure on active measures calculated as the sum of Categories 2 to 7 in the *OECD/Eurostat Labour Market Programme Database* (in Panel B). For more details about the categories, see Grubb and Puymoyen (2008).

a) Data refer to fiscal years 2010/11 for Australia, 2009/10 for the United Kingdom, and to the year 2011 for Ireland.

b) Data include federal expenditure on programmes implemented by the P/Ts, but generally do not include the provinces' additional or complementary funding of these programmes.

c) The sum of expenditures in ALMP Category 1 (Panel A) and Categories 2 to 7 (Panel B) does not correspond to the expenditures in actives measures (in Figure 5.6) because the latter includes the Aboriginal Human Resources Development Agreements, which have not been allocated across the main categories.

d) The sum of expenditures in ALMP Category 1 (Panel A) and Categories 2 to 7 (Panel B) does not correspond to the expenditures in actives measures (in Figure 5.6) because the latter includes work-related activities of Temporary Assistance for Needy Families (estimated as 0.02% of GDP), which have not been allocated across the main categories.

Figure 5.7. **The decline in labour market spending in Canada partly reflects the devolution of responsibilities** *(cont.)*

Public expenditure per unemployed, as a percentage of GDP per capita (Panels A and B) and percentages (Panel B), by category of spending, 2002 and 2012[a]

Source: OECD/Eurostat Labour Market Programme Database, http://dx.doi.org/10.1787/data-00312-en; *OECD Population and Labour Force Dataset*, a subset of the *Annual Labour Force Statistics (ALFS) Database*, http://dotstat.oecd.org/Index.aspx?DataSetCode=ALFS_POP_LABOUR; and Grubb, D. and A. Puymoyen (2008), "Long time series for public expenditure on labour market programmes", *OECD Social, Employment and Migration Working Papers*, No. 73, OECD Publishing, Paris, http://dx.doi.org/10.1787/230128514343.

StatLink http://dx.doi.org/10.1787/888933238926

Canada invested in skills development and training during the crisis

Canada has placed considerable emphasis over many years on skills development and training, and further increased its investments in this area during the crisis (Figure 5.8). Scaling up existing skills development programmes and training courses in response to the crisis was a valuable response according to evaluations of training. Nevertheless, the level of expenditure in training, measured as the share of GDP, remains quite low relative to other OECD countries (Figure 5.7), around six times less than the highest spending European countries, such as Denmark. At the same time, expenditure on employer-sponsored training in Canada, most of which is non-formal, has also been declining (Burleton et al., 2013). ILO (2014) examines what countries have learned from the implementation of training and retraining programmes as part of their recovery strategies in response to the GFC of 2008–09, and their results suggest that programmes that were demand driven and involved employers in the design and delivery of training at the workplace produced more immediate results.

Figure 5.8. **Canada has increased spending on training in response to the crisis**

Evolution of expenditure in ALMP Categories 2 to 7, percentage of GDP, 2000-12

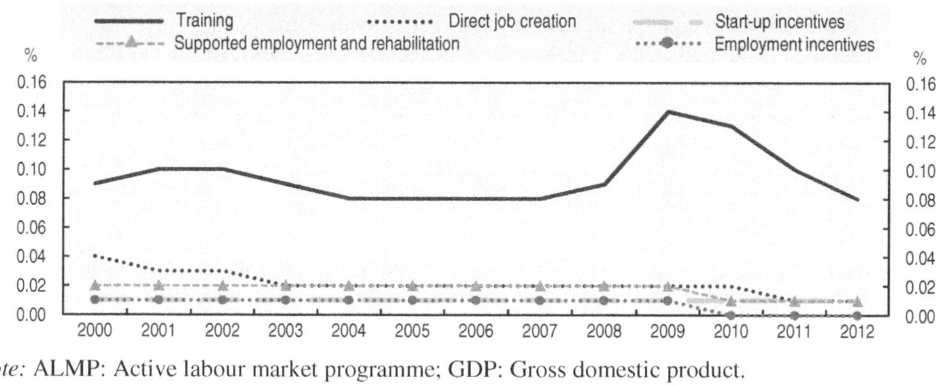

Note: ALMP: Active labour market programme; GDP: Gross domestic product.

Source: OECD/Eurostat Labour Market Programme Database, http://dx.doi.org/10.1787/data-00312-en.

StatLink http://dx.doi.org/10.1787/888933238938

Moving towards an employer-driven training approach

In 2013, the federal government announced its intention to renew and transform the LMAs into the Canada Job Fund (CJF) Agreements to make them more responsive to labour market demand (see Chapter 2). CJF includes the Canada Job Grant (CJG), an employer-driven approach designed to help Canadians gain the skills and training they need to fill available jobs (see Box 5.1).

Box 5.1. **Canada Job Grant**

The renegotiation of LMAs with P/Ts into the Canada Job Fund agreements (CJF, see Chapter 2) reaffirmed the federal commitment to introduce the Canada Job Grant (CJG) initiative and to more directly connect skills training with employers. By the time of its full implementation, planned for 2017-18, CAD 300 million per year (out of the total CAD 500 million CJF agreements with P/Ts) will be invested in the new CJG. Each province is responsible for the design and delivery of CJG in its own jurisdiction:

- Ontario signed the Canada-Ontario Job Fund Agreement with the federal government in March 2014. This agreement will provide Ontario with CAD 192 million per year for the next six years and is a key source of funding for new employer-led training.
- Quebec's training system already included the key principles of the Canada Job Grant. In March 2014, Quebec signed the Canada-Quebec Agreement 2014-20 ensuring the transfer of funds from the Canada Job Fund agreement (CJF, see Chapter 2), for an approximate amount of CAD 116 million per year for six years. The agreement aims to improve employment inclusion of underrepresented groups and workers with a significant deficit in basic training.

CJG cover part of the costs to employers of training provided by eligible third-party trainers. CJG is also available for an unemployed worker in contact with a potential employer, when the former needs to acquire specific skills to get a position the latter is offering. The total cost of training is shared with employers who contribute one-third in addition to the government contribution of up to CAD 10 000). Training can take various forms including formal classroom training, on-the-job training at an employer's workplace or online training, and other training costs (tuition fees or fees charged by training providers; mandatory student fees; textbooks, software and other required materials; as well as examination fees). Eligible third-party trainers are determined by P/Ts. They include actors such as community or career colleges, trade union centres or private trainers.

Employers, regardless of their size, industry or region, are eligible to participate in CJG. Flexible arrangements apply to small businesses (50 or fewer employees), such as allowing to count wages as part of the employer's contribution, and aims at increasing their employees' access to training.

Source: Economic Action Plan (2013), "Jobs growth and long-term prosperity", Ministry of Finance, March, http://actionplan.gc.ca/en/page/economic-action-plan-2013.

This innovative approach relies on sharing training costs between the government and employers who are providing training to potential or existing employees for new or better jobs. While this initiative appears well suited to help employers, initial concern was expressed by P/Ts and stakeholders that the proposed CJG would reduce training resources available to improve the employability of vulnerable groups such as recipients of social assistance benefits and the long-term unemployed. In response, the Government of Canada worked closely with P/Ts to retain flexibility in the agreements so that P/Ts can design and deliver programmes that meet their local labour market needs.[4] As part of the CJG, employers decide who gets training, and what type of it, and are required to have a job available at the end of training. Employers can use the Grant to provide training to individuals who are currently unemployed, but who could be a good fit for the firm with a few additional skills. Employers can also apply to train current employees who require up-skilling or re-skilling for either their current job or another position in the firm.

The CJG initiative is not free from deadweight costs, creating a windfall opportunity for employers to subsidise training they already provide (Mendelson and Zon, 2013). While P/Ts strongly support the involvement of employers in improving the skills of their current and future employees, consistent with the Grant, they expressed concern (at the early stages of the negotiations with the federal government) that many SME employees could miss out on Grant training because their employers do not have the means to pay their share of the total training costs (including the employee's absence) or would find the Grant administratively burdensome (Carey, 2014). Therefore, SMEs can now benefit from flexible arrangements, such as contribute a minimum of 15% or make up to 50% of their contribution in wages or wage replacement. Targeting CJF subsidies at the low-skilled (both unemployed and workers) is crucial to limit deadweight costs. For that reason, funding under the CJF agreements continues to be transferred to P/Ts to support other employment services and supports, similar to those they offered under the LMAs with priority given to low-skilled employed and unemployed individuals ineligible for EI.

The CJG could possibly become a useful resource for displaced workers perhaps particularly in the case of mass layoffs, but this would require linking CJG with the early intervention scheme (see Chapter 3). Action centres/CAR/CREC have an important role to play in gathering information on skills needs, potential employers and the corresponding training courses available to fill the skill gaps that displaced workers might have to qualify for a new position. Here, labour market information and access to information about employers' skill and recruitment needs are crucial for CJG to efficiently serve the specific population of displaced workers.

The sooner these potentially recruiting employers are identified by Action centres or caseworkers in local PES agencies, the sooner they can put these employers in contact with displaced workers (possibly even before displacement takes place). This retraining option could thus create important opportunities for displaced workers coming from shrinking industries to retrain and access jobs in growing industries and occupations.

In addition, early warning of public authorities in the case of large-scale dismissals is crucial because the subsequent sudden increase in local training demand might require adapting the training supply from VET institutions. For example, RIM (maker of Blackberry) was able to approach the Ontarian provincial government and local community in 2012 about the mass dismissal of more than 2 000 of their workers in Waterloo. This early assessment enabled the creation of a partnership between the Government of Ontario with the employer, as well as universities and colleges which were able to add spaces in entrepreneurship and business programmes to help displaced workers develop skills to start their own businesses.

Further efforts are required to link training to other employment services and harmonise certifications across P/Ts

ILO (2014) highlights the need for training and retraining to be further connected to other labour market interventions and employment services. It suggests that connecting training initiatives with pre-training counselling services might increase post-training employment rates. In the case of Canada, the employment services delivery model in Ontario makes it difficult to connect more closely employment counselling and training (see Chapter 2). The more integrated way employment services are delivered in Quebec is an advantage for addressing this issue. Temporary arrangements for reducing working times and wages were implemented in Canada in combination with job training (see Chapter 3), which allowed employers not only to avoid displacement but also to retrain qualified workers and use downtime to upgrade their employees' skills.

Accrediting on a national basis the competencies acquired by training participants is a major challenge in Canada. Until recently, accreditations and certifications were set up at the provincial level, creating a barrier to geographic mobility. The negotiations Canada engaged with Europe on this topic were exclusively the occasion to address this issue also at a national level. Recent initiatives to develop common provincial standards are therefore welcome. OECD (2014) highlights the progress made in this direction, for example by the Red Seal Program which contributed to some harmonisation of the scope of trades occupations, however inconsistencies remain. The federal government should continue to work with P/Ts to harmonise the content of training courses and the certification requirements of both apprenticeship and training programmes.

Strengthen the activation strategy in Canada

The Canadian "work-first" approach relies on the provision of job-matching services on a self-service basis...

The general employment services available to the unemployed in Canada reflect a "work-first" philosophy that emphasises a speedy return to work and also expects most unemployed persons to search for a new job in a relatively autonomous manner, in part by taking advantage of the core job-search assistance that the PES offers in a largely self-service way, such as vacancy listings and other labour market information. The work-first approach is reinforced by the modest replacement rates and relatively short time limits attached to EI benefits (see Chapter 4), and more recently by increased efforts to communicate and enforce job-availability requirements. Some jobseekers need more help than the core job-search assistance, and this is especially likely to be the case for older long-tenured displaced workers, but intensive services are used quite sparingly. In particular, intensive counselling by caseworkers (case management) is not available to the majority of the unemployed and only a small share of displaced workers will benefit from intensive job counselling. Targeting therefore needs to be well adapted to the specific needs of displaced workers.

...by providing job offers and labour market information to the unemployed through the Job Bank...

Employment and Social Development Canada (ESDC) administers the main job-matching service in Canada through the "Job Bank" job-posting website (www.jobbank.gc.ca). Employers from all P/Ts are able to post job offers online free of charge (see Box 5.2), reaching over 6 million visitors monthly. Job Bank now also disseminates free Labour Market Information (LMI) resources to the public accessing these services on a self-service basis. By allowing users to access relevant job postings and produce a variety of detailed reports on wages, education and career paths, Job Bank helps Canadian jobseekers (including displaced workers) connect with employers. These free online services improve the collection and dissemination of labour market information and reduce duplication, thereby improving the quality of information, and making online information more accessible and easier to use.[5] Federal LMI services are complemented by P/T LMI services like the "*information sur le marché du travail*" in Quebec, providing more local information.

Box 5.2. Job Bank and Labour Market Information (LMI)

Job Bank website (www.jobbank.gc.ca) provides employers with a tool to advertise their vacancies for free, in both English and French, and also features specialised online tools, such as Job Match, Job Alerts and Job Search. In addition, the site provides visitors with basic information on how to acquire the skills needed to pursue their chosen career. Job Bank also favours the dissemination of labour market information resources, providing visitors with access to job opportunities, as well as occupational and career information, a skill and knowledge checklist, and a Career Tool. Job Bank leverages labour market information from 30 sources and can generate more than 32 000 unique LMI reports based on a client's occupation and location. Job Bank reports provide targeted, comprehensive information on job postings, wage rates, employment trends and outlooks, licensing and certification requirements, job skills, and relevant educational and training programmes for occupations at the regional, provincial and national levels. In 2013/14, Job Bank received more than 59 million visits, and provided access to about one million job postings.

Information sur le marché du travail (Labour Market Information, http://imt.emploiquebec.gouv.qc.ca). Since June 2011, Quebec implemented personalised job placement and LMI services through a specific website called "*information sur le marché du travail*" (IMT). This website provides information about wages, working conditions, occupations in demand, training and careers, job prospects, growing sectors of activity, potential employers, available manpower and other labour market topics. In addition, newsletters called "*bulletin sur le marché du travail au Québec*" provide monthly updates on changes in employment, the labour force and unemployment. Local labour market information is given at regional, sectorial and occupational levels, and comparisons with the situations in Ontario and Canada as a whole are presented.

Source: CEIC (2014), "EI monitoring and assessment report 2012/13", Canada Employment Insurance Commission, Employment and Social Development Canada, March, http://www12.hrsdc.gc.ca/servlet/sgpp-pmps-pub?lang=eng&curjsp=p.5bd.2t.1.3ls@-eng.jsp&curactn=dwnld&pid=7982&did=1.

… and by clarifying job-search requirements

Connecting Canadians with Available Jobs (CCAJ) is a new ESDC initiative implemented in 2014, whose objective is to improve the labour market information delivered to EI claimants and better enforce the conditionality of EI benefit receipt on active job search. This initiative consists of three components:

- First, Service Canada provides EI beneficiaries with more and better tailored information about job vacancies. In particular, they now send twice daily emails to beneficiaries, listing job vacancies near where they live that appear to match their qualifications. These vacancies are culled from both vacancies employers list with Service Canada and those obtained from commercial placement services, such as Monster.[6]

- Second, CCAJ more clearly defines what constitute a "reasonable and ongoing job search".[7] Service Canada also takes into account the availability of jobs in the community when assessing whether a claimant is conducting a reasonable and ongoing job search.
- Third, ESDC has encouraged P/T employment services to set up pilot programmes offering new EI beneficiaries prompt access to re-employment services, including training. Results of these pilots are expected in late 2015. The Government of Canada will continue to work with P/Ts to encourage earlier activation as part of ongoing discussions. However, displaced workers still need to contact separately Service Canada to apply for EI and a P/T employment office to enquire about re-employment assistance and training support.

Jobseekers are now required to look for a job every day while claiming EI, and the suitability of a job offer now depends on the EI recipient's claim history, with repeat users being subject to more stringent conditionality.[8] This clarification of reasonable job offers and job-search requirements should not be particularly onerous for displaced worker. Indeed, many among them are likely to fulfil the conditions to be considered long-tenured workers[9] and therefore will have less restrictive requirements in terms of jobs to be accepted. This might reduce the wage losses displaced workers have to accept to get back to work and give them more time to find a suitable (and better paid) job. There is nevertheless a risk that these new job-search requirements may remain ineffective in the absence of significant face-to-face engagement with jobseekers, for example through the development of an agreed individual action plan.[10]

The Canadian activation system is not very strict…

Eligibility criteria for unemployment benefits may require recipients (either displaced workers or other job separators) to actively look for work, take up suitable job offers or take part in active labour market programmes (ALMPs), or risk benefit sanctions. These eligibility criteria can play an important role in offsetting the negative impact of unemployment benefits on employment incentives. Venn (2012) presents a composite indicator of the strictness of eligibility criteria for unemployment benefits in 2011 for OECD (and EU) member countries. In Canada, depending on provincial practices, registration with placement services is not necessarily a precondition for benefit payment (OECD, 2007; and Venn, 2012). Jobseekers who wish to receive EI benefits must register at Service Canada, after which there is a two-week waiting period to receive benefits. Compared with other OECD countries, job-search requirements and subsequent monitoring of individual obligations as well as sanctions appear to be particularly weak in Canada. As was discussed above, some of these eligibility criteria were tightened in 2013 when the CCAJ was implemented.

When displaced workers apply for EI benefits at Service Canada, they are informed of their obligations to search for work and to accept suitable job offers. Jobseekers are required to confirm their availability for work and report their job-search activities every two weeks to Service Canada, but evidence of job-search activity is only needed if requested. This job-search monitoring consists of a "tick-the-box" exercise that jobseekers have to carry out online each fortnight, but which leaves out information about the type of jobs or the frequency of the search. In addition, the disconnection between job-search assistance provided by the provincial/territorial PES and job-search monitoring under the responsibility of Service Canada may undermine the effectiveness of the Canadian activation strategy. Moreover, there are no legislative provisions that govern the number and type of applications for work that must be made, the format for a job search or the frequency of reporting job-search activities (Venn, 2012). CCAJ filled part of the gap by specifying what constitutes a reasonable job-search effort (see above) but monitoring of the job-search intensity remains poor.

... and requires further improvements to adapt job-search monitoring and make more effective use of sanctions.

The Integrity Services Branch of Service Canada is responsible for explaining job search and job availability rules to beneficiaries and monitoring compliance with these requirements. New EI beneficiaries can therefore be required to attend a Client Information Session (CIS) where their obligations as a beneficiary are explained.[11] Follow up by the CIS is quite limited but beneficiaries may be called in for additional interviews where they must provide more detailed proof of their job-search activities than the usual online tick-the-box exercise. Service Canada can also call in longer-term beneficiaries for a CIS or a one-on-one interview, if they suspect a problem and want to check compliance with the rules. In some provinces, these CIS can be jointly organised by Service Canada and the local employment office.[12]

Reforming and making more systematic the monitoring of compliance with job-search requirements, combined with a credible sanctions regime, may be a way to improve activation in Canada. According to *Statistics Canada's Key Socioeconomic Database* (CANSIM), in 2013 only 210 EI benefit disqualifications were pronounced for refusal of a suitable job, and another 600 for failure to search for work. In comparison to the number of jobseekers in Canada, these figures are extremely low, leaving room for more effective use of sanctions. CCAJ goes in this direction, as the number of disqualifications for failure to search for work has already doubled in the first semester of 2014.[13]

Relevant mainstream programmes for displaced workers

Access to employment services by displaced workers needs to be facilitated

Canada provides a large range of ALMPs…

Beyond the self-service job-search assistance, Public Employment Service (PES) interventions usually include direct job placement by employment counsellors, help to tackle or address barriers that decrease employability and capacity to take jobs, and referrals to different types of Active Labour Market Programmes (ALMP), called Employment Benefit and Support Measures (EBSM) in Canada. These ALMPs are established to assist the unemployed (including displaced workers) in preparing for, obtaining and maintaining employment. They are delivered mostly by P/Ts and financed through Labour Market Development Agreements (LMDAs), CJF and P/Ts own funding. Unemployment benefits are available only to EI-insured clients (active and former claimants), while Support Measures are available to all unemployed individuals in Canada, including non-insured clients. CEIC (2014) provides a detailed national overview of EBSM delivered by the Government of Canada and EBSM-similar programmes delivered by P/Ts. For simplicity, all EBSM-similar programmes delivered by P/Ts and EBSM programmes are called ALMP in the rest of this review (see Chapter 2 and Annex 5.A1).

… requiring information sessions early on in the unemployment spell to ease access for displaced workers

As seen in Chapters 2 and 4, the employment service system can be difficult to navigate for displaced workers and severance pay can delay EI claims and consequently the access of displaced workers to employment support considerably, especially for the older long-tenured ones. In order to prevent labour market detachment and intervene early in the unemployment spell, systematic early information should be provided to displaced workers on income support, mainstream employment services and targeted programmes available to help them find a new suitable job. Canada can build on the existing Client Information Session (see below) to improve further the access by displaced workers to early and relevant information on the wide variety of services they can get access to.

Early information sessions for displaced workers should: i) occur preferably during the notice period and no later than two weeks after displacement; ii) take place either on the workplace (i.e. before displacement) in the case of large dismissals or in a "one-stop-shop" in the case of small-scale and individual dismissals (see also Chapter 2); iii) become the entry door to employment support by making registration to the PES during these information sessions compulsory in order to speed up access to employment support; iv) present the large set of services available to displaced workers, ranging from the self-service mode to mainstream ALMP, and special programmes targeted to certain categories of displaced workers. The low take-up rate of these programmes has been identified as being partly caused by the lack of timely referral to them; information sessions can fill this gap.

Who gets what and how is ALMP provision decided?

Displaced workers' access to ALMP can be further improved

As described in Chapter 4, Canadian displaced workers qualify much more often for EI (62%) than when job losses occur for other reasons (26%) and therefore are likely to have better access to the suite of EI-related ALMPs operated by P/Ts. Displaced workers who are not (or not yet) eligible to receive EI benefits have access to the self-service online job assistance and may also be able to access the range of services not targeted on EI beneficiaries (notably employment assistance services, which can include job-search support, résumé writing, etc.). However, these ALMPs appear to be largely targeted on very disadvantaged groups such as social assistance recipients, early school leavers, aboriginals and persons with disabilities, and may not fit well the needs of displaced workers. Even for active EI claimants, access to proper job-search counselling is not automatic as 24% do not access programmes until six months or more into their EI claim (CEIC, 2014).

ESDC (2014b) presents a comprehensive analysis of ALMP procurement in Canada in 13 P/Ts over the period 2002-05, and of their effectiveness for different groups. All other things equal, workers who lost their job due to layoff or a shortage of work (very similar to the definition of displaced workers used in this report) have better access to ALMP programmes than when the job loss is not labour market related (Figure 5.9, Panel A), but more restrictive access than in the case of voluntary quits or dismissal. Access to ALMP is also negatively correlated with age, in particular for skills development access (Figure 5.9, Panel B). There seems to be some room for further easing ALMP access for older long-tenured displaced workers, who suffer the largest displacement losses.

Figure 5.9. Access to labour market programmes in Canada varies by individual characteristics

Likelihood of receiving ALMP in Canada, marginal effects in percentage points, 2002-05

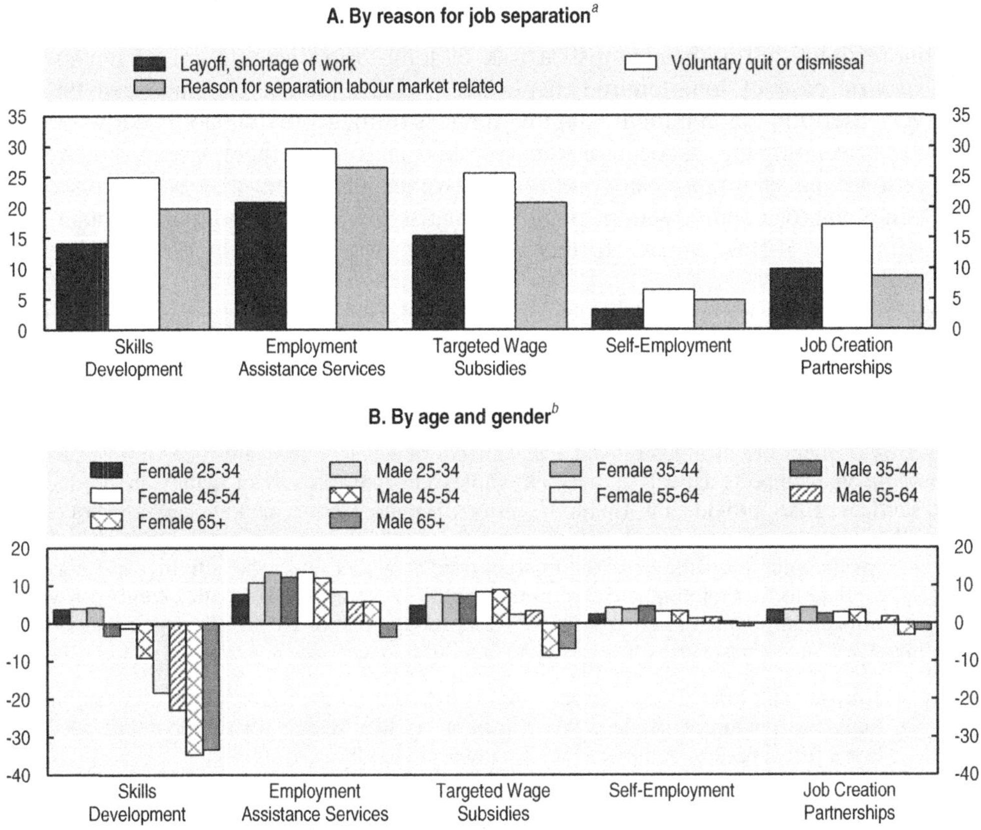

a) Marginal effects compared to the reference reason for separation "not labour market related".

b) Marginal effects compared to the reference youth population (less than 24 years old).

Source: OECD calculations based on ESDC (2014), "Analysis of national Employment Benefits and Support Measures (EBSM) profile, outcomes and incremental impacts", Technical Report (draft), Cycle II of the Evaluation of the Labour Market Development Agreements (LMDAs), Evaluation directorate, 11 March.

StatLink http://dx.doi.org/10.1787/888933238944

Even though EI is financed federally, some provinces such as Quebec have a reputation of being proactive about establishing contact with new claimants (see Box 5.3). Quebec has worked closely with the Government of Canada to maintain a Targeting, Referral and Feedback (TRF) application that proactively targets EI claimants likely to face employment barriers and those in demand occupations. However, with the exception of Quebec targeting EI clients for early intervention, no P/T operates a systematic early needs' assessment of displaced workers that would ease access to more frequent meetings with a caseworker and to active measures relevant for those identified as being most at risk of long-term unemployment. In the specific case of long-tenured displaced workers, job-search clubs can be very useful in helping them "mourn" the loss of their previous job, deal with the psychological aspects of the job loss and help them expand their professional horizon. Networking with other displaced workers is also beneficial to socialise with peers, de-dramatise the job loss and make contact with new firms where former displaced workers were successfully re-employed.

Box 5.3. **Employment Assistance Services in Quebec**

In Quebec, *Emploi-Québec* provides Employment Assistance Services (EAS) that are potentially available to all unemployed (irrespective of whether they are receiving or not any form of income support) as well as persons employed or still in school if they are in need of such services. EAS provide information sessions on the labour market, career advice and counselling, job-search, and its job-placement assistance activities. An employment assistance officer helps the unemployed review their career trajectory and select the activities and services most appropriate to find a job quickly, retrain or change occupation. Activities can be provided either by a local employment centre (CLE) of *Emploi-Québec* or by third-party partners. EAS are generally short-term services, lasting less than 180 hours. Examples of EAS include:

- **Job-search clubs**: These support groups help carrying out job search and finding the tools and resources needed. When joining a club, search for employment becomes like a full-time job, completed within a workplace-like setting.
- **Job-hunting strategies**: These include the provision of support and advices to help the unemployed get started on their job search, as well as assist them with organising their search.
- **Multi-service rooms**: These are available in all local employment agencies in Quebec, gathering under the same roof self-service tools (such as computers, phones, printers) and access to online Labour Market Information and information on in-demand careers and jobs. A caseworker is also available to answer questions, guide jobseekers in their searches and counsel them on how to use the various tools at their disposal.

Source: Emploi-Québec (2010), "Rapport global – Enquête sur la situation post-intervention des participantes et participants aux interventions des services publics d'emploi", http://emploiquebec.gouv.qc.ca/fileadmin/fichiers/pdf/Publications/00_enquete_PI_emp_global.pdf.

Are displaced workers benefiting from the profiling tools identifying the need for more intensive employment support?

Most employment service providers limit one-to-one intensive counselling or job-placement services to hard-to-help clients (i.e. those judged to be furthest away from the labour market). The selection into more intensive services is made either by statistical or subjective profiling tools, varying across P/Ts. In Ontario for example, referral relies on the expertise of caseworkers (based on the client needs assessment) and on a quantitative profiling tool, the Employment Service (ES) suitability indicators, that considers 12 potential barriers to employment, including "labour market change" defined as "having suffered a recent job loss (within the last six months) as a results of company/plant downsizing closure layoff" (MTCU, 2014). Displaced workers may qualify for more intensive services under this ES suitability indicator, which is also used as a reporting tool to ensure that service providers are providing services to those clients with the greatest needs.

However the profiling is made, a careful evaluation is required to measure how adequately the profiling and assessment methods used to select unemployed persons for more intensive assistance pick up the specific barriers and obstacles displaced workers face in getting back into jobs. As discussed in Chapter 1, older long-tenured displaced workers suffer from large earnings losses and have weak re-employment outcomes. They should therefore be considered as a target group for more intensive re-employment support. Caseworkers need to consider the specific situation of displaced workers as regards their delay in actually receiving EI due to severance pay when considering referral for training as well as for other types of ALMP. In France, for example, some caseworkers are dedicated to displaced workers in specific teams (*contrat de sécurisation professionnelle*, see Box 3.4), allowing them to get to know each displaced worker's specific circumstances and better assess their needs, and therefore offer them a more tailored approach of re-employment support.

Implement systematic early needs assessment for displaced workers

Not all displaced workers require intensive employment support. Indeed, a large share of them find jobs quickly after displacement, without any (or with limited) support from the PES. To prevent deadweight costs that systematic case management would induce, early needs assessment for displaced workers can be introduced so as to i) better identify the jobseeker's skills, relevant experience and opportunities on the labour market; ii) explore options for alternative career paths, iii) identify skills development needs and barriers to re-employment; and iv) refer to early interventions (such as intensive individual counselling or training) only when specific barriers to re-employment have been identified. This needs assessment, formalised in an individual action plan (Tubb, 2012) would be the occasion for displaced workers to discuss their professional plans, retraining options and job-search methods with a caseworker. If not compulsory, Individual Action Plans (IAP) could be made available on a voluntary basis to all displaced workers, and presented as one of the options during the information session (see above).

Are ALMPs cost-effective in helping displaced workers getting back to work?

What can we learn from the international literature?

Consistent with the work-first philosophy, the international evaluation literature shows that job-search assistance and job-matching services are among the most cost-effective active labour market measures that governments can adopt to help the unemployed get back to work (Card et al., 2010; Martin and Grubb, 2001; Card, 2014; and Parent and Sautory, 2014). These types of programmes have also been shown to be most effective for the unemployed close to the labour market. This is likely to be the case for the majority of displaced workers, who are more job-ready than many other unemployed (especially long-term unemployed), given their recent work experience.

Intensive job-search counselling is among the most effective measures to help the unemployed get back to work. In France, and based on the specific population of displaced workers, Dares (2009) analysed the effects of two different intensive counselling programmes and compared them with the mainstream PES assistance. In 2008, 60% of displaced workers were in "stable work" (permanent job or temporary jobs with a duration of six months and over) after participating in the most intensive counselling programme (*contrat de transition professionnelle*), compared with 55% of those who benefited from a less intensive programme (*convention de reclassement personnalisé*) and 46% of those who did not receive any specific programme but the basic PES assistance.

In Europe, evaluations of training programmes suggest that they are likely to have positive effects for specific target groups. In particular, they appear to raise employment rates for unemployed people with better labour market prospects like women re-entering the labour market, and for educated people with migrant background (European Commission, 2013). Two main factors seem to condition the positive effects of training: i) it needs to provide vocational skills demanded by employers; and ii) the duration of training should not be too short for the skills gain to display positive employment outcomes. However, when labour demand is low and large segments of the economy are restructuring like during an economic crisis, the effects of training are mitigated, as it becomes difficult to accurately assess future or current skill needs. In such conditions, the European Commission (2013) suggests that training in general skills may be useful to maintain or increase the employability of the unemployed, even though the results on employment rates are less visible. Training also appears to offer a more sustainable impact on labour market outcomes in the medium run.

How effective are the Canadian ALMPs in helping displaced workers into work?

In Canada, ESDC (2014b) provides an impact analysis of the effectiveness of ALMPs in ten P/Ts for a treatment group including 42% of long-tenured workers which concludes that participation in Skills Development (SD), Targeted Wage Subsidies (TWS), Job Creation Partnerships (JCP) and Employment Assistance Services (EAS) improved significantly workers' labour market situation: more than if they had not taken any employment programme or service or if they had only received minimal employment services (Table 5.1). Participation in ALMP is also found to be particularly beneficial for older workers compared to their prime-age counterparts. When costs and durations of these programmes are taken into consideration, the cost-effectiveness analysis would recommend to favour EAS and TWS, especially for older workers, as no lock-in effect is observed on the short-term and large significant impacts are found on the long-term, increasing re-employment rates for older participants up to 7.7 percentage points in the case of EAS (for an average cost of CAD 700) and up to 15.2 percentage points for TWS (for an average cost of CAD 4 700).

ESDC (2014d) investigated further what the best timing is to participate in these programmes. Individuals who started their participation within four weeks following the start of their EI benefit claim had larger post-programme impacts on both earnings and re-employment rates. In the second and third month of an EI claim, participating in ALMP still has a positive impact on earnings but not on re-employment, and starting from the second quarter, both outcomes become significantly negative. These findings confirm the need for i) early needs assessment and ii) earlier targeting of re-employment services to displaced workers, in particular older long-tenured workers.

Table 5.1. **The cost-effectiveness of active labour market programmes in Canada**

A. Net impact of receiving ALMP, 2002-05

Percentage points (pp)

Lock-in effect or negative employment outcome

No lock-in effect or positive employment outcome

	Skills Development	Employment Assistance Services only	Targeted Wage Subsidies	Self-Employment	Job Creation Partnerships
All active claimants compared with their non-participant counterparts					
Lock-in effect during participation (decreasing incidence of employment during in-programme period)	Lock-in (-4.5pp to -4.7pp)	Small lock-in (-0.5pp)	No lock-in (+4.4pp to +7.2pp)	Lock-in (-12.4pp to -29.1pp)	..
Increasing incidence of employment after participation (annual incidence, over five years)	+2.4pp to +4.4pp	+0.8pp to +1.8pp	+4.9pp to +5.1pp	-12.3pp to -21.9pp	+5.5pp to +6.3pp
Increasing employment earnings after participation (over five years)	+ CAD 13 156	Starting 3rd year	+ CAD 7 125	- CAD 43 066	+ CAD 16 552
Average annual employment rate post-programme	86%	84%	85%	64%	85%
All older workers active claimants compared with their non-participant counterparts					
Lock-in effect during participation (decreasing incidence of employment during in-programme period)	Mixed (-2.4pp to +3.6 pp)	No lock-in (+0.9 pp)	No lock-in (+8.2pp to +15.6pp)	Lock-in (-9.6pp to -20pp)	..
Increasing incidence of employment after participation (annual incidence, over five years)	+9.6pp to +13pp	+3.8pp to +7.7pp	+13.3pp to +15.2pp	-5.2pp to -13.8pp	+5.5pp to +11.6pp
Increasing employment earnings after participation (over five years)	+ CAD 20 498	+ CAD 6 173	+ CAD 16 335	- CAD 16 081	+ CAD 16 788
Average annual employment rate post-programme	72%	73%	71%	50%	68%

B. Cost and duration of ALMP, 2002-05

Canadian dollars (CAD) and weeks

	Skills Development	Employment Assistance Services only	Targeted Wage Subsidies	Self-Employment	Job Creation Partnerships
Average cost of these interventions (CAD)	7 150	700	4 700	11 100	8 400
Median duration of the corresponding action plan (weeks)	40	7	28	52	26

Source: Author's own work based on ESDC (2014), "Analysis of national Employment Benefits and Support Measures (EBSM) profile, outcomes and incremental impacts", Technical Report (draft), Cycle II of the Evaluation of the Labour Market Development Agreements (LMDAs), Evaluation directorate, 11 March.

StatLink *http://dx.doi.org/10.1787/888933238988*

Jones (2012) analyses the effectiveness of training for displaced workers with long prior job tenure and finds that the returns to training are quite low for this population, even lower than the returns to formal schooling. On a cost-benefit basis, the evidence suggests that training does not pay off for most of the displaced workers population. Jones suggests alternative means to compensate the losers from economic adjustment including modified or expanded EI coverage and Wage Insurance (see Chapter 4). Connecting further training and retraining with other labour market interventions, employment services and temporary arrangements for reducing working time and wages might also help to improve training outcomes.

Increase the use of case management, especially for older long-tenured displaced workers

ESDC (2014c) provides an evaluation of Employment Assistance Services (EAS) in Canada, including three types of intervention: i) employment services ranging from job-search assistance for job-ready participants to the implementation of more intense return-to-work action plans for participants facing multiple employment barriers; ii) group services focusing on short-term job search and re-entry activities; and iii) a case management process including individual counselling in order to address more complex issues, particularly when participants face multiple employment barriers. The evaluation, based on a reference population that includes 58% of displaced workers, highlights the importance of providing a "participant-centred holistic approach involving the provision of counselling, assurance, motivation, building self-esteem and assisting participants in choosing a career path".

These results confirms the need for increased access to more intensive and tailored counselling for older long-tenured displaced workers as well as displaced workers with specific barriers. Increasing face-to-face counselling for this group would increase labour market expenditure, but appears to be cost effective. Moreover the higher cost of easing access to case management has to be seen against the rather low level of Canada's current public expenditure on active measures in international comparison.

Specific programmes targeted to displaced workers

Targeted Initiative for Older Workers

The Targeted Initiative for Older Workers (TIOW) is a federal-provincial/territorial cost-shared initiative designed to support unemployed older workers (typically ages 55-64) living in small, vulnerable communities of less than 250 000 inhabitants which have been affected by high unemployment, significant downsizing/closures, unfulfilled employer demand and/or skills mismatches (see Box 5.4).

Box 5.4. **Targeted Initiative for Older Workers (TIOW)**

First announced in 2006, Canada's Targeted Initiative for Older Workers (TIOW) programme is a federal-provincial/territorial cost-shared initiative specifically designed to support unemployed older workers in re-integrating into employment and/or becoming more employable. TIOW targets unemployed aged 55 to 64, living in small, vulnerable communities of 250 000 inhabitants or less, and affected by high unemployment or significant downsizing or firm closures. TIOW was first implemented as a temporary measure scheduled for a three-year period (in 2006 in Quebec and in 2009 in Ontario) In all provinces, the programme has been renewed since for successive periods of three years, the last renewal being made by *Budget 2014* represented a federal investment of CAD 75 million for the period 2014-17 and broadened the eligibility criteria to also support communities experiencing unfulfilled employer demand and/or skills mismatches. Since 2007, TIOW has provided support to over 35 500 unemployed older workers (as of April 2015) and the average cost per programme participant is estimated at about CAD 7 000.

Under TIOW agreements, the Government of Canada contributes up to 70% of programme costs and each province and/or territory contributes a minimum of 30%. Workers in the age groups 50-54 and 65 and over who meet all other TIOW criteria may also be eligible, provided that their participation is not at the expense of those in the core age group. The majority of TIOW projects are delivered by third-party community-based organisations, but the precise delivery model varies across provinces and territories.

TIOW projects provide group-based skills training and employment assistance services. TIOW participants are also offered income support in the form of allowances during the training. TIOW projects offer at least 25 hours of training per week, and must include employment assistance services (such as job-search techniques, résumé writing, interview technique and counselling) and at least two employability improvement activities (such as basic skills upgrading, vocational skill training, work-experience, direct marketing to employers and preparation for self-employment). Under TIOW, projects in all jurisdictions must include group-based activities and income support in the form of allowances (except when a P/T has legislation governing eligibility for income support). Best practices and lessons learned from the "Older Workers Pilot Projects Initiative" (1999-2006) were collected and used when designing and implementing the TIOW programme.

Source: Economic Action Plan (2014), "Targeted Initiative for Older Workers", http://actionplan.gc.ca/en/initiative/targeted-initiative-older-workers.

ESDC (2014e) provides an impact evaluation of TIOW for all provinces except Quebec, while MESS (2010) provides a qualitative evaluation of this initiative in Quebec based on a survey of participants and interviews with representatives of regional and promoter organisation conducted in 2007-08. ESDC (2014e) indicates that 75% of all participants found paid employment following their participation in TIOW (respectively 70% in Quebec; MESS, 2010). In comparison with a group of unemployed receiving the mainstream Employment

Assistance Services, the net impact of the programme on employment is positive (TIOW increases re-employment rates by six percentages points) but it has no impact on earnings and the use of Employment Insurance or Social Assistance. The programme is equally successful for men and women and all age categories (50-54, 55-59, 60-64 and 65+).

The programme also succeeds in reaching vulnerable older workers: half of TIOW participants had not attained more than a high school diploma (including 24% not having completed high school) and half of the participants experienced a recent job loss, either in the year they started the TIOW programme (24%) or the year prior to starting the programme (31%; ESDC, 2014e). In Quebec, 20% were on social assistance and 13% had access to no public income support at all (MESS, 2010).Satisfaction is also very high among TIOW participants in Quebec: while feeling at first that they needed to learn job-search techniques, identify their skill needs and receive support from the PES, they most appreciated guidance from caseworkers, group support and job-search assistance. The main obstacles to their re-employment that they identified were their lack of job-search experience (59%), their age (53%), the lack of training for available jobs (50%), available jobs being too far away (29%), outdated vocational skills (20%), health problems (19%) and trouble reading and writing (5%). The obstacles to re-employment identified by caseworkers included unrealistic expectations regarding wages in some cases, pointing to the need for good quality labour market information and physical limitations in other cases, calling for a comprehensive approach for some displaced workers facing greater barriers to return to work (MESS, 2010).

In view of these results, TIOW can be regarded as a good practice worth to be shared with countries facing similar job displacement issues. The recent third renewal of the Canadian initiative is therefore welcome, but consideration should be given to funding the programme on a more permanent basis.

Career Transition Assistance initiative

The Career Transition Assistance (CTA) initiative was a temporary measure introduced in 2009 to help displaced workers update and acquire new skills in the context of the GFC (see Box 5.5). CTA offered long-tenured displaced workers the opportunity to receive earlier or extended EI regular benefits if they undertook longer-term training early in their claim (CEIC, 2014). The CTA initiative was introduced based on the assumption that many long-tenured workers affected by the GFC had been employed in declining industries and were likely to suffer large and persistent earning losses and, therefore, in need of skills upgrading to find a new job (ESDC, 2014a). These assumptions are consistent with the empirical evidence presented in this review (see Chapter 1).

Box 5.5. **Career Transition Assistance (CTA)**

The CTA initiative was introduced as part of Economic Action Plan 2009 in response to the economic downturn, and was designed to support long-tenured workers who engage in full-time, long-term training to update and acquire new skills. The CTA initiative was offered to EI claimants who met the definition of a long-tenured worker and who established a claim between January 2009 and May 2010. As of 31 May 2012, any CTA training had to be completed.

A **Long-Tenured Worker** is someone who: i) has contributed to the EI program for at least seven out of the ten calendar years immediately preceding the start date of the EI claim; and ii) has received no more than 35 weeks of EI regular benefits in the five years immediately preceding the start date of the EI claim. Long-tenured workers received a letter from Service Canada notifying them of their eligibility for the CTA initiative. The letter also provided a description of the initiative and encouraged long-tenured workers to visit their local employment agency (either PES or private provider) for more information. With the assistance of their local service provider, interested claimants identified appropriate training and established a Return to Work Action Plan (RTWAP) and/or received a referral allowing them to continue to receive EI benefits during the period they are participating in the referred training programme.

CTA included two non-mutually exclusive components:

- The first component of the CTA initiative, the **Extended Employment Insurance and Training Incentive** (EEITI) increased the duration of income support (up to a maximum of 104 weeks) by providing additional weeks of EI regular benefits to long-tenured workers who enrolled in long-term training early in their claim. The training had to meet the following criteria: i) be full time; ii) last for 20 weeks or more; iii) be purchased by participants or financed by the P/T under EI Part II; and iv) start within the first year of the benefit period.
- The second component of the CTA initiative, the **Severance Investment for Training Initiative** (SITI), provided earlier access to EI regular benefits to long-tenured workers who invested in their own training using all or part of their severance package and enrolled in training early in their claim. To benefit from the SITI, claimants had to receive separation payments and a referral for eligible training had to be given while receiving severance pay or within six weeks of notice. The training had to meet the following criteria: i) be full time; ii) last at least ten weeks or cost a minimum of CAD 5 000 or 80% of the separation payments; iii) be purchased by participants; and *iv)* start within the first year of the benefit period.

Despite a higher initial target, a little less than 12 000 individuals engaged in longer-term training as part of the CTA initiative between 2009-10 and 2012-13, for a total amount of extended EI regular benefits slightly below CAD 190 million. Both the take-up rate and the total spending were lower than initially expected.

Source: ESDC (2014), "Evaluation of the career transition assistance initiative", Final Report, Strategic Policy and Research Branch, March, http://www.esdc.gc.ca/eng/publications/evaluations/skills_and_employment/2014/ctai.shtml.

A comprehensive evaluation of CTA – relying on two econometric studies, a descriptive analysis, a literature review, a cost study analysis and interviews with key informants – highlights the following main results (ESDC, 2014a):

- **Take-up rate**: The CTA take up rate was quite low (about 2% of eligible claimants), but similar to other long-lasting training programmes in Canada. This lower-than-expected participation rate has been partly attributed to the initial eligibility criteria that required clients to have a "referral to training" within the first 20 weeks of an EI claim. This criterion is not in line with the way long-tenured workers begin their unemployment spell after being displaced. Long-tenured displaced workers are more likely to exhaust their severance package first, before seeking help to find employment. For those who were interested in training, the increase in the number of unemployed early in the downturn made it difficult to get referrals to training within the time limit to qualify for CTA. In response to feedback from P/Ts, ESDC adapted CTA eligibility to require only an active Return to Work Action Plan to qualify, rather than a referral for training.
- **Reasons for participation**: Participants enrolled in the CTA initiative so as to: upgrade their skills or obtain a certificate (35%), increase their chances of finding a job (34%) or change occupation or industry (27%).
- **Reasons for non-participation**: Low take-up was partly attributable to work-related reasons. About one-third of eligible long-tenured displaced workers either were already working, decided to work instead of upgrading their skills, or expected to return to the same employer. One out of four non-participants did not feel the need for training, while 13% said the available training did not fit their needs, or their duration was too long. According to PES providers, the complexity of the second scheme (SITI, see Box 5.7) could also explain low take-up.
- **The CTA initiative has met its targeted population**: CTA participants were mostly workers with limited EI history (half of them are first time EI users) and long tenure in their previous job (claimants with five years or more of job tenure with the same employer are over-represented). Many had been displaced from a declining industry (29% from manufacturing and 22% from trade and transport industries).
- **CTA training**: The training sponsored by CTA had longer durations than usual trainings (44 weeks on average compared with 16 for the training typically followed by long-tenured displaced workers outside CTA). The training was also mostly full-time, compared with part-time for other training programmes.
- **Training outcomes**: Almost all CTA training (93%) led to a new certification, a key requirement for finding a new job. In 65% of the cases, it was a trade or community college diploma.

The objectives of CTA seemed to be met, as CTA managed to enrol long-tenured workers displaced from industries where the acquired skills may not be transferable to growing industries and occupations. However, a large discrepancy arises around possible deadweight effects. Almost half of the CTA participants declared they would not have participated in training in the absence of CTA, whereas the econometric study suggests that the EI extension (EEITI) had no significant impact on training participation while the earlier access to EI conditioned on the use of severance package (SITI) increased participation by a modest 0.05 percentage points.

Second Career programme in Ontario

Launched in June 2008, Ontario's Second Career (SC) programme is a permanent programme targeted at displaced workers. It aims to help laid-off workers train for new careers in high-demand fields, by providing them with skills training and related needs-based income support. SC is a cost-sharing grant and laid-off workers are asked to contribute to their training or education according to their means. A profiling system based on seven criteria enables the programme to favour high-tenured and low-skilled displaced workers (see Box 5.6).

Box 5.6. **Ontario's Second Career programme**

To be eligible for the Second Career programme, individuals must meet three criteria:

- Have been laid-off on or after 1 January 2005;
- Be unemployed; and
- Demonstrate occupational demand for the training requested with evidence of good employment prospects locally or within Ontario. This could be made by providing proof such as job ads in local newspapers or a letter from an employer who intends to hire.

This programme allocates grants of up to CAD 28 000 per displaced worker for tuition, books, and other instruction costs such as manuals or workbooks, transportation, or a basic living allowance. Additional funds may be available for people who need help to pay for academic upgrading, the costs of living away from home, disability needs or child care.

Whenever eligibility criteria are fulfilled, the Employment Ontario caseworker proceeds to a suitability assessment of the displaced worker's application, based on seven criteria: length of previous active job search, duration of the unemployment spell, educational attainment, work history, labour market prospects, type of desired training and experience (see table below).

Box 5.6. **Ontario's Second Career programme** *(cont.)*

Up to three points are attributed for each criterion. A minimum test score of 16 is necessary to qualify for the Second Career programme. The Ontario Ministry of Training, Colleges and Universities (MTCU) then assesses the financial needs of the individual to determine the share of the total cost that will be asked of the displaced worker. A score below 16 leads displaced workers to be directed towards other EO services or programmes and/or other community services.

This way of profiling favours displaced workers with low skills and low educational attainment, high tenure, long-term unemployment, and work experience in occupations requiring low qualifications and with few opportunities for sustainable, long-term employment.

Ontario's Second Career programme eligibility and suitability assessment

	Programme suitability		
Criteria	**High** (3 points)	**Medium** (2 points)	**Low** (1 point)
Active job search	More than 26 weeks of active job search, with documentation	13 to 26 weeks of active job search, with documentation	Less than 13 weeks of active job search, with documentation
Duration of unemployment	More than 26 weeks unemployed	13 to 26 weeks unemployed	Less than 13 weeks unemployed
Educational attainment	High school completion or less; or post-secondary completion not recognised in Ontario	High school completion with some post-secondary; or some apprenticeship training	Post-secondary completion; or apprenticeship completion
Work history	More than 7 years in the same occupation	3 to 7 years in the same occupation	Less than 3 years in the same occupation
Labour market prospects	Credential/license needed for chosen employment	No credential or license needed for chosen employment	
Type of training	Leads to certificate/diploma; occupationally-specific training in NOC B or C	Provides upgrading/language training to qualify for occupationally-specific training in NOC B or C that leads to certificate/ diploma	
Experience: occupational skills	Work experience in NOC D occupations and there are few opportunities for sustainable, long-term employment; and/or a disability prevents the applicant from using existing occupational skills	Work experience is in NOC B and/or NOC C occupations and there are few opportunities for sustainable, long-term employment; and/or a disability prevents the applicant from using existing occupational skills	

Note: Canada uses the National Occupational Classification (NOC) system to classify occupations in its labour market. The NOC consists of four broad skill levels identified as A through D. These levels correspond to the kind and/or amount of training or education required for entering an occupation:

Skill level A: Occupations usually require university education.

Skill level B: Occupations usually require college education or apprenticeship training.

Skill level C: Occupations usually require secondary school and/or occupationally-specific training.

Skill level D: On-the-job training is usually provided for occupations.

Source: MTCU (2012), "Second Career (SC) guidelines", Ministry of Training, Colleges and Universities, June, http://www.tcu.gov.on.ca/eng/eopg/publications/2012_sc_guidelines.pdf.

The initial three-year target of helping 20 000 laid-off workers was achieved after only 16 months, and since 2008 SC assisted over 76 000 displaced workers. A government survey conducted in 2010 on SC students showed that 93% of them have graduated. The average length of training was nine months with average funding of approximately CAD 17 500. Over 61% had found jobs within three months, and three-quarters within one year of graduation (compared with half of all displaced workers as defined in Chapter 1).

This programme provides a useful scheme for Ontarian displaced workers to access training, retrain and increase their occupational mobility after displacement. One of the weaknesses of SC is the lack of mandatory workplace training as part of the programme which might lead some workers to undertake training without having the work experience to help them find a job after the training is completed. SC is an important but costly provincial government intervention: more evaluation is required to quantify the net effects (incremental) of the programme and its costs and benefits, considering this high level of subsidy.

Conclusion

All unemployed in Canada can access job-matching services by contacting Service Canada and entering a local PES agency. However, the fact that ALMPs are organised (and funded) on the assumption that most unemployed workers can and should find a job with little or no re-employment assistance from the government might limit the assistance received by displaced workers. Due to the interaction between severance payments and eligibility to EI (see Chapter 4), displaced workers may delay their contact with Service Canada, and consequently with a service provider. This would delay their access to basic re-employment support such as job-matching services. And even when they contact a PES agency, only workers deemed to face severe barriers to re-employment will be offered more intensive forms of assistance, such as close case management and training, due to the rather limited labour market expenditures. This system avoids large deadweight losses, but also prevents long-tenured displaced workers from accessing tailored intensive counselling early enough in their unemployment spell.

This chapter has shown that displaced workers are generally strongly motivated to search intensely for another job and likely to do well with the self-service model generally used to provide job-search assistance to EI beneficiaries in Canada. Indeed, many displaced workers find a new job relatively quickly after displacement, either by themselves or with limited assistance from their local PES agency, through a listing of job vacancies or the provision of basic job-search training. However, an important minority of displaced workers perceive that they have poor re-employment prospects or need retraining and this group - which are disproportionally older and long-tenured workers – would benefit from more intensive re-employment assistance, especially job-search counselling and training, to help them get back to work quickly. Some displaced workers will be able to access intensive re-employment support from the core active labour market programmes in their province, but many probably do not since these services are tightly rationed. This could help to explain why 52% of displaced workers do not find a job in the first year after displacement. Thus, one key challenge is to improve the access of displaced workers who encounter particular adjustment difficulties to more intensive employment services.

In recent years, several targeted programmes for select groups of displaced workers have been created and they have shown promise. For example, the Second Career programme in Ontario and the Career Transition Assistance and Targeted Initiative for Older Workers at the federal level, which all provide additional adjustment assistance for older and/or long-tenured workers affected by economic restructuring. The targeting of these programmes and the range of services that they offer differ somewhat, but they illustrate how a well-designed package of income and re-employment support can help to reduce the adjustment costs associated with displacement. These targeted programmes are useful initiatives that address some of the gaps in general re-employment programmes, but some of them reached relatively few displaced workers (CTA for example) and despite a third renewal in 2014 and promising evaluation results, TIOW remains a temporary measure the durability of which is not ensured in the future. Attention should be devoted to making the services offered by these programmes readily available on a more permanent basis to a greater number of older and/or long-tenured displaced workers who face similar difficulties with their reintegration into the labour market. Canada would benefit from building upon the lessons from TIOW and SC programmes in order to increase further the access of older long-tenured displaced workers to case management and training.

Another context in which extra re-employment services for displaced workers is likely to be required is in an economic downturn when the number of workers experiencing layoffs increases and their job-search prospects are poor. It is important that governments quickly scale up ALMPs in a recession, while also shifting the mix of services towards more general types of training and job-search counselling. Following the GFC, the federal and provincial governments managed to reorient and expand existing employment and training programmes in an effective manner that should be held in ready for future downturns. The Canadian programmes that were introduced in response to the crisis are also good examples for other countries to follow.

Notes

1. Parent (2014a) analyses which are the main factors penalising re-employment prospects of older displaced workers in France. Lacking an internet access for the search of a new job is one of the most penalising factors identified in the specific case of displaced workers (but not for other unemployed). These long-tenured displaced workers compensate their lack of internet use through looking at job ads (+3 percentage points compared with short-tenured counterparts), and employment agencies (+3 percentage points).
2. EICS data is not limited to ILO unemployed nor to unemployed eligible to EI (see Chapter 4 for more details on this dataset), therefore displaced workers out of work are included in the survey even if they are not actively looking for work.
3. PES and administration (Category 1) includes placement and related services for employers and the employed as well as the unemployed, including any similar services delivered by private providers but with public financing, and the administration costs of implementing these services and the active and passive programmes in Categories 2 to 9.
4. P/Ts have the added flexibility to fund the CJG from their CJF allocation, Labour Market Development Agreement, or their own P/T funding source. P/Ts will be phasing in their investments in the CJG by annual increments of 15% of their CJF allocation until they reach an investment target of 60% and onwards in the fourth year of the agreements (2017-18).
5. Service Canada has also transformed its service delivery model through increased automation and now relies on multi-channel services: online, by phone or in-person. Since the crisis and the rise in EI claimants, the use of electronic reporting for EI has almost reached 100% (CEIC, 2014).
6. Moreover, starting in February 2013, Claimant Information sessions are tailored to each of the three EI claimant groups: Frequent Claimants, Occasional Claimants and Long-Tenured Workers, improving the quality and targeting of the labour market information delivered.
7. It now states that job search should include the following activities: assessing employment opportunities (by searching for vacancies online, in newspapers); preparing a CV or cover letter; registering for job-search tools or with electronic job banks or employment agencies (for example by signing up with Job Alerts or registering with a temporary agency or a head hunter); attending job-search workshops or job fairs (events bringing together recruiters for employers, admission officers, and employment counsellors with jobseekers looking for immediate work or who may be thinking about developing their skills to find work); networking (by contacting former colleagues, associates, and friends for information on expected hiring needs in their organisations); contacting prospective employers; submitting job applications; attending interviews; or undergoing competency evaluations.

8. Long-tenured workers and other occasional users of the programme are expected to accept jobs in their usual occupation paying 90% (or more) of their previous wages for, respectively, the first 18 weeks and six weeks on EI. Subsequently, they are expected to accept "similar" jobs paying at least 70% of their former wage (80% for occasional users during weeks 7-18). Frequent claimants must immediately look for and accept jobs in similar occupations that pay 80% or more of their previous wage, and, from the 7th week, accept any type of job paying at least 70% of their previous wage.

9. A long-tenured worker is an individual who has contributed to the EI programme (paying at least 30% of the annual maximum EI premiums) for at least seven out of the last ten calendar years and has received no more than 35 weeks of EI regular benefits in the last five years (see Chapter 4 for more details).

10. In almost all OECD countries (apart from Turkey), an individual action plan can be set up following the diagnostic and needs assessment made during the first meeting of an unemployed person with his or her caseworker. These individual action plans are either established for all newly registering unemployed (or at least a large majority) or targeted to particular groups. Canada (along with the Czech Republic and Japan) is quite unique among OECD countries in the sense that jobseeker participation in developing and agreeing to an individual action plan is not mandatory (OECD, 2007; Tubb, 2012; and Konle-Seidl, 2012).

11. Moreover, since February 2013, CIS became tailored to three EI claimant groups: frequent claimants; occasional claimants; and long-tenured workers, allowing for a graduated control over an EI recipient's job search, depending on their EI history.

12. Nevertheless, the fact that the Integrity Services Branch of Service Canada is mostly known by Canadians for bringing criminal cases against persons who defraud the federal government could lead to misleading results in its role in activation. Even though the CIS is supposed to be an informational session, trade unions note that the "threat effect" of being convoked to a meeting by Integrity Services, leads to counterproductive results, as jobseekers assume they are the object of a criminal investigation.

13. Parent (2014b) presents a literature review of the main European experiences and micro-econometric evaluations of job-search monitoring and sanctions. These evaluations show that monitoring and sanctions have positive effects on the return to work of the unemployed, but negative ones on the quality of the jobs found which are less stable and lower paid. They may also have penalising effects on the subsequent career of sanctioned individuals and can lead to labour market exit.

References

Burleton, D., S. Gulati, C. Mc Donald, S. Scarfone (2013), "Jobs in Canada. Where, what and for whom?", Special Report, TD Economics, October, http://www.td.com/document/PDF/economics/special/JobsInCanada.pdf.

Card, D. (2014), "Evaluating active labor market programs: What have we learned?", *TRAVAIL ET EMPLOI*, No. 139, pp. 15-23 (available in French only), http://travail-emploi.gouv.fr/etudes-recherches-statistiques-de,76/etudes-et-recherches,77/publications-dares,98/revue-travail-et-emploi,103/tous-les-numeros,2100/no139-revue-travail-et-emploi,18442.html, and Summary available in English, p. 117.

Card, D., J. Kluve and A. Weber (2010), "Active labour market policy evaluations: A meta-analysis", *Economic Journal*, Royal Economic Society, Vol. 120, No. 548.

Carey, D. (2014), "Overcoming skills shortages in Canada", *OECD Economics Department Working Papers*, No. 1143, OECD Publishing, Paris, http://dx.doi.org/10.1787/5jz123fgkxjl-en.

CEIC – Canada Employment and Insurance Commission (2014), *2012/13 Employment Insurance Monitoring and Assessment Report*, Canada Employment Insurance Commission, Employment and Social Development Canada [ESDC], March, www.esdc.gc.ca/en/reports/ei/monitoring2013/index.page.

Dares (2009), "Le reclassement professionnel des salariés licenciés pour motif économique : Comparaison entre le contrat de transition professionnelle, la convention de reclassement personnalisée et l'accompagnement classique de l'ANPE", *Premières Synthèses Informations*, No. 43.3, October, http://travail-emploi.gouv.fr/IMG/pdf/2009-10-43-3-2.pdf.

Economic Action Plan (2014), "Targeted Initiative for Older Workers", http://actionplan.gc.ca/en/initiative/targeted-initiative-older-workers.

Economic Action Plan (2013), "Jobs growth and long-term prosperity", Ministry of Finance, 21 March, www.budget.gc.ca/2013/doc/plan/budget2013-eng.pdf.

Emploi-Québec (2010), "Rapport global – Enquête sur la situation post-intervention des participantes et participants aux interventions des services publics d'emploi", http://emploiquebec.gouv.qc.ca/fileadmin/fichiers/pdf/Publications/00_enquete_PI_emp_global.pdf.

ESDC – Employment and Social Development Canada (2014a), "Evaluation of the career transition assistance initiative", Final Report, Strategic Policy and Research Branch, March, http://www.esdc.gc.ca/eng/publications/evaluations/skills_and_employment/2014/ctai.shtml.

ESDC (2014b), "Analysis of national Employment Benefits and Support Measures (EBSM) profile, outcomes and incremental impacts", Technical Report (draft), Cycle II of the Evaluation of the Labour Market Development Agreements (LMDAs), Evaluation directorate, 11 March.

ESDC (2014c), "Study on Employment Assistance Services", Final Technical Report, Cycle II of the Evaluation of the Labour Market Development Agreements (LMDAs), Evaluation directorate, Strategic Policy and Research Branch, 28 May.

ESDC (2014d), "Effects of the timing of participation in Employment Assistance Services", Report on National Results, Cycle II of the Evaluation of the Labour Market Development Agreements (LMDAs), Partnership Evaluation, Evaluation directorate, 13 November.

ESDC (2014e), "Summative Evaluation of the Targeted Initiative for Older Workers", Final Report, Partnership Evaluation, Evaluation directorate Strategic Policy and Research Branch, 5 May, http://www12.edsc.gc.ca/sgpe-pmps/p.5bd.2t.1.3ls@-eng.jsp?pid=8638.

European Commission (2013), "Active labour market policies", http://ec.europa.eu/europe2020/pdf/themes/24_almp_and_employment_services.pdf.

Government of Canada (2010), *Canada's Economic Action Plan: A sixth report to Canadians*, September, http://www.fin.gc.ca/pub/report-rapport/2010-09-27/pdf/ceap-paec-2010-09-eng.pdf.

Grubb, D. and A. Puymoyen (2008), "Long time series for public expenditure on labour market programmes", *OECD Social, Employment and Migration Working Papers*, No. 73, OECD Publishing, Paris, http://dx.doi.org/10.1787/230128514343.

ILO – International Labour Office (2014), "Lessons from the implementation of training and retraining programmes in response to the Great Recession", Skills for Employment, *Research Brief*, 23 May, Geneva, http://www.ilo.org/wcmsp5/groups/public/---ed_emp/---ifp_skills/documents/publication/wcms_244381.pdf.

Jones, S.R.G. (2012), "The effectiveness of training for displaced workers with long prior job tenure", Canadian Labour Market and Skills Researcher Network, *CLSRN Working Papers*, No. 92, January, http://www.clsrn.econ.ubc.ca/workingpapers/CLSRN%20Working%20Paper%20no.%2092%20-%20Stephen%20Jones.pdf.

Konle-Seidl, R. (2012) "Activation and integration: Working with individual action plans. Monitoring and follow-up of IAPs and their outcomes in selected EU countries", *PES to PES Dialogue*, The European Commission Mutual Learning Programme for Public Employment Services, DG Employment, Social Affairs and Inclusion, European Commission, http://ec.europa.eu/social/main.jsp?langId=en&catId=105&newsId=1208&furtherNews=yes.

Martin, J.P. and D. Grubb (2001), "What works and for whom: A review of OECD countries' experiences with active labour market policies", Institute for Evaluation of Labour Market and Education Policy, *IFAU Working Papers*, No. 2001:14.

Mendelson, M. and N. Zon (2013), "The training wheels are off: A closer look at the Canada Job Grant", Caledon Institute of Social Policy, MOWAT, School of Public Policy & Governance, University of Toronto, http://vibrantcanada.ca/files/training_wheels_are_off_canada_job_grant_review.pdf.

MESS – Ministère de l'Emploi et de la Solidarité sociale (2013), "Les pratiques du recrutement des entreprises au Québec", http://emploiquebec.gouv.qc.ca/publications/pdf/Enquete-pratiques-recrutement-MESS.pdf.

MESS (2010), "Support for older workers", Direction des politiques d'emploi et de main-d'œuvre, Presentation from Marie Grenon at the Canada's Public Policy Forum, 28 October, Ottawa, www.ppforum.ca/sites/default/files/m_grenon_eng.pdf.

MTCU – Ministry of Training, Colleges and Universities (2014), "Employment Service – Service providers guideline", http://www.tcu.gov.on.ca/eng/eopg/publications/es_2014_2015_sp_guidelines.pdf.

MTCU (2012), "Second Career (SC) guidelines" (Effective 1 June 2012), 25 May, www.tcu.gov.on.ca/eng/eopg/publications/2012_sc_guidelines.pdf.

OECD (2014), *OECD Economic Surveys: Canada 2014*, OECD Publishing, Paris, http://dx.doi.org/10.1787/eco_surveys-can-2014-en.

OECD (2007), "Activating the unemployed: What countries do?", in *OECD Employment Outlook 2007*, OECD Publishing, Paris, http://dx.doi.org/10.1787/empl_outlook-2007-en.

Parent, G. (2014a), "Retour à l'emploi des chômeurs seniors français ayant bénéficié d'un accompagnement renforcé vers l'emploi en 2009 et 2010: Enquête auprès des salariés licenciés pour motif économique et des publics en difficulté d'insertion", *OECD Social, Employment and Migration Working Papers*, No. 156, OECD Publishing, Paris, http://dx.doi.org/10.1787/5jz2fnj84vd4-fr.

Parent, G. (2014b), "Job search monitoring and sanctions", *TRAVAIL ET EMPLOI*, No. 139 (juillet-septembre 2014), pp. 91-104 (available in French only), http://travail-emploi.gouv.fr/etudes-recherches-statistiques-de,76/etudes-et-recherches,77/publications-dares,98/revue-travail-et-emploi,103/tous-les-numeros,2100/no139-revue-travail-et-emploi,18442.html, and Summary available in English, p. 118.

Parent, G. and O. Sautory (2014), "Employment support for the unemployed: Effects of strengthening and outsourcing", *TRAVAIL ET EMPLOI*, No. 139 (juillet-septembre 2014), pp. 75-89 (available in French only), http://travail-emploi.gouv.fr/etudes-recherches-statistiques-de,76/etudes-et-recherches,77/publications-dares,98/revue-travail-et-emploi,103/tous-les-numeros,2100/no139-revue-travail-et-emploi,18442.html, and Summary available in English p. 118.

Tubb, H. (2012) "Activation and integration: Working with individual action plans. Toolkit for public employment services", *PES to PES dialogue*, The European Commission Mutual Learning Programme for Public Employment Services, DG Employment, Social Affairs and Inclusion, European Commission, http://ec.europa.eu/social/main.jsp?langId=en&catId=105&newsId=1208&furtherNews=yes.

Venn, D. (2012), "Eligibility criteria for unemployment benefits: Quantitative indicators for OECD and EU countries", *OECD Social, Employment and Migration Working Papers*, No. 131, OECD Publishing, Paris, http://dx.doi.org/10.1787/5k9h43kgkvr4-en.

Database references

Employment Insurance Coverage Survey (EICS), Statistics Canada http://www23.statcan.gc.ca/imdb/p2SV.pl?Function=getSurvey&SDDS=4428.

OECD/Eurostat Labour Market Programme Database, http://dx.doi.org/10.1787/data-00312-en.

OECD Population and Labour Force Dataset, a subset of the *Annual Labour Force Statistics (ALFS) Database*, http://dotstat.oecd.org/Index.aspx?DataSetCode=ALFS_POP_LABOUR).

Statistics Canada Key Socioeconomic Database (CANSIM), http://www5.statcan.gc.ca/cansim/a01?lang=eng.

Annex 5.A1

Employment benefits and support measures (EBSM) in Canada

The LMDAs grant considerable flexibility in the design and delivery of EBSM-similar programmes to P/Ts in order to ensure that programming can respond to local and regional labour market needs. The Government of Canada provides a framework under which the ALMP are delivered and focuses on accountability, evaluation and policy development. Through EBSM, EI-eligible unemployed persons are able to receive different kind of support (see Table 5.A1.1). Canada spent around CAD 2 billion in EBSM in 2012-13, mostly concentrated on Skills Development (CAD 915 million) and Employment Assistance Services (CAD 575 million). Due to lower unit costs, Employment Assistance Services (essentially job-search assistance) serves many more people. Individual counselling only represent a small share of these employment services, but different ways of reporting from the P/Ts prevent further analysis of the use of intensive counselling for displaced workers.

Quebec and Ontario provide EBSM-similar programmes to the highest number of clients in Canada, with respectively around 200 000 and 150 000 clients served in 2012-13 (CEIC, 2014). The composition of EBSM clients varies a lot across P/Ts, with three Quebec clients out of four being EI-recipients, while it's only the case for around half of the Ontario clients. In order to improve its cost-effectiveness, Quebec revised the methods used to select clients for EBSM participation by: 1) proactively targeting EI claimants likely to face employment barriers and those in high-demand occupations, and 2) implementing in 2008 the *Pacte pour l'emploi*, designed to increase participation in Employment Assistance Services, better identify and target client needs, and expand access to Skills Development and Targeted Wage Subsidies.

Table 5.A1.1. **Employment Benefits and Support Measures (EBSM)**

Expenditure and interventions in 2012-13

EBSM category	Programme	Programme characteristics	Share of total expenditure	Share of total interventions
Employment Benefits (available only to insured clients, active and former EI claimants)	Targeted Wage Subsidies (TWS)	Assist eligible unemployed individuals to obtain on-the-job work experience by providing employers with financial assistance towards the wages of insured participants whom they hire.	3.4	1.2
	Self-Employment assistance (SE)	Provides financial assistance and business planning advice to EI-eligible participants to help them start their own business (covers personal living expenses and other expenses during the initial stages of the business.)	5.8	0.8
	Job Creation Partnerships (JCP)	Provides insured participants with opportunities to gain work experience that will lead to ongoing employment. Also aimed at developing the community and the local economy.	1.2	0.3
	Skills Development (SD)	Helps insured participants obtain employment skills through direct financial assistance that enables them to select and pay for their own training.	45.2	11.1
	Targeted Earnings Supplement (TES)	Temporarily topping-up wages to enable people currently on EI or the longer-term unemployed to accept low-wage jobs (the *Supplément de retour au travail* in Quebec is the only intervention currently in place that is similar to this programme.)	0.1	0.5
Support Measures (available to all unemployed individuals including no-insured clients)	Employment Assistance Services (EAS)	Assists organisations in the provision of employment services to unemployed persons, including counselling, action planning, job-search skills, job-finding clubs, job-placement services, provision of labour market information, case management and follow-up.	28.4	83.7
	Labour Market Partnerships (LMPs)	Provides funding to help employers, employee and employer associations, and communities to improve their capacity for dealing with human resource requirements and to implement labour force adjustments. Involves developing plans and strategies and implementing adjustment measures.	7.7	n.a.
	Research and Innovation measure (R&I)	Supports activities that identify better ways of helping people to prepare for or keep employment and to be productive participants in the labour force. Funds are provided to eligible recipients to enable them to carry out demonstration projects and research for this purpose.	0.6	n.a.
Pan-Canadian Activities	Aboriginal Skills and Employment Training Strategy (ASETS), Pan-Canadian Labour Market Partnerships, Pan-Canadian Research and Innovation		7.6	2.4

Note: LMPs and R&I are generally not associated with direct client service and therefore do not have participants or interventions. N.a.: Not available.

Figures 5.6 and 5.7 rely on the active labour market programme categories of the *OECD/Eurostat Labour Market Programme Database*, while this table presents expenditures in EBSM using the Canadian reporting of CEIC (2014). Both classifications are not completely comparable, thus caution is needed in comparing this table with the international figures presented above.

Source: CEIC (2014), "EI monitoring and assessment report 2012/13", Canada Employment Insurance Commission, Employment and Social Development Canada, March, http://www12.hrsdc.gc.ca/servlet/sgpp-pmps-pub?lang=eng&curjsp=p.5bd.2t.1.3ls@-eng.jsp&curactn=dwnld&pid=7982&did=1, Annexes 3.6 and 3.12.

StatLink http://dx.doi.org/10.1787/888933238995

ORGANISATION FOR ECONOMIC CO-OPERATION AND DEVELOPMENT

The OECD is a unique forum where governments work together to address the economic, social and environmental challenges of globalisation. The OECD is also at the forefront of efforts to understand and to help governments respond to new developments and concerns, such as corporate governance, the information economy and the challenges of an ageing population. The Organisation provides a setting where governments can compare policy experiences, seek answers to common problems, identify good practice and work to co-ordinate domestic and international policies.

The OECD member countries are: Australia, Austria, Belgium, Canada, Chile, the Czech Republic, Denmark, Estonia, Finland, France, Germany, Greece, Hungary, Iceland, Ireland, Israel, Italy, Japan, Korea, Luxembourg, Mexico, the Netherlands, New Zealand, Norway, Poland, Portugal, the Slovak Republic, Slovenia, Spain, Sweden, Switzerland, Turkey, the United Kingdom and the United States. The European Union takes part in the work of the OECD.

OECD Publishing disseminates widely the results of the Organisation's statistics gathering and research on economic, social and environmental issues, as well as the conventions, guidelines and standards agreed by its members.

OECD PUBLISHING, 2, rue André-Pascal, 75775 PARIS CEDEX 16
(81 2014 35 1 P) ISBN 978-92-64-23323-2 – 2015-16

Made in the USA
Las Vegas, NV
06 November 2024

11119650R00103